This is my book !
Believe me

START AND RUN A PROFITABLE BED AND BREAKFAST

Your step-by-step business plan

Monica Taylor and
Richard Taylor

Self-Counsel Press
(*a division of*)
International Self-Counsel Press Ltd.
Canada U.S.A.

Printed in Canada

First edition: August, 1992
Reprinted: March, 1993; February, 1994; November, 1994; September, 1996

Canadian Cataloguing in Publication Data
Taylor, Monica, 1930-
Start and run a profitable bed and breakfast

   (Self-counsel business series)
   ISBN 0-88908-989-2
   1. Bed and breakfast accommodations — Management.
I. Taylor, Richard, 1932-   II. Title.   III. Series.
TX911.2.T39 1992   647.94   C92-091401-2

Inset cover photo by Gary Ritchie, Gary Ritchie Photography, Vancouver
Background cover photo by Corel Professional Photos — Corel Corporation

Self-Counsel Press
(a division of)
International Self-Counsel Press Ltd.

1481 Charlotte Road	1704 N. State Street
North Vancouver, British Columbia	Bellingham, Washington
V7J 1H1	98225

CONTENTS

SAMPLES

ACKNOWLEDGMENTS

We wish to express our thanks to the following people who gave their support and assistance during the preparation of this book:

To Ruth Wilson at Self-Counsel Press, who gave us so much helpful advice and encouragement during the early stages of the manuscript.

To Ken Bridgman of Bridgman and Durksen, Chartered Accountants, St. Catharines, Ontario, who kindly agreed to review the financial chapters.

To our fellow bed and breakfast operators, who were always ready to share their knowledge and their expertise.

And finally to our customers, who put up with our mistakes and, ultimately, became our friends.

INTRODUCTION

Have you ever thought about operating your own bed and breakfast? Perhaps you have just taken early retirement and want to run a small business to supplement your pension. Or you may have family obligations that keep you at home and you are looking for a home-based source of income. Maybe you have stayed at a B & B and were attracted to the lifestyle of the owner. If you already live in a tourist area, you are ideally situated to cash in on the passing trade, and if you like talking to people, you probably have the right type of temperament to become a successful B & B host. If you have a nice home and one or two extra bedrooms, why not give it a try? We did!

We took early retirement and purchased an old Victorian home in a small tourist town. We quickly realized that we were in an ideal spot to open a B & B but we didn't know how to start. We looked in libraries and bookstores for a how-to book, but there weren't any. We talked to a few B & B operators, but they all had different points of view. In the end, we opened for business not fully understanding how to proceed, and we were blissfully unaware of the many pitfalls and problems that we would face. We wasted time, energy, and money, and we learned the trade by trial and error. Thank goodness we had forgiving guests that put up with our mistakes, and some of them even offered helpful suggestions and gentle encouragement.

After our first year in business, we realized how simple the whole process would have been if we could have hired an experienced B & B operator to guide us. As we gained expertise and confidence, many of our guests began to ask advice on how they could start their own B & B. In response to this evident need, we decided to write a book for anyone who was thinking of starting a B & B business.

Operating a bed and breakfast can be a very interesting career and it can be financially rewarding. For most people the start-up cost is within reason, since they can use their existing home. But if you are thinking about starting a B & B, you owe it to yourself to investigate all the pros and cons and to consider all the implications before you proceed. After you have read this book, you will have a thorough understanding of the B & B trade, you will have assessed your skills as a potential B & B host, and you will have calculated the dollars needed to start your business.

With your enthusiasm and our help, we know that you will become a very successful B & B host. Recipes for some of our own house specialties precede each chapter: enjoy!

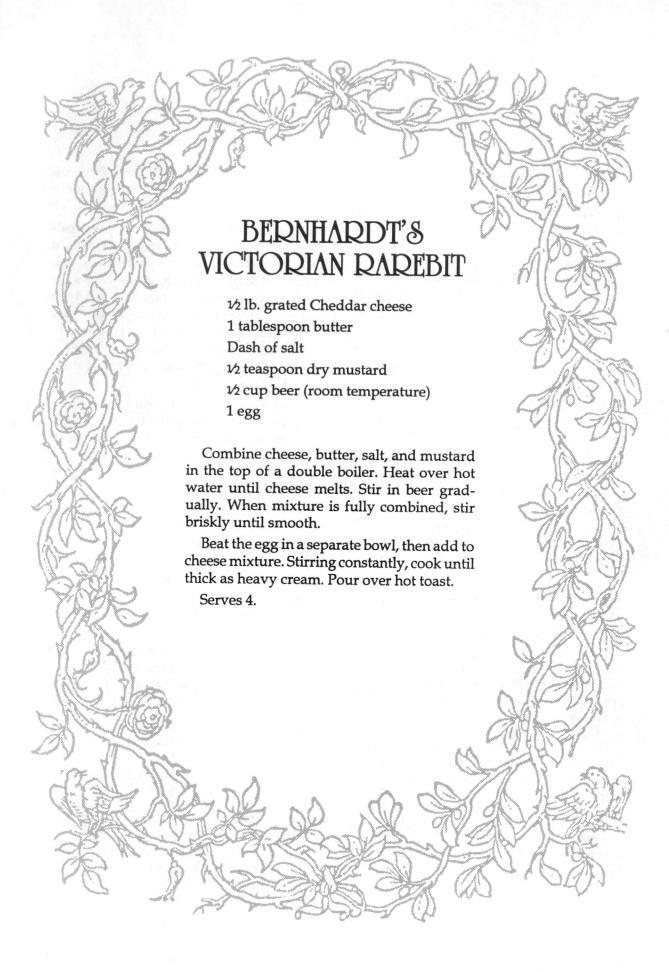

BERNHARDT'S VICTORIAN RAREBIT

½ lb. grated Cheddar cheese

1 tablespoon butter

Dash of salt

½ teaspoon dry mustard

½ cup beer (room temperature)

1 egg

Combine cheese, butter, salt, and mustard in the top of a double boiler. Heat over hot water until cheese melts. Stir in beer gradually. When mixture is fully combined, stir briskly until smooth.

Beat the egg in a separate bowl, then add to cheese mixture. Stirring constantly, cook until thick as heavy cream. Pour over hot toast.

Serves 4.

1

THE BUSINESS OF BED AND BREAKFAST

a. WHAT IS BED AND BREAKFAST?

Bed and breakfast (B & B) has its roots in ancient times. In parts of the countryside where public inns were not always available, weary travelers would be accommodated by a local family who would provide food and lodging for a fee.

B & Bs have been popular in Britain and Europe for many years, but only recently have they gained wide acceptance in North America as a legitimate and popular type of accommodation.

The modern B & B provides the same type of environment as its ancient counterpart. The emphasis is on hospitality in a family setting. The visitor is greeted by the host and is given overnight accommodation in one of the spare bedrooms. In the morning, the visitor usually joins the host family for a leisurely breakfast and social conversation. The breakfast menu varies from house to house, but guests are offered selection and quality. The cost is usually less than comparable accommodation in a hotel or motel, especially when the price of the breakfast is included.

Because of the increased popularity of B & Bs, a range of services are now offered in the name of bed and breakfast. Most of them are legitimate, but some vary greatly from the original concept of this special type of accommodation.

The following are brief descriptions of different establishments that may call themselves B & Bs.

1. Private homes

The true B & B falls into this category, and it usually consists of a home situated in a residential area with one or two family members running the business. Spare bedrooms are set aside for guests and breakfast is served by the hosts.

From the guest's point of view, the emphasis is on visiting a local family, enjoying their companionship, and sharing their home. Meals other than breakfast may or may not be available.

2. Family-run operations

Family-run establishments consist of small lodges or inns that are owned and operated by a host family. The hosts live on site and might join the guests for breakfast. Although these establishments are operated on a larger scale, they can provide an alternative to a private home, but guests should not expect the same level of interaction with the host family. Additional meals may or may not be served.

3. Commercial operations

Larger commercial establishments consist of blocks of apartment suites, cabins, motels, or hotels. The owners usually don't live on site, and there is no interaction with a host family. All these operations have some form of lobby or front desk, where the visitor checks in and out. Breakfast can vary from coffee and muffins available in the lobby to a prepared breakfast in a coffee shop.

These establishments actively advertise themselves as B & Bs in order to attract that part of the marketplace, and although they do, technically, provide a bed and a breakfast, they do not offer the friendly family environment that gives a true B & B its unique appeal.

4. Other variations

There are a number of other variations of B & B that don't seem to fall into any particular category. They offer a variety of unusual sleeping accommodations followed by a fairly standard breakfast. Houseboats, camping trailers, recreational vehicles, and tents have all been offered as B & Bs.

b. TAKE A LOOK AT YOUR COMPETITORS

If you are thinking about opening your own B & B, you have probably stayed at a few establishments and have your own ideas of what you would like to do to make yours unique. It's a good idea to explore other B & Bs to share ideas with other hosts or just to see how others have set up shop.

If you want to find out more about other B & Bs, the following references will be helpful. You will also want to consider having your own B & B listed or advertised in one or more of these publications.

1. Government publications

Free pamphlets listing B & Bs or reservation services are available from most government tourist offices. A list of tourist offices along with the titles of their B & B brochures is provided in Appendix 1.

2. Bed-and-breakfast guide books

There are numerous guide books that provide detailed descriptions and sometimes pictures of B & Bs. Specific features of each home are pointed out, and a coding system tells you what services are available and what restrictions may apply (e.g., no smoking or no children under 12).

Book stores and libraries generally carry a large selection of bed-and-breakfast guide books, which are regularly updated and revised. Appendix 2 provides a list of guide books covering Canada and the United States.

3. Reservation services

Reservation services act on behalf of groups of B & B hosts and match a customer's requirements to one of the homes registered with the service. Each B & B pays an annual membership fee to be listed with the reservation service, which will actively seek customers for their members by advertising in government brochures, travel publications, newspapers, etc. Most reservation services will inspect each B & B to ensure a certain standard is maintained.

There are two general types of reservation services available: booking agencies and B & B associations.

A booking agency does *all* the reservation tasks on behalf of its members. The agency will record the visitor's name, address, telephone number, and estimated time of arrival. Some agencies will collect a room deposit or guarantee the reservation by credit card. Many of them will arrange restaurant or theater ticket reservations as well. B & Bs are usually charged a fee for each room booked through an agency.

B & B associations are composed of individual operators who have collected together to promote business by focusing on some common service. They may all be located in a specific area, or they may have a common type of customer (e.g., hunters, hikers, canoers, etc). These associations will match a customer's requirements to one of their members, but it is up to the traveler to contact the B & B directly to make reservations and deposit payments.

4. Other sources

To assist travelers in locating B & Bs there are a number of other sources of information:

(a) Chambers of commerce often have listings of local B & Bs. Some of them also provide reservation services.

(b) Tourist information centers may provide help locating B & Bs. Many of these centers are operated by government personnel who have access to the government publications mentioned previously.

(c) Private advertising is conducted by many B & B operators. They distribute business cards and brochures to various tourist locations, and they often advertise in selected magazines or tourist attraction pamphlets.

(d) Signs identifying B & Bs are permitted in some municipalities. Signs are usually located directly outside each establishment. In areas that have stricter bylaws, there may be a small, inconspicuous logo attached to the front of the building.

(e) Word of mouth is considered the best form of advertising, and it is an excellent way to find out about good quality B & Bs in a particular area. It is very reassuring to have a personal endorsement from another guest.

c. WHO ARE THE B & B CUSTOMERS?

The prevailing attitude in western culture over the last 40 years has been "more is better." As we all strived to acquire more wealth and more possessions, and as we succumbed to the images of success that advertisers would have us accept as "normal," we set ourselves unrealistic and sometimes unattainable goals. In striving for these goals, we have wasted our resources, polluted our environment, and sacrificed quality time with our loved ones, our friends, and our fellow citizens.

Fortunately, these attitudes are changing; many of us now recognize that our resources need to be managed, our environment needs protection, and people need to be the top priority in any civilized society. Many people now search for "quality in life" rather than "quantity in life." These people are interested in community involvement, the search for their historical roots, and the general pursuit of the arts. It is from these people with a new outlook that B & Bs draw many of their customers.

Many travelers are tired of staying in look-alike hotel or motel rooms. They seek out the friendlier atmosphere of a home, and they are interested in meeting local people and sharing in a family environment. They often are looking for a B & B host that has similar interests to them, such as a fellow antique collector, gardening enthusiast, or craftsperson. Some customers are attracted to a particular style of accommodation, such as an historic home in a small village, a townhouse close to the center of a large city, or a farmhouse in the peaceful countryside. Some visitors seek the companionship of a particular culture or language. Whatever the requirements of the traveler, they can be met by the diverse variety of B & B homes now operating across North America.

d. CAN YOU OPERATE A B & B?

The vast majority of B & Bs are conducted from existing residential homes, and there are no "rules" about who may run one. Any adult member of the family can take it upon him or herself to operate a B & B as long as local zoning and licensing bylaws are complied with. There is such a wide variety of people running B & B establishments that it would be impossible to document them all, but the following list shows some of the more common operators:

(a) Homemakers

(b) Widows or widowers

(c) Adults caring for a family member

(d) Retired people

(e) People seeking a career change

Larger B & Bs usually require the full-time attention of couples or even entire families. In addition, they often hire employees to help ease the workload.

Of course, you must genuinely like people and be prepared for the type of work required in running a B & B. The attributes necessary for success are explored in chapter 2.

e. HOW WILL THIS BOOK HELP YOU?

With the increase in demand for this type of accommodation, there has been a corresponding increase in the number of people converting their homes to a B & B operation. Some of these new businesses have succeeded, but many have not. The lack of proper planning, the absence of reliable reference material, and the risk of doing business by trial and error, prove too much for many new operators.

If you are contemplating starting your own B & B, this book will get you started and keep you going successfully. Each chapter has been organized to represent one step of a complete start-up plan. As you progress through each step and each chapter, you will develop your own plan for your unique B & B. Information from each chapter is used in the following chapters to gradually build the total start-up plan, so be sure to work through the book in the order presented.

We follow a "case study" of an imaginary couple, Carol and Bob Morris, who are preparing to start a B & B. This couple encounter and conquer the same problems that you will face as you try to start your business, and we use information they gather to develop sample business forms and cost sheets — the same forms that you will need to complete in preparing your plan. Blank, tear-out worksheets are included at the back of the book. You may photocopy these forms as needed for your personal use. The forms shown are actual examples used by existing B & Bs and their usefulness has been tested through experience.

We have included helpful tips from our own experience and from other B & B operators — tips that will steer you away from potential pitfalls. As well, reference material is included to keep your business on track during its initial years.

Ultimately, your success as a bed-and-breakfast operator is up to you, but using this book will greatly reduce the amount of trial and error you will have to suffer in those first exciting but difficult months.

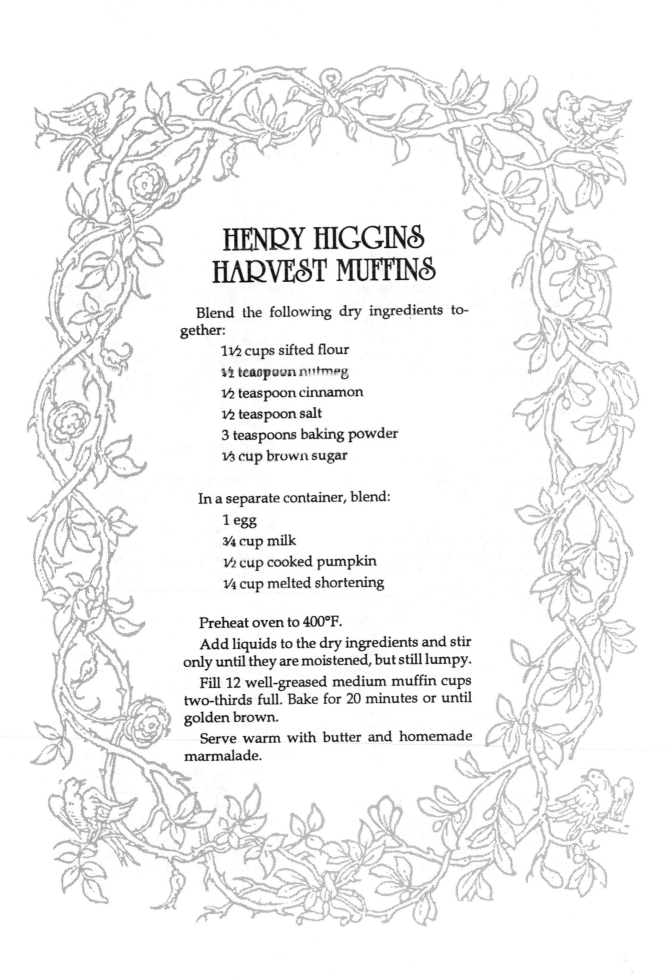

HENRY HIGGINS HARVEST MUFFINS

Blend the following dry ingredients to-gether:

1½ cups sifted flour

½ teaspoon nutmeg

½ teaspoon cinnamon

½ teaspoon salt

3 teaspoons baking powder

⅓ cup brown sugar

In a separate container, blend:

1 egg

¾ cup milk

½ cup cooked pumpkin

¼ cup melted shortening

Preheat oven to 400°F.

Add liquids to the dry ingredients and stir only until they are moistened, but still lumpy.

Fill 12 well-greased medium muffin cups two-thirds full. Bake for 20 minutes or until golden brown.

Serve warm with butter and homemade marmalade.

2

BECOMING A BED AND BREAKFAST HOST

There are both advantages and disadvantages to operating a B & B, and if you want to be successful, you need to be aware of both. This chapter explores those advantages and disadvantages as well as the personal qualities and skills that are most desirable in a B & B host. We then provide you with a method of measuring your own skills and show you how to create an "action plan" to improve those skills.

a. ADVANTAGES

There are many advantages to starting a B & B. Some of them relate to running your own business generally, and some to the unique nature of a B & B.

(a) *Be your own boss:* You have complete control over all work-related activities. You can decide when to take a day off, when to go on vacation, or whether to shut down for a season. You also get to set your own working standards and don't have to answer to anyone else (acknowledging, of course, certain minimum standards set by municipalities and health authorities).

(b) *Earn extra money:* The extra revenue earned through a B & B can be a powerful incentive, and it can provide a meaningful contribution to a family's income.

(c) *Gain a tax advantage:* A B & B can produce considerable tax advantages by allowing a wide range of deductions for business expenses including a portion of your house expenses.

(d) *Work at home:* As a B & B host, you work in your home. You eliminate the need to battle heavy traffic or bad weather in order to reach your workplace, which allows you to begin your day in a more relaxed frame of mind.

(e) *More family time:* A B & B business allows you to spend more time at home, which can be very important if you have young children or if you are caring for a family member at home.

(f) *Continue other interests:* By conducting your business at home, you have the opportunity to continue other interests during the day. For example, you may have an existing home-based business that can be blended with your B & B business, or you may have a craft or hobby that can be carried on in conjunction with your B & B enterprise.

(g) *Meet new people:* B & B hosts meet many diverse and interesting people. This can be a very rewarding experience, particularly for hosts who live alone. Sharing your hospitality with your guests can result in many personal and business benefits.

(h) *Choose your customers:* B & B hosts can specify the type of customer that they accept into their home. A host that speaks one particular language may decide to accept only visitors who can speak that language. A female host who lives alone may decide to accept only female guests or family groups.

b. DISADVANTAGES

Just as there are many advantages to being a B & B host, there are some disadvantages that should be considered.

(a) *Less family privacy:* Conducting business inside your home makes it more difficult to separate family from business. Some guests may require your assistance during family time, so you need to organize your home and business operations to minimize these problems. You also need your family's full support if you are to be successful.

(b) *Work load:* Running a B & B requires extra effort in addition to your regular household duties. You must prepare and serve additional meals, and bed linen needs to be changed and washed after each guest has checked out. All areas that are used by your guests require a higher-than-normal level of housekeeping.

(c) *Repetition:* There is a lot of repetition to the work involved in running a B & B. Every morning that you have guests you must rise early to prepare and serve breakfast. Every day you must clean effectively and quickly. Your client and business records will need daily updating. You must be prepared for these daily routines without exception.

(d) *Income fluctuations:* Depending on the traffic pattern of visitors to your area, you could experience sporadic or seasonal fluctuations in the income derived from your business. If you are relying on this extra income, keep these variations in mind.

c. SKILLS AND QUALITIES THAT BEST SUIT THE JOB

For the moment, let's visualize the "perfect" B & B hosts. Below is a list of the most desirable skills and personal qualities that these imaginary hosts would possess. This list is *not* in order of importance because all these skills are equally important. Don't get discouraged when you read this list — remember these are "perfect" hosts, and nobody is perfect.

(a) Friendly: Perfect hosts are very friendly and always smiling. They have a natural love of people, and they are relaxed and at ease with strangers. They welcome each and every guest as if they were old friends.

(b) Tolerant: Perfect hosts show compassion for their guests' problems. They are tolerant of race and religion and open minded and flexible in providing for their guests' comfort.

(c) Clean: Perfect hosts exhibit acceptable dress code, good grooming, and excellent personal hygiene. Their house exhibits outstanding cleanliness in all areas, but particularly in guest bedrooms, bathrooms, and dining areas.

(d) Diplomatic: Perfect hosts are courteous and tactful when talking to guests. They are peacemakers by nature, but if a guest's behavior needs to be addressed, they are firm but fair.

(e) Hospitable: When perfect hosts start their day, they are "on stage." They forget all their own troubles and concentrate on providing the highest level of hospitality possible. They anticipate the needs of their guests and proceed accordingly. They serve meals that feature high quality, variety, and eye appeal.

(f) Organized: Perfect hosts are very well organized and conduct their business efficiently, using thoughtfully prepared operating procedures. Their client and business records are well organized, accurate, and neat.

(g) Prepared: Perfect hosts are prepared for all emergencies. They have medical and fire procedures in place, and they are able to carry out those procedures in a calm and orderly manner. In addition, they have back-up plans for operating problems such as power outages, etc.

(h) Communicators: Perfect hosts have excellent verbal and written communication skills. They have systems in place to encourage good communication between them and their customers. They are good listeners.

(i) Informative: Perfect hosts are very well informed about local matters including history of the area, local events, tourist attractions, retail shops, and restaurants. They keep available current copies of all train, bus, and plane schedules.

(j) Motivated: Perfect hosts are self-starters and achievers, and they often set themselves goals and deadlines. They get satisfaction and enjoyment from operating their B & B.

(k) Hard workers: Perfect hosts have excellent work ethics, and they tackle extra duties and work routines with enthusiasm. They maintain their work ethic through proper diet and adequate rest. Their standards are very high, and they maintain those standards.

The skills and qualities that perfect hosts possess help them be successful. These are the same skills and qualities that you should aim for as you plan your own B & B. You may not be able to achieve the same level of perfection as our imaginary hosts, but if you use them as a target — something to aim at — you can greatly improve your chances of success.

d. SKILL ASSESSMENT

1. Why do a skill assessment?

Successful businesses know the value of assessing the skills of their employees. They use the information to target employee training so that their business can continue to grow. As future B & B operators, you will need to document all the skills you will bring to your new business. If other people are going to support you in the running of your B & B, their skills should also be assessed. By doing a skills assessment during the planning stages, you will be able to identify any areas that require improvement.

Nobody is skilled in all aspects of running a B & B. As we said before, nobody is perfect, but if everyone involved in the running of your B & B pools their skills, the overall results can be very good.

In certain highly specialized areas, such as accounting or legal matters, you may decide to seek outside assistance from professionals. You may need them for some start-up advice, or you might want to retain them steadily for continuing help.

Carol and Bob have decided to run their B & B as a team, and since both of them will be sharing the duties, each completed an assessment worksheet separately so that neither influenced the other. Sample #1 shows a completed skill assessment for Carol.

Once they had independently answered all the questions, they looked for any statements they had marked "no." They then transferred their N answers into the Team columns on Carol's worksheet, opposite those statements. See the Team column on Carol's worksheet in Sample #1.

2. Do your own skill assessment

The results of Carol and Bob's assessment are discussed below, but before examining them, take the time now to complete your own skill assessment by completing Worksheet A in Appendix 3 at the back of this book. There are three copies provided, one for each partner and one for the final, common form. If more than two people are going to participate, you should photocopy the form and distribute one copy to each person. It is better to work individually on

SKILL GROUP	SKILL STATEMENTS	Carol No	Carol Yes	TEAM Carol	TEAM Bob
FRIENDLINESS	You prefer to be around people.	☐	☒		
	You enjoy talking to strangers.	☐	☒		
	You usually speak first.	☐	☒		N
	You are always ready to smile.	☐	☒		
TOLERANCE	You tolerate all age groups.	☐	☒		
	You tolerate religions & races.	☐	☒		
	You are open minded and flexible.	☐	☒		
	You help people in distress.	☐	☒		
CLEANLINESS	You are a tidy person.	☐	☒		
	You don't mind housework.	☐	☒		N
	You have good personal hygiene.	☐	☒		
	You are always well groomed.	☐	☒		N
DIPLOMACY	You seldom lose your temper.	☐	☒		
	You can accept criticism.	☐	☒		
	You are a peacemaker.	☐	☒		
	You can be firm if necessary.	☒	☐	N	
HOSPITALITY	You like to entertain guests.	☐	☒		
	You anticipate their needs.	☐	☒		
	You seldom moan and groan.	☐	☒		
	You are a good cook.	☐	☒		N
ORGANIZATION	You like to be organized	☒	☐	N	
	You like to make lists.	☒	☐	N	
	You like record keeping.	☒	☐	N	N
	You like to work with figures.	☒	☐	N	N
PREPARATION	You plan for emergencies.	☒	☐	N	
	You know First Aid and C.P.R.	☒	☐	N	
	You can put out a grease fire.	☐	☒		
	You act calmly in an emergency.	☒	☐	N	
COMMUNICATION	You think before you speak.	☒	☐	N	
	You speak clearly.	☐	☒		
	You are a good listener.	☐	☒		
	You enjoy letter writing.	☐	☒		
INFORMATION	You are interested in history.	☒	☐	N	
	You know your area businesses.	☐	☒		
	You are aware of local events.	☐	☒		
	You know public transportation.	☐	☒		N
MOTIVATION	You are a self starter.	☐	☒		
	You set goals & deadlines.	☐	☒		
	You always meet those goals.	☒	☐	N	
	You want to operate a B & B.	☐	☒		
WORK ETHIC	You don't mind hard work.	☐	☒		
	You don't mind extra duties.	☐	☒		
	You are in good health.	☐	☒		
	You maintain high standards.	☐	☒		

the assessment, so that your answers are not influenced by anyone else. When all team members have participated, you can mark the individual N votes onto a common form under the "Team" column.

Remember the rules:

(a) Study each statement carefully.

(b) If you mostly agree, put a Y under the Yes column.

(c) If you mostly disagree, put an N under the No column.

(d) If you are part of a team, transfer your N votes to a common worksheet after you have each completed your individual forms.

Be absolutely honest in your answers. Don't try to hide your feelings. All of us have strengths and weaknesses, and we wouldn't be human without them. By recognizing your likes and dislikes, and by determining how strongly you feel about each of them, you will be in a better position to identify the skills that you already possess, and the ones that require improvement.

e. ACTION PLAN TO IMPROVE YOUR SKILLS

1. Analyzing the skills assessment

By referring to Carol and Bob's skill assessment in Sample #1, you can analyze the results of the team by examining the collective results. As a team, Carol and Bob have a high level of skill in areas such as friendliness, tolerance, diplomacy, hospitality, communications, motivation, and work ethic. These are all excellent qualities to have when running a B & B.

Both Carol and Bob need to make an effort to improve certain skills to achieve their true potential as good B & B hosts. Whatever they answered *no* to on their individual assessments requires improvement. As a team, they need some improvement in cleanliness, preparation, and information. The skill group that needs the most improvement is organization, which involves preparing operating procedures and setting up client and business records. Because they are operating as a team, Carol and Bob may decide to assign bookkeeping to only one member of the team. This would release the other to concentrate on other aspects of the business.

Sample #2 shows an action plan for Bob. He took all the skill statements that he personally marked as *no* and wrote them down on his action plan under the heading "Statements Needing Improvement." He then thought about the steps he could take to improve those skills, and he wrote those down under the heading "Action Plan For Improvement." Carol completed her own action plan, and together they worked to improve their skills.

2. Make your own action plan

Now create your own action plan by completing Worksheet B in Appendix 3. (Two copies are provided; make photocopies if you need more.) Write down the skill statements that you need to improve based on your own skill assessment. Then write down your action plan for improving each of those skills.

Refer to your action plan regularly to monitor your progress, and when you feel that you have conquered a skill, strike it off your list.

STATEMENTS NEEDING IMPROVEMENT	ACTION PLAN FOR IMPROVEMENT
1. You usually speak first (to strangers).	Strike up conversations with strangers whenever possible.
2. You don't mind housework.	Start doing some of the repetitive household cleaning jobs.
3. You are always well groomed.	Buy a good pair of workpants t shirt. Upgrade my wardrobe.
4. You are a good cook	Start cooking breakfast
5. You like record keeping	Start to keep detailed records of all house and car repairs.
6. You like to work with figures	Buy a calculator t learn how to use it. Make a household budget.
7. You know public transportation	Obtain all train, bus, and plane schedules. List all taxi
8.	companies and their phone numbers.
9.	
10.	
11.	
12.	

"APPLE CART" APPLE BUTTER

10 lbs. apples
4 lbs. brown sugar
6 quarts apple cider
2 tablespoons cinnamon
2 tablespoons ground cloves
2 tablespoons allspice

Core and quarter apples, but do not peel. Boil apples in the cider until soft.

Remove apples and force through a seive back into the cider.

Add spices and brown sugar. Stir constantly and continue to cook until the mixture reaches a thick consistency.

Bottle, store, and serve like jam.

3

MARKET RESEARCH

You have now completed your skill assessment and you are ready to tackle the planning process for the B & B itself. Your first step is to research your market carefully. As you read through this chapter, take the time to study the examples and complete all the corresponding worksheets in Appendix 3. Don't rush through this very important chapter because the information you gather here will influence many other decisions later.

a. WHY DO MARKET RESEARCH?

You may have specific ideas about who will come to your B & B and what facilities will attract them, but your ideas need to be backed up by solid market research. Your customers may be attracted to your locale because of tourist attractions, such as historical sites or theater festivals, or they may be seeking a relaxing weekend "get-away." The reputation of the B & B itself is also important (although it usually takes some time to build up the kind of reputation that attracts customers to your B & B by name alone).

It is in your best interest to do market research *before* you open for business, otherwise you may be trying to attract customers who do not exist, or you may be offering facilities and services that are not in demand.

You need to collect enough information to answer the following four basic questions:

(a) What attracts visitors to your area?

(b) How many of these visitors are potential B & B customers?

(c) What facilities and services do they want?

(d) What local competition do you face?

When you have answered these questions, you will have completed your market research. Keep a record of all costs encountered during your research and keep all your receipts; you will be documenting these costs at the end of this chapter.

b. SOURCES OF INFORMATION

Since you are contemplating a tourist-oriented business, you will be happy to know that there is a huge amount of information available. Most of this material is produced by various levels of government that are always trying to capture a larger piece of the lucrative tourist trade. To obtain market research information on your particular area, the following sources are suggested:

(a) Provincial or state government travel offices.

- Travel brochures
- Accommodation listings (see list in Appendix 1)
- Provincial or state tourist studies

(b) Municipal government offices

- Local tourist studies
- Seasonal visitor patterns
- Traffic studies

(c) Chamber of commerce

- Local business statistics
- Tourist services available
- Accommodations available

(d) Nearby tourist attractions

- Attendance records
- Types of visitors
- Operating season

(e) Local B & B associations

- Local competition
- Styles of accommodation
- Tariff structures

(f) B & B guide books (see list in Appendix 2)

- Styles of accommodations
- Tariff structures
- Services offered

(g) B & B reservation services

- Listing and booking fees charged
- Tariff structures
- Average bookings placed in your area

(h) Brochures from local B & Bs

- Types of accommodation
- Tariff structures
- Meals provided
- Services provided

(i) Brochures from local hotels, motels, inns, lodges

- Types of accommodation
- Tariff structure
- Services provided

c. WHAT TOURIST ATTRACTIONS ARE IN YOUR AREA?

A considerable number of customers to your bed and breakfast home will be visitors to one of the local tourist attractions in your area. It is useful, therefore, to do a survey of these attractions so that you will have a better understanding of the length of stay, the age range, and the interests of these visitors. You will also be able to determine the specific months of the year when people are most likely to travel through your area.

1. The tourist attraction survey

Sample #3 shows Carol and Bob's completed tourist attraction survey. Let's review each section of the sample:

(a) The first column shows the name of the local attraction (and any further comments needed to clarify the nature of the attraction), the distance to the attraction from your B & B, and the gate total, or yearly attendance record, for the attraction.

(b) The second, third, and fourth columns define your target customers. They indicate how long the average visitor would spend at this attraction, the age group most likely to attend, and the range of interests of the customers to that particular attraction. When answering some of these questions on your own attraction survey, you will have to use your own judgment unless the attraction has published statistics available.

(c) Visitor patterns indicates the operating season of each attraction and shows the number of days in each month that the attraction is open for business. For the sake of simplicity, consider each month to have 30 days (including 4 weekends).

2. Do your own tourist attraction survey

Complete Worksheet C provided in Appendix 3 to do your own tourist attraction survey. Phone or visit each attraction in your area and get their descriptive brochures, information on their operating season, and their yearly attendance figures.

When you select local attractions for your survey, start with the one closest to your B & B and move geographically outward from there. It is more likely that the closer attractions will provide the most customers for your business.

SAMPLE #3
TOURIST ATTRACTION SURVEY

LOCAL ATTRACTION NAME / DISTANCE & GATE TOTAL	TARGET CUSTOMERS		
	LENGTH OF STAY	AGE RANGES	INTERESTS
1. Bell Theatre (live performance) Distance 1/4 mile Gate Total 200,000	Few Hours ☒ / Day Tour ☐ / Overnight ☐ / Long Stay ☐	Children ☐ / Teenagers ☐ / Adults ☒ / Elderly ☒	Sporting ☐ / Artistic ☒ / Cultural ☒ / General ☐
2. Yacht Club (large boats) Distance 1/4 mile Gate Total 1,000	Few Hours ☐ / Day Tour ☐ / Overnight ☒ / Long Stay ☐	Children ☐ / Teenagers ☐ / Adults ☒ / Elderly ☒	Sporting ☒ / Artistic ☐ / Cultural ☐ / General ☐
3. Fort Penn (historic site) Distance 1 mile Gate Total 100,000	Few Hours ☒ / Day Tour ☒ / Overnight ☐ / Long Stay ☐	Children ☒ / Teenagers ☒ / Adults ☒ / Elderly ☒	Sporting ☐ / Artistic ☐ / Cultural ☒ / General ☒
4. Pine Park (day use only) Distance 3 miles Gate Total 200,000	Few Hours ☐ / Day Tour ☒ / Overnight ☐ / Long Stay ☐	Children ☒ / Teenagers ☒ / Adults ☒ / Elderly ☒	Sporting ☒ / Artistic ☐ / Cultural ☐ / General ☒
5. Ship Canal (lift locks) Distance 5 miles Gate Total 200,000	Few Hours ☒ / Day Tour ☐ / Overnight ☐ / Long Stay ☐	Children ☒ / Teenagers ☒ / Adults ☒ / Elderly ☒	Sporting ☐ / Artistic ☐ / Cultural ☐ / General ☒
6. Long Beach (swimming/picnics) Distance 6 miles Gate Total 400,000	Few Hours ☐ / Day Tour ☒ / Overnight ☐ / Long Stay ☐	Children ☒ / Teenagers ☒ / Adults ☒ / Elderly ☒	Sporting ☒ / Artistic ☐ / Cultural ☐ / General ☐

VISITOR PATTERNS TO LOCAL ATTRACTIONS
OPERATING DAYS

LOCAL ATTRACTIONS	Jan	Feb	Mar	Apr	May	Jun	Jul	Aug	Sep	Oct	Nov	Dec
1. Bell Theatre					15	30	30	30	15			
2. Yacht Club					15	30	30	30	15			
3. Fort Penn					15	30	30	30	30	15		
4. Pine Park			30	30	30	30	30	30	30	30		
5. Ship Canal				30	30	30	30	30	30	30		
6. Long Beach						30	30	30	15			

Make sure you fill in the operating day patterns for each attraction. We suggest that you survey no more than six attractions. As with all the completed worksheets, keep your tourist survey close at hand for future reference.

d. KNOW YOUR POTENTIAL CUSTOMERS

1. Who are your potential customers?

No matter how many tourists your area attracts, not all of them will be potential customers for your B & B. You need to separate potential customers from unlikely customers by researching how people visit your area. For example, if you live in a popular tourist area with annual summer festivals, arts celebrations, etc., the potential for customers throughout the high tourist season is greater. If, however, you live off the beaten track, your customers may be more likely to be weekend "getaway" seekers.

Review the following list of unlikely customers and remove them from your plan for your potential market. Then review the list of potential customers and keep the variety in mind when you are thinking about attracting clientele to your B & B.

Unlikely customers:

(a) Organized tours with pre-planned itineraries and standard hotel arrangements

(b) Sightseers who spend a few hours only in each location and then move on

(c) Day-trippers who spend the day in your area but do not require overnight accommodation

(d) Campers who bring their own sleeping quarters so they don't need your accommodation

(e) High rollers who are looking for action and are attracted to luxury hotels with fitness clubs, tennis courts, and other amenities

Potential customers:

(a) Families who are looking for a home environment that can provide safe and friendly accommodations for their children

(b) Single parents who are looking for a similar home environment and who welcome the extra support that a friendly host family can provide

(c) Business travelers who are looking for a comfortable rest and a good home-cooked meal — usually in a downtown location

(d) Women travelers who are looking for safety and security and who appreciate the added protection of a family setting

(e) People traveling alone who enjoy the companionship of a B & B

(f) Retired people who have plenty of time to travel and to pursue their interests and who often seek the less-hurried atmosphere of a B & B

(g) People pursuing a particular sport or hobby who are looking for facilities that can cater to their particular needs

(h) People attending cultural attractions who enjoy the study of history, science, or the arts, and who are seeking the company of hosts who appreciate those values

(i) Professional people who are looking for clean and comfortable surroundings, friendly hosts, and interesting conversation

(j) People visiting local friends or family who need nearby accommodations

(k) Personal friends and "friends of friends" who want to visit you

(l) People who have heard about your B & B either through word-of-mouth or written advertising

As well as all those listed above, you should include any other local visitors you think would be potential customers. Each local area has a different mix of visitors and accommodations. Your B & B may attract other types of customers not mentioned here.

2. What facilities and services do your customers want?

Once you have determined your potential customers, you need to carefully consider what each type of customer is looking for in accommodation. You can do this by completing a customer survey for each type of potential customer you anticipate accommodating. Sample #4 shows how Carol and Bob completed a customer survey for families with young children.

Let's review each section of Sample #4:

(a) Beside potential customer, Carol and Bob have indicated they are considering families with young children. They have noted the age range as 1 to 40 because young children could be defined as 1 to 10 years, and parents could be 18 to 40 (approximately). This statistic is useful when thinking about the facilities and services that this type of customer might want.

(b) Customer availability indicates the monthly visiting pattern normally expected for this type of customer and the reasons for this pattern. You may get this information from existing statistical data or you can give your best estimate based on common sense and a knowledge of your own area. For the sake of simplicity, consider each month to have 30 days (including 4 weekends).

(c) Booking days available indicates the total days in any one year that you could reasonably expect to book this type of customer. Add the estimated days for each month to get this figure.

(d) Actual number shows the number of this type of customer that visit your

area in any one year. You may get this figure from existing tourist statistics; however, an actual number is often difficult to obtain. Personal observations of the types and volume of tourists in your local area may provide you with an estimate of the percentage of tourists that fall into this category. If you cannot obtain this figure, leave the space blank. Carol and Bob estimated that there are about 1,200 families with young children visiting the area each year.

(e) Overnight facilities needed are the furnishings and room arrangements normally required by this type of customer, specifically bedrooms and bathrooms. Imagine that you are a young family who has just arrived at overnight accommodations. What facilities and services would you like to have?

(f) Food services include the variety of food, serving facilities, equipment, and refreshments required. In Sample #4, Bob and Carol have included a bottle warmer and high chair for the convenience of families with infants.

(g) Other facilities needed is where any extra facilities or services needed for this type of customer should be listed. Bob and Carol's B & B would probably need a play area and children's games, for example.

(h) Preferred attractions can be determined by referring to your tourist attraction survey. Transfer those attractions that would appeal to this type of customer from your tourist survey onto your customer survey form. In Sample #4, Carol and Bob circled 3, 4, 5, and 6.

Now do your own customer survey by using Worksheet D in Appendix 3. We have provided two copies of this form, but you should photocopy as many as you need, so that you can fill one out for each type of potential customer that visits your local area.

SAMPLE #4
CUSTOMER SURVEY FORM

Potential Customer **Family with young children** Age Range **1 to 40**

CUSTOMER AVAILABILITY

Month	Est. Days	Reasons for Estimate of Days
January	—	Bad weather
February	—	Children at school
March	—	Parents at work
April	—	
May	6	Better weekend weather
June	20	
July	30	Summer holidays
August	30	
September	6	Occasional weekend
October	—	
November	—	Deteriorating weather
December	—	

Booking Days Avail. **92** Actual No. **1,200**

OVERNIGHT FACILITIES NEEDED

	REASONS
King, queen, or double bed	Parents
Twin beds or rollout cots	Children
Crib	Baby
Small step stool	Children at sink
Covered waste basket	Diapers

FOOD SERVICES NEEDED

	REASONS
Adult and children's menu	Parents and children
High chair	Baby
Bottle warmer	Baby
Non-breakable glasses	Safety
Pack picnic lunch	Next day

OTHER FACILITIES NEEDED

	REASONS
Safe play area + games	Children
Common sitting area	Family get-togethers
Babysitting service	Parents' night out
Info. on family attractions	Next day

PREFERRED ATTRACTIONS   1.   2.   ③   ④   ⑤   ⑥

It is very important that you gather statistics on all types of potential customers. Don't restrict your list to those types that you personally prefer. You should survey your total potential customer base so that you will have all the necessary information to make informed decisions in the next chapter.

Keep all completed copies of your customer surveys for future reference.

e. KNOW YOUR COMPETITION

One essential market research task is to study your competition. Take a look at existing establishments already offering accommodation and meals to your potential customers. By knowing what your competition is and is not doing, you will be able to design a more competitive B & B.

1. Other B & Bs

The majority of your direct competition will come from any existing B & Bs close to you. If you are in the countryside, the distance of direct competition will probably be many miles in all directions. If you are in a small town, the town boundaries will mark out your area of direct competition. In very large cities, you need to look at existing B & Bs within your own neighborhood.

2. Local small inns

Small, family-run inns or lodges will also compete directly with your B & B because they offer many of the same attractions. For the purpose of your market survey, consider any inn or lodge with ten rooms or less to be classed as small. Larger inns and lodges should be classed as commercial establishments.

3. Local commercial establishments

Commercial establishments are defined as large blocks of apartment suites or cabins, large inns and lodges, and hotels or motels. Generally speaking, these commercial establishments do not present a serious competitive threat to a B & B. The service

provided and the overall atmosphere of these types of commercial businesses is quite different.

However, larger commercial establishments will present some competition if they are within sight of your B & B. A closely situated inn, hotel, or motel may distract passing customers who are seeking overnight accommodation.

You can overcome this difficulty by cultivating a customer base that is not dependent on the "passing trade." You can also make yourself known to the management of these commercial businesses and offer to take overflow guests.

4. The competitor survey

Now you need to collect information on existing B & Bs, small inns, and those commercial establishments in your immediate area that will compete with you. Sample #5 shows Carol and Bob's survey of Laker House, a competing B & B close to theirs.

After reviewing Sample #5, do your own competitor surveys by using the blank forms supplied as Worksheet E in Appendix 3. Photocopy enough copies for your needs plus two extra copies which you will need later in chapter 4.

To simplify the survey procedure, you should follow these guidelines:

(a) Confine your surveys to establishments in your local area.

(b) Limit your research to about ten surveys.

(c) Survey no more than two commercial establishments.

(d) Survey no more than three small inns.

(e) Survey at least five B & Bs.

If there are more than five B & Bs in your area, classify them into similar groups: for example, all historic homes or all homes with swimming pools, etc. Then survey the best example from each group.

SAMPLE #5
COMPETITOR SURVEY

ESTABLISHMENT Name _Laker House_   B & B home ☒
                                                       Small inn ☐
                                                       Commercial ☐

HOST/MANAGER Name _Jane & Fred Laker_
                  Address _100 Province Circle_
                  Phone (555) _456-7890_   Postal/Zip code _14411_

STYLE

FACILITIES AND SERVICES

Air conditioning	☒	Handicap access	☐
Swimming	☐	Walk to shops	☒
Sauna or gym	☐	Child play area	☐
Tennis court	☐	Patio or gardens	☒
Guest lounge	☒	Television	☒
Public transit	☐	Fax service	☒
Taxi service	☒	Babysitting	☐
Parking	☒	Pet sitting	☐
Boat mooring	☐	Laundry service	☐
Other_____		Room service	☐

BEDROOMS

Numbers Upstairs _3_   No. of stairs up _10_
         Downstairs_____   No. of stairs down _____
         Main floor _____   Adjoining rooms _2_

Beds King _____   Single _1_   Other_____
      Queen _____   Crib _____   _____
      Double _1_   Roll-out _1_   _____
      Twin _1_   Waterbed _____ _____

BATHROOMS

En-suite _____   Bathtubs _1_
Private _____   Showers _1_
Shared _1_   Other_____

BREAKFAST

Menu Continental ☐   Buffet ☒
      Hot food ☒   Served by host ☐
      Cold food ☐   Cook your own ☐
      Other_____

Location Dining room ☒   Kitchen ☐
          Guest room ☐   Lounge or lobby ☐
          Other_____

OTHER FOODS AVAILABLE

Extra meals	☐	Hot/cold drinks	☒
Snacks	☐	Special diets	☐
Packed lunch	☒	Ethnic	☐
Fruit	☐	Other_____	

OPERATING RULES

Min. stay (days) _1_   No children ☐
Check-in time _1 p.m._   No pets ☐
Check-out time _11 a.m._   No alcohol ☐
Season from _Jan_ to _Dec_ No smoking ☒

ROOM TARIFFS

Single occupancy _$80_   Group rate ☐
Double occupancy _$80_   Weekly rate ☐
Personal checks ☒   Off season ☐
                            Extra person _$10_

Credit cards: MC ☒ Visa ☒ AE ☐   Other_____

Following are some notes on completing your surveys:

(a) *Establishment* and *Host/Manager*: Name the establishment and indicate what type it is. It is also helpful to include the name, address, and phone number of the hosts or managers. "Style" indicates the general character: historic, quaint, modern, motel, hotel, etc.

(b) *Facilities and services*: Check off those services offered by the competitor.

(c) *Bedrooms* and *Bathrooms*: Note the number of bedrooms and bathrooms, the location of those rooms, the type of beds available, and convenience factors such as number of stairs.

(d) *Breakfast*: Indicate the variety of menu offered, the food services provided, and the location where the breakfast is served.

(e) *Other foods available*: Note any other foods and refreshments made available.

(f) *Operating rules*: Describe the operating rules and restrictions of the establishment.

(g) *Room tariffs*: List the room rates and the methods of payment accepted. Everybody accepts cash, so this method of payment is not shown. Room rates are quoted in dollars per day and they imply that the cost of breakfast is included. Single occupancy means one person per room. Double occupancy means two people in one room. Extra person means the charge for accommodating a third person in a room. Discount rates are listed under Group, Weekly, or Off Season.

Keep all completed survey worksheets for future reference.

Once you have looked closely at your competitors, you probably have some additional ideas on the facilities and services needed by your customers. You should look again at your customer surveys (Worksheet D) and update them with any new ideas.

f. DOCUMENT YOUR MARKET RESEARCH COSTS

Cost Sheet #1 in Appendix 4 is provided to document all the costs that you might have encountered during your market research. Make sure that you make all relevant entries onto this cost sheet before you proceed to the next chapter. Memories tend to fade with time, and loose receipts tend to get lost. It is important to cultivate the habit of recording expenses as they occur and keep all receipts. You don't need to worry about a sophisticated bookkeeping system at this point; it is enough to sort your receipts and store them in envelopes labeled with the month and year..

Do not total Cost Sheet #1 because other entries will be made after you have completed chapter 4.

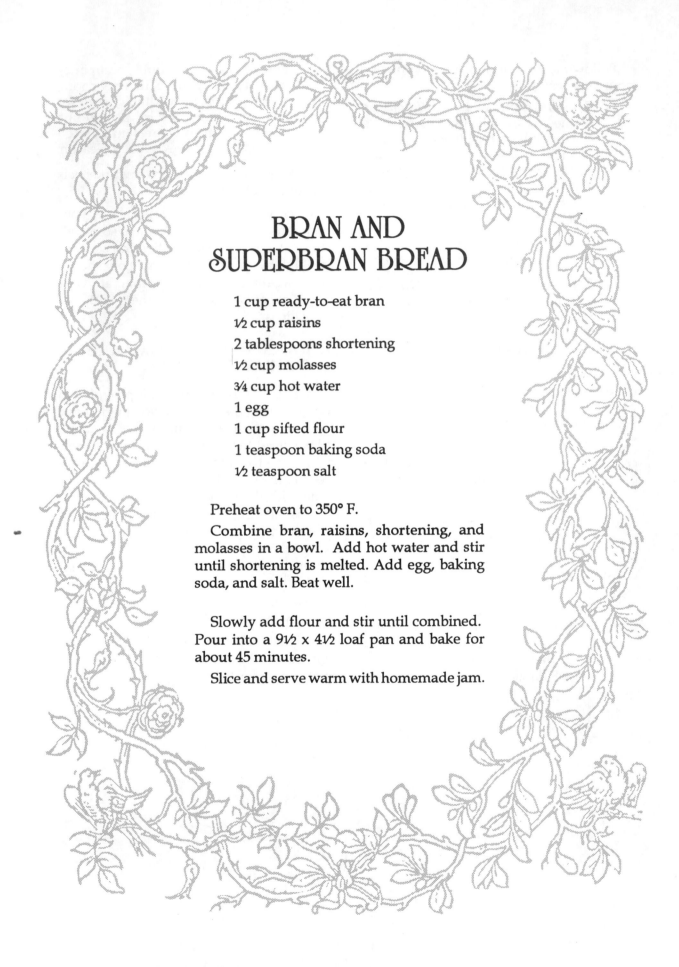

BRAN AND
SUPERBRAN BREAD

1 cup ready-to-eat bran
½ cup raisins
2 tablespoons shortening
½ cup molasses
¾ cup hot water
1 egg
1 cup sifted flour
1 teaspoon baking soda
½ teaspoon salt

Preheat oven to 350° F.

Combine bran, raisins, shortening, and molasses in a bowl. Add hot water and stir until shortening is melted. Add egg, baking soda, and salt. Beat well.

Slowly add flour and stir until combined. Pour into a 9½ x 4½ loaf pan and bake for about 45 minutes.

Slice and serve warm with homemade jam.

4

USING YOUR MARKET RESEARCH

By now you have conducted a number of surveys in the name of market research. Now you need to analyze this information and to effectively establish the start-up parameters for your B & B. In the process, you will make your final customer selections and then visit an established B & B home that caters to the same types of customers.

Before you begin, assemble all the surveys that you have completed in the previous chapter. Spread them out in front of you, and make sure you have the following:

(a) Tourist attraction surveys

(b) Customer surveys

(c) Competitor surveys

a. SUMMARIZE YOUR MARKET RESEARCH SURVEYS

1. Choose your start-up customers

Prior to conducting the customer surveys in chapter 3, you had looked at the total range of visitors to your area, and had carefully weeded out any types of visitors that could be deemed unlikely to want to stay at a B & B. Therefore, your customer surveys represent only those visitors considered to be potential customers.

Now it is time to re-examine these potential customers and to select a suitable range of start-up customers for your business. When you select your clientele, it is important not to restrict your choices to only one or two types, otherwise you may not have enough customers to make your business viable. On the other hand, you should avoid selecting all customer types because some of them may be incompatible. Guests that have good reason to complain about your other customers will not recommend or return to your establishment.

(a) Expense

You have already listed the facilities and the services required by each customer on the customer survey forms. If you compare their requirements to the facilities you already have in place, you can get a rough idea of the cost involved in servicing that particular customer. You may decide that some of these customer types are too expensive to consider as start-up clientele and, therefore, you should set them aside for now. You may decide to broaden your customer base after a year or two in business. (Home renovation and equipment costs are discussed in later chapters.)

(b) Acceptability

When you run a B & B, you learn very quickly to set your own house rules. You have no obligation to accept guests who make you feel personally uncomfortable. You may decide that you do not want to cater to families with children under a certain age, or smokers, or travelers with pets.

Study each of your customer surveys carefully and try to imagine yourself inviting that customer into your home. Try to visualize yourself welcoming them at the door, engaging in polite conversation and serving them refreshments. Think about arranging their sleeping accommodations, cooking their food, and joining them for breakfast. If you determine that you would not feel comfortable hosting that particular customer type, declare them as unacceptable for your B & B.

(c) Compatibility

Take all your "acceptable" customer surveys and see if any would be incompatible with the rest. For example, small children may present a problem to adult guests seeking a quiet weekend unless you have a separate wing of the house where either of them could stay. A steady stream of early-rising business travelers could present a problem to customers trying to sleep later unless you can provide soundproof facilities.

If you foresee any incompatibilities that cannot be corrected, then you may need to reject one or more customer types.

2. List your final customer choices

Sample #6 shows Carol and Bob's market research summary form. Complete your own summary by using Worksheet F provided in Appendix 3.

You can see that the form is designed to sort chosen customers in order of booking days available (as shown on each customer survey). Enter all the choices in that order, then enter the total and monthly booking days available for each customer type.

Your tourist attraction surveys show the local attractions that would generate tourist traffic in your area. Summarize only those attractions that would be preferred by your chosen customers. List them in order of popularity.

Finally, your competitor surveys, which show a sampling of private and commercial competition in your local area, should be summarized. Using only the B & B and small inn surveys, fill in Worksheet F by adding the information from all the B & B and small inn surveys. For the minimum and maximum rates, find the lowest and highest rates among all the survey forms.

Separate the commercial surveys from the others. You don't need to summarize this information, but keep it for future reference. You may be able to provide a few of the "extras" that they offer in your B & B.

b. WHAT DOES YOUR MARKET RESEARCH SUMMARY TELL YOU?

Refer to your completed market research summary. You now have a list of final customer choices for your B & B. This clientele is both acceptable to you and compatible with each other. You can now plan your facilities and services to attract these customers. Your market research summary will help you in this process.

The total available booking days will give you an idea of the amount of business you should expect from each customer. If Customer A is twice as available as Customer B, then it is reasonable to expect that your B & B will have more Customer As. You may not see exactly twice as many, but you should see considerably more of them. This statistic will help you provide the type of facilities that the majority of your future customers will want.

The available booking day pattern will tell you when you should expect each customer type to be in your area. This statistic can be used to adjust your business to meet the requirements of different customers arriving at different times of the year. You can also use this information when establishing your operating season, planning your vacations, offering special rates, etc.

The inventory of local attractions tells you what is likely to entice your chosen customers to travel to your area. The order of popularity indicates which attractions appeal to the majority of your future customers. You should consider advertising in brochures issued by the more popular attractions.

The operating days of each attraction will indicate the months that you will feel the impact of these attractions. These figures will help you forecast the busy or slack months of your business.

Finally, the summary of your competitors shows the most popular and the least popular facilities and services offered by

SAMPLE #6
MARKET RESEARCH SUMMARY

FINAL CUSTOMER CHOICE BY AVAILABILITY / AVAILABLE BOOKING DAYS

	Total	Jan	Feb	Mar	Apr	May	Jun	Jul	Aug	Sep	Oct	Nov	Dec
a) *Retired people*	172		2	6	8	30	30	30	30	30	4	2	
b) *Family & children*	92				6	20	30	30	6				
c) *Women travelers*	82			1	6	8	30	30	6	1			
d) *Single parents*	72				2	8	30	30	2				
e)													
f)													
g)													
h)													
i)													

PREFERRED ATTRACTIONS BY POPULARITY / OPERATING DAYS

	Gate Totals	Jan	Feb	Mar	Apr	May	Jun	Jul	Aug	Sep	Oct	Nov	Dec
3. *Fort Penn*	100,000					15	30	30	30	30	15		
6. *Long Beach*	400,000						30	30	30	15			
5. *Ship Canal*	200,000			30	30	30	30	30	30	30			
4. *Pine Park*	200,000			30	30	30	30	30	30	30	30		

SUMMARY OF COMPETITORS OF SIMILAR SIZE

Total surveyed	8	Bedrooms up	8	Dining room	6
B & B homes	5	Bedrooms down		Guest room	2
Small inns	3	Bedrooms main	3	Kitchen	
Historic	2			Lounge/lobby	
Quaint	4	King size	4		
Modern	2	Queen size	6	Extra meals	1
		Double size	8	Snacks	4
Air conditioning	7	Twin beds	8	Packed lunch	4
Swimming	2	Single bed	2	Fruit	6
Sauna or gym		Crib	2	Hot/Cold drink	6
Tennis court		Rollout	1	Special diets	3
Guest lounge	4	Waterbed		Ethnic	2
Public transit	8				
Taxi service	8	Ensuite bath	6	No children	4
Parking	8	Private bath	2	No pets	6
Boat mooring	1	Shared	7	No alcohol	2
Handicap access	3	Tubs	6	No smoking	7
Walk to Shops	8	Showers	8	Min. single rate	$65
Child play area	2			Max. single rate	$95
Patio or gardens	6	Continental	2	Min. double rate	$75
Television	4	Hot food	6	Max. double rate	$105
Fax service	1	Cold food			
Babysitting	2				
Pet sitting	2	Buffet	6	Discount rates	3
Laundry service	1	Served by host	2	Credit cards	4
Room service	4	Cook your own		Personal checks	8

your direct competitors. Study these statistics carefully. What would your customers want? What can you offer them that your competitors are lacking? Can you fill a need that currently isn't being satisfied? Think about all the little extras.

Study your competitors' rates. Think about the type and style of B & B that your clientele would want. What tariff rate would be appropriate for your B & B?

c. DO A TRIAL BED AND BREAKFAST VISIT

Now that you have chosen your range of start-up clientele, you are probably beginning to visualize the type of facilities and services that would best meet the needs of these customers. It is important to take a close look at a B & B that is already servicing your type of clientele. You need to look "behind the scenes" to get a better feel for the facilities that are required and the duties and responsibilities of the hosts.

Even though you may have already stayed at a B & B, you probably thought only in terms of being the visitor, not the host. Now is the time to go visiting again, but this time with your eye to the competition.

1. Choosing the home

We suggest that you pick a home in another town by using a B & B guide book. Choose a home that has the same style and range of customers as your proposed business. Pick one that charges a rate that seems correct (compare it to your competitor surveys). Descriptions in guide books can sometimes be misleading, but rates usually point to the truth.

Book into the home for one night, and plan to arrive in the early afternoon so that you can get a good look at the house exterior. If the B & B is quite close to your home area, don't be concerned about fabricating elaborate excuses for your overnight stay. Just say that you want to get away for a day. Most hosts won't even bring up the subject, because they have found, as you will, that the best policy is never to ask personal questions of their guests.

2. Inspecting the home

When you make your trial visit, imagine that you are an inspector for a B & B booking agency. You are there to look at every facet of the operation (without the knowledge of the owner).

Begin your inspection by doing a survey of the facilities and services. Use a copy of the competitor survey (Worksheet E) that you used in chapter 3 and fill in as much as you can by reading the description in the guide book. Take the worksheet with you when you visit the home so that you can complete your survey.

To complete the inspection, you must document the level of hospitality that you receive. We define hospitality as *the open and friendly reception of guests, followed by a high level of continuous care and attention, given in pleasant surroundings*. This means that a hospitable B & B will have hosts who are friendly and approachable and that the level of care will not deteriorate during your stay. As well, the surroundings will be comfortable, clean, and pleasant.

Sample #7 shows an example of a B & B hospitality rating. The top of the form allows you to apply a rating of poor, fair, or good to specific features of the home. The bottom of the form allows you to document your personal observations and to suggest how you would improve the hospitality. A blank form, Worksheet G, is provided in Appendix 3. Two copies are provided in case two of you want to complete your own forms and compare, or if you do more than one trial visit.

Note the following during your visit:

(a) *Exterior*: What are your impressions of the exterior of the house? Was it easy to locate? Note if parking is a problem, and rate the general condition of the structure, landscaping, and neighborhood. What exterior guest areas are provided (e.g., patios

SAMPLE #7
HOSPITALITY RATING FORM

HOUSE NAME _River Glen House_   DATE VISITED _April 16, 1992_

		Poor	Fair	Good
EXTERIOR	Signage	X		
	Parking		X	
	House condition			X
	Landscaping		X	
	Trash & garbage			X
	Ext. guest areas		X	
	Neighborhood			X
CHECK IN	Welcome		X	
	Baggage	X		
	Tariff payment			X
	Check in routine		X	
	Tour of facilities	X		
	House rules			X
	Advice offered	X		
	Host attitude		X	
BEDROOM	Layout			X
	Cleanliness			X
	Decoration			X
	Comfortable chairs			X
	Clothes storage		X	
	Bed comfort			X
	Reading material	X		
	Writing space			X
	Lighting			X
	Privacy			X
	Security			X
	Room refreshments	X		

		Poor	Fair	Good
BATHROOM	Fixtures			X
	Lighting			X
	Decoration			X
	Cleanliness			X
	Towels			X
	Ventilation			X
	Privacy			X
	Convenience			X
BREAKFAST	Welcome	X		
	Time slot			X
	Presentation			X
	Food variety			X
	Food quality			X
	Cleanliness			X
	Host hygiene			X
	Host attitude		X	
CHECK OUT	Routine			X
	Time slot			X
	Baggage	X		
	Host attitude		X	
	Travel advice	X		
HOSPITALITY RATING		X		

COMMENTS: Difficult to locate house – no sign. No tour of facilities; no local advice offered

Excellent bedroom decor – good security

Host attitude poor at breakfast; we felt we were intruding

Would not recommend this B & B

or gardens)? Was trash or garbage in view?

(b) *Check-in:* Did you feel welcome and did the hosts help with your baggage? How efficient was the check-in routine and tariff payment? Did the hosts show you all the guest areas and did they explain the house rules? Did they offer advice on places to eat or visit and was their general attitude friendly and helpful?

(c) *Bedroom:* Rate the layout, cleanliness, and decoration in the bedroom. Look for comfortable surroundings and functional furniture. What extra features and services are there, and how would you rate privacy and security?

(d) *Bathroom:* Rate the overall cleanliness and decoration. Are the fixtures, lighting, ventilation, and towels of good quality? How private and convenient is it?

(e) *Breakfast:* How welcome do you feel? Rate the overall presentation and cleanliness of the eating area. How convenient is the breakfast time? Rate the food quality and variety and the host's attitude and hygiene.

(f) *Check-out:* Was the check-out time convenient? How efficient was their check-out routine? Did the hosts help with the baggage, and what was their general attitude? Would you stay there again?

(g) *Hospitality rating:* Give an overall hospitality rating to the home.

As you do your own rating, think about things that could be changed to improve the level of service you are receiving. Try to think both as a guest and as a host.

Don't forget to ask the host for a receipt for payment, and keep track of any transportation costs, etc.

3. Document your costs

Locate your Cost Sheet #1 in Appendix 4 and enter any costs associated with your trial visit. Remember to include any transportation, parking, and tariff costs, and put all your receipts into a labeled envelope. Get into the habit of documenting all costs no matter how small. Your accountant will ultimately advise you on what is deductible and what is not.

d. ESTABLISH START-UP PARAMETERS

It is time to take a "snapshot" of how you visualize your B & B. To do this, take a blank copy of a competitor survey (Worksheet E) and complete it as if you were looking at your own B & B. This preliminary survey is not cast in concrete, of course, because you will be making further decisions in later chapters of this book. It is useful, however, to establish a preliminary list of facilities and services that you would like to offer to your chosen customers.

Your preliminary survey will help point you in the right direction. Fill in each entry carefully and pay particular attention to the following points:

(a) Think about a name for your new business. In the next chapter we discuss the pros and cons of legally registering your business name. For now, you should be thinking about some suitable names that could be used for your establishment. B & Bs often use the same name as the host family. For example, our imaginary couple, Carol and Bob Morris, have decided to name their B & B Morris House. Others make use of local features such as Willow Beach Lodge or River Glen House. Historic homes are often named after the original owners such as The Carnochan House.

To get more ideas on typical B & B names, refer to any one of the guide books or government brochures listed in Appendixes 1 and 2.

(b) Refer to the list of facilities and services your customers will need.

What facilities and services were needed during your trial visit? Also note the facilities and services offered by your direct competition and by local commercial establishments.

(c) What bedroom arrangements would you probably use? Consider your chosen customer types and your existing home layout. What bathroom facilities could be provided for your guests?

(d) What style of breakfast will best suit your chosen customers? Where will they eat breakfast, and what other food services do you propose? What extra refreshments would you have preferred during your trial visit?

(e) Decide when your operating season will probably be based on the availability of your chosen customers. Also think about any customer restrictions you might apply.

(f) Check your market research summary information, and determine a realistic rate for your B & B. Make some preliminary decisions on any special rates you might offer.

These preliminary parameters will prove to be a useful first step in your total planning process. As you continue to study each of the remaining chapters, you will adjust these parameters to develop your final start-up plan.

OSCAR'S
WILDE CHILI SAUCE

1 teaspoon allspice

1 teapsoon whole cloves

1 teaspoon cinnamon

10 large tomatoes

1 hot red pepper

2 medium apples

2 large onions

1 cup white sugar

½ cup vinegar

Place allspice, cloves, and cinnamon into a cheese cloth bag and tie closed.

Peel and cut up tomatoes and place in a large saucepan. Add chopped onion and chopped red peppers (without seeds).

Peel, core, and chop apples and add to the onions and pepper. Add sugar, vinegar, and the spice bag.

Boil the mixture for one hour or until thick, stirring occasionally. Remove spice bag.

Cool and pour into sterilized jars.

Serve as a condiment with any egg dish.

5

MAKING IT LEGAL

When you open a B & B, you provide a service to the general public for a fee. When you provide this service, you must follow specific regulations designed to safeguard the general public. Similarly, when you collect a fee for the service, you must obey all the tax rules that apply to that fee. These rules and regulations are established by one or more levels of government and you need to be aware of their implications.

a. SOURCES OF INFORMATION

To obtain reliable information on starting a B & B, the following sources should be consulted:

(a) *Municipal government:* Municipal governments will be concerned with and have information on the location and facilities of your proposed B & B. Bylaws, zoning, and municipal licenses fall under their jurisdiction. Visit the planning department or clerk's office of your municipality and ask for any pertinent information.

(b) *Regional government:* Depending where you live, there may be another level of government that has jurisdiction over a group of municipalities. Generally, regional governments coordinate services that stretch across a number of municipalities. Health and fire regulations could be regional concerns, for example.

(c) *State or provincial government:* This level of government is interested in the collection of some taxes and in the registration of the business. They are also good sources of general information on how to start a small business,

and they may have grants available to the small business entrepreneur.

(d) *Federal government:* The federal government is concerned with the collection of income taxes and federal sales taxes. They will also be interested in the tax impact of any additional revenue obtained through your customer fees. The federal government may also have grants available to small businesses.

(e) *Your accountant:* We highly recommend that you seek the advice of a knowledgeable, professional accountant early in your planning stage. His or her advice will allow you to gain the best tax advantages during both the planning and operational stages. An accountant can also advise you on the advantage or necessity of registering your business with the government.

When you are choosing an accountant, select one that has other B & B operators on his or her client list. Ask other B & B operators for their recommendations. Remember that some or all of your accountant's fees can be charged as a business expense.

(f) *Your lawyer:* If you seek the advice of a knowledgeable accountant and follow all the zoning and bylaw requirements of your local government, then you probably do not need the services of a lawyer. However, you are in the best position to evaluate your own situation. If you are planning a very large operation or if you are going to form a corporation, we recommend the services of a lawyer.

b. YOUR BUSINESS STRUCTURE

Your accountant can provide advice on the advantages and disadvantages of selecting a particular business structure. He or she will be familiar with the tax and liability implications associated with each form of organization. There are three basic forms your business structure can take:

(a) Sole proprietorship

(b) Partnership

(c) Corporation

A sole proprietorship is the most common form of business structure for small business, including B & B operators. A sole proprietorship has the following features:

- Tax advantages for the small operator
- Owner has complete control
- Low start-up costs
- Unlimited liability
- Difficult to raise capital (from banks, etc.)

In a partnership, you share the ownership of the business with one or more people. A partnership has the following features:

- Tax advantages for the partners
- Liability depends on type of partnership
- Low start-up costs
- May have better success raising capital
- Control must be shared

The corporation is a form of organization more often used by larger businesses. Most B & Bs would not normally choose to incorporate their business. Corporations have the following features:

- Better tax advantages in certain higher tax brackets
- Limited liability
- Easiest to raise capital

- Expensive to organize
- Extensive accounting required

If you are interested in incorporating your business, incorporation guides and kits are available for many states and provinces. Self-Counsel Press publishes incorporation guides for British Columbia, Alberta, Saskatchewan and Manitoba, and Ontario, as well as for Washington State, Oregon, and Florida.

c. REGISTERING YOUR BUSINESS NAME

In the previous chapter we talked briefly about naming your B & B. You should give a lot of thought to the name as you will be using it in your advertising to attract customers. You want to think of a name that is easy for your customers to remember, but unique to your business as well. You certainly don't want to copy the name of a business close by as that could cause misunderstandings and confusion.

Most jurisdictions require that your business name be registered. This is done by filing a fictitious name statement with county or provincial authorities. The only exception is when you use your own name, for example "Carol Morris Bed and Breakfast." Even in this circumstance, you can choose to register the name if you wish.

When you register a fictitious name, it will be checked against those previously filed to ensure the name has not been taken by another business. This is for your protection, too. Once your name is on file, it cannot be used by anyone else.

It is a good idea to have two or even three names ready before you register. That way, if your first choice is rejected, you have another name ready, and you won't have to start all over again. In Canada, you can have a name search done through the provincial ministry that handles incorporations. This will also tell you if the name is registered out of province. This process takes about a week and there is a small fee, generally under $50. In the United State, your city or county clerk will tell you if the name you have chosen is available for use.

We recommend that you register the name of your B & B because this will define it as a legal entity, and will establish a recognized start date for your business. It can be a costly mistake to not register your name. You may operate for a few months or longer, all the while spending time and money to get the name of your B & B recognized and respected, then one day you receive a registered letter telling you to stop using it. Too late, you find out that the name is already used and protected by someone else. You may even be liable for damages.

d. LEVELS OF TAXATION

As consumers, we are constantly faced with ever-increasing taxes, and we have very few ways of recovering those taxes. By starting a B & B, you will join the world of small business, and you will find additional deductions that can be claimed as legitimate business expenses, thus relieving your total tax burden.

As part of your business responsibilities, you will be asked to collect certain taxes and to remit them to various levels of government. Tax regulations are complex and inconsistent, and they vary from one area of the country to another. We strongly urge you to consult your accountant, your municipality, your provincial or state, and federal government to make sure that you are aware of your total tax rights and responsibilities.

The areas of taxation generally fall into the following categories.

(a) *Income tax:* The federal government is interested in the total revenue of your B & B operation. How they tax that total revenue depends on the structure of your business; an accountant can provide the best advice on effective tax planning.

(b) *Sales tax:* Most state and provincial governments have some form of taxation on sales of goods or services. These taxes are not consistent among jurisdictions, and some governments have chosen to exempt B & Bs from collecting sales tax.

Check with your state or provincial government taxation authorities, and if you are required to collect sales tax, make sure that you register with the appropriate authority and obtain the correct permits.

(c) *Room tax:* Municipal governments often impose a hotel/motel room tax to generate additional revenues. You should check with your municipality to see if they impose this tax. Some municipalities exempt B & Bs.

(d) *Goods and Services Tax (Canada):* You may have to register with the Goods and Services Tax and therefore you may have to charge your customers the GST and remit the tax to the government. The current legislation states that any business in Canada that has a gross income of more than $30,000 per year must register and collect the tax. Any business with a gross income of less than $30,000 per year has the option of registering. Your accountant can help you make an informed decision.

If you register and collect the tax, you can recover any of the GST you pay on your business expenses. However, the collection and remittance of the GST will add to your paperwork.

If your gross income allows you the option not to register and not to collect the tax, you cannot recover any of the GST, but you can deduct the tax as a business expense.

Most groceries are exempt from the tax, so you will not have to pay the tax on the large quantities of food supplies that you purchase, but you will have to pay the tax on other supplies such as paper products, garbage bags, cleaning products, etc. You will also require the services of accountants, booking agents, and contractors, who will charge you GST.

Most B & B operators in our area have chosen not to collect the GST. You must be the final judge, but let your accountant be your guide. For more information on the GST, you might want to refer to *The GST Handbook,* another title in the Self-Counsel Series.

e. BYLAWS AND ZONING

There are many regulations you must adhere to before you can open your doors for business; it is not enough to register your name. You must also consider local bylaws and zoning requirements that affect your business.

Municipal bylaws specifically regarding B & Bs are strikingly similar across North America. Most municipalities regard B & Bs as a special type of business, different from hotels and motels. The majority of bylaws concerning B&Bs reflect some or all of the following limitations:

- The dwelling is residential
- No more than one meal per day is served
- No guest cooking facilities permitted
- Length of stay is limited
- The number of guest rooms is limited
- Off-street parking is required
- Must be owner operated
- Any building changes must be reversible to the original residential use
- Its operation must not affect the characteristic of the neighborhood.
- It must be licensed and inspected.

Zoning bylaws exist to control the type of activity allowed on any piece of property. You must check with your municipality to determine if a B & B is allowed on your property. Most municipalities do allow this type of business in a residential zone. If they do not, you can and should apply to your council for a "zoning variance" before you proceed with your plans.

f. BUSINESS LICENSES AND INSPECTIONS

Before you are granted a business license, the municipality will probably require your premises to undergo fire, building, and health inspections. Even if your municipality does not require a license or inspections, it is useful to look at the details of typical inspections to identify how you can make your home as safe as possible. Any steps you can take in this direction will also help your insurance premiums.

1. Fire inspection

You should contact your local fire department for advice on the best way to meet specific code requirements. A fire inspection will concentrate on the following criteria:

(a) *Containment* is the ability of the structure to resist the spread of a fire so that the occupants can escape. The building materials used in the floors, walls, and ceilings need to have a specific rating of fire resistance. Typically, the local fire code would require these materials to have a fire resistance rating of three-quarters of an hour.

(b) *Egress* refers to the number and type of escape routes available to occupants during a fire. The fire codes in your area will specify the number of stairways and exit doors required for your home. A typical code would require one fire exit from each of the first and second floors, and two fire exits from the third floor. In a B & B, the interior stairway is usually considered to be a fire exit.

(c) *Detection* specifies the number, locations, and types of fire and smoke detectors needed in your B & B to adequately warn your customers. Typical codes call for smoke detectors on all levels of the house and heat detectors at special locations.

(d) *Suppression* refers to the number, locations, and types of fire extinguishers needed to meet your local fire code. Typical codes call for five-pound multi-purpose dry chemical extinguishers on all levels and at all exits.

2. Building inspection

A building inspection will first concentrate on the physical integrity of a house and its general state of repair. If you have kept your home well maintained, you should have no problem. An inspection will also review the availability of proper customer accommodations. Your municipality may have guidelines that specify the number of bedrooms allowed, the washroom facilities needed, and the eating arrangements required.

Safety concerns include anything that could present a hazard to your guests. Typical problems could be loose floor boards, unsafe electrical wiring, etc.

The inspector will also review any regulations about signage: the type, size, and location of any signs advertising your business. You can contact your local building department to find out the standards.

3. Health inspection

A health inspection will be concerned with the following:

(a) What is the availability and quality of water, light, and heat? Generally, water must be potable (drinkable), and the temperature of the hot water must be restricted to avoid scalding. Light levels for bathrooms and hallways will have to meet minimum standards and room air temperatures must meet minimum and maximum allowable limits. A typical code specifies a maximum bath or shower water temperature of 120 °F (48.9°C) and light levels of 30 footcandles in the bathrooms and 10 footcandles in the hallways. The minimum winter room temperature might be set at 68 °F (20°C).

(b) Your house may have to meet minimum size requirements for the guest bedrooms, bathrooms, sitting rooms, and eating areas. The location of these rooms is also important. Typical codes specify bedrooms to be a minimum of 65 square feet (6 m^2), with dining and sitting areas to be a minimum of 15 square feet (1.4 m^2) per person. The codes might also note that furnace or utility rooms cannot be used for sleeping areas, and that bathrooms cannot open directly into any food-preparation or dining area.

(c) Bathroom specifications cover the health and safety of guest bathrooms. Typical codes specify that grab bars and non-skid surfaces for tubs and showers must be in place. Other requirements might include mechanical ventilation and lockable doors for privacy.

(d) Linen requirements deal with the availability of private towels and washcloths and the minimum number of bed linen changes. Generally, bed linen must be changed after each visitor, or once per week, whichever is less, and clean towels and facecloths must be provided for each guest.

(e) You must consider the proper storage, preparation, and disposal of guest food. Typical codes require that the refrigerator maintain a minimum temperature of 45 °F (7.2°C) and that sanitary procedures for food preparation areas be carried out. The code might also specify adequate garbage storage and disposal.

g. INSURANCE

What would happen if one of your guests fell and broke an ankle on your front walk? Or if a guest fell ill because of accidental food contamination? You must protect yourself against any liability arising as a result of conducting your B & B business.

You are probably not covered under your existing homeowners' policy, so you should check with your insurance company to see what special conditions they require to provide the extra coverage.

If you are having your premises inspected by the fire, building, and health authorities, you should receive a better premium. It is also wise to shop around. Many insurance companies don't want to get involved in the B & B business, so they will quote you a high premium in the hope that you will go elsewhere. A few insurance companies specialize in the small business field, and they can quote very competitive rates, particularly if you belong to a business group. Contact your nearest chamber of commerce or bed and breakfast association for advice.

h. DOCUMENT YOUR COSTS

Cost Sheet #2 in Appendix 4 is provided to document any costs associated with the rules and regulations that affect the establishment of your B & B. Enter all of the costs that you have paid to date. Do not total your cost sheet at this time because some of the expenses will probably occur later in your start-up plans.

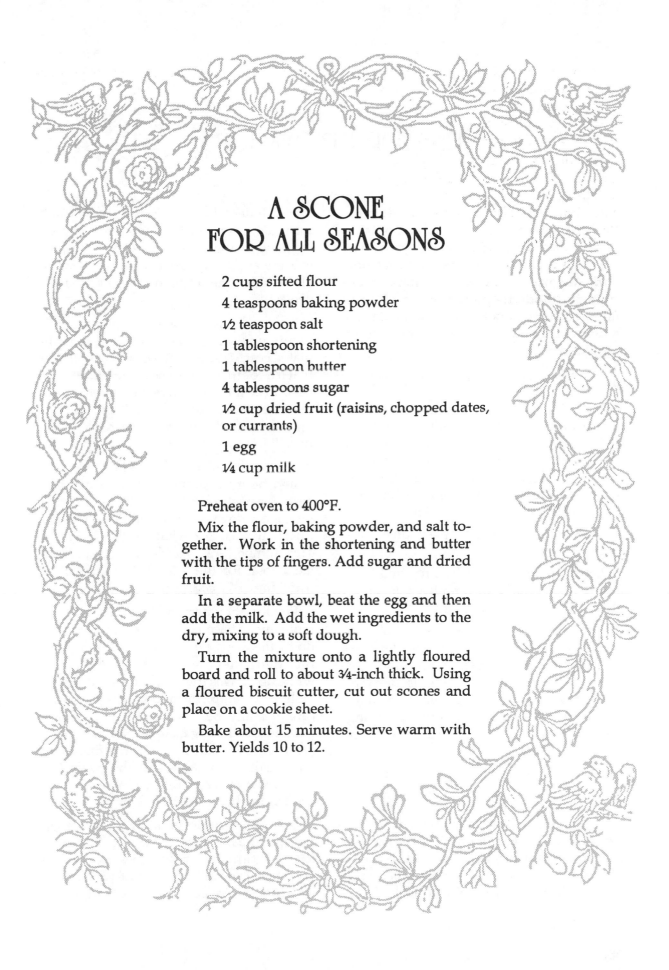

A SCONE
FOR ALL SEASONS

2 cups sifted flour

4 teaspoons baking powder

½ teaspoon salt

1 tablespoon shortening

1 tablespoon butter

4 tablespoons sugar

½ cup dried fruit (raisins, chopped dates, or currants)

1 egg

¼ cup milk

Preheat oven to 400°F.

Mix the flour, baking powder, and salt together. Work in the shortening and butter with the tips of fingers. Add sugar and dried fruit.

In a separate bowl, beat the egg and then add the milk. Add the wet ingredients to the dry, mixing to a soft dough.

Turn the mixture onto a lightly floured board and roll to about ¾-inch thick. Using a floured biscuit cutter, cut out scones and place on a cookie sheet.

Bake about 15 minutes. Serve warm with butter. Yields 10 to 12.

6

TIME FOR RENOVATIONS?

This chapter is meant to guide you through your house — inside and outside — to help you decide what, if any, renovations are needed to establish an efficient B & B. As you do your renovation survey, keep in mind the requirements of your targeted customers and pay particular attention to any areas covered by rules or regulations.

a. THE RENOVATION SURVEY

Sample #8 shows a renovation survey done by Carol and Bob for one of the bedrooms in their home. One sheet is used for each area being surveyed. Sample #8 is a survey of one of the guest bedrooms, identified by the twin beds. (Their other guest bedrooms have different bed configurations.)

Let's look at their survey section by section.

Under "Renovation," Carol and Bob listed each renovation required to bring this bedroom up to standard.

Next, under "Labor required," Bob and Carol wrote down the separate steps required to complete each renovation. For example, "paint ceiling/walls" is a job that requires a number of steps such as removing the furniture from the room, stripping old wallpaper, patching the drywall, purchasing the paint, etc.

Opposite each step, in the column titled "Hours," they wrote down an estimate of the time needed to complete that step. If they planned to hire a contractor to do the work, as in the case of replacing the carpeting, some additional time would be spent choosing and purchasing the carpet, and the contractor will do all the rest of the labor. Under labor required, Bob and Carol included "Purchasing" and provided an estimate of the time needed for the purchasing and transportation of task materials, as this time adds to the length of the project.

Their next step was to list all materials required for each renovation and the estimated cost of those materials. You will note that if a contractor is to be hired, those costs need to be included here. For example, for the recarpeting, the cost will include not only the actual cost of the carpet, but the installation cost as well.

Bob and Carol then totalled the estimated hours of labor and the estimated costs for each renovation. The total costs for each renovation is listed beside "Total Costs Task #1" (or whatever Task # it is). This number is also added to the accumulated total for the whole room, which is listed under "Accumulated Costs."

Finally, they assigned an order to the renovations based on a logical approach to doing the work. For example, although the first thing they noticed in the room and wrote down was the decrepit old bookcase, table, and lamp, installing new furniture cannot really be done until the room is painted and the rug installed. So they made installing new furniture #4, the final item on their list. Similarly, it is impractical to put down new carpeting before you paint, so painting became #1 on their list.

You can now do your own renovation surveys by using Worksheet H in Appendix 3. Make as many photocopies as you will need to survey all the areas of your home. You will require at least one worksheet for

SAMPLE #8
RENOVATION SURVEY

ROOM Twin beds bedroom   SHEET # 1

Task #	Renovation	Labor Required	Hours	Materials Required	Costs	Accumulated Costs
4	Replace bookcase, side table, & lamp	Purchasing	3	Bookcase Table Lamp	$70 50 50	
		Total Labor for Task # 4	3	Total Costs for Task # 4	170.	$170.00
2	Replace rug	Purchasing Installation by contractor	1.5 6.0	Carpeting 15 yd^2 & installation	$600	
		Total Labor for Task # 2	7.5	Total Costs for Task # 2	$600	$770.00
3	Replace outlets, plates, fixture	Remove old items Install new items Purchasing	1 1 1.5	Outlets-3 Plates-2 Fixture	15 10 50	
		Total Labor for Task # 3	3.5	Total Costs for Task # 3	75	$845.06
1	Repair, repaint ceiling, walls, woodwork	Remove furniture Strip wallpaper Patch Paint Stain woodwork Purchasing	1 3 1 2.5 2.0 1.5	Plaster Stripper Paint - 2 gallons Stain 1 quart Sandpaper	7 5 40 10 10	
		Total Labor for Task # 1	11	Total Costs for Task # 1	72	$917

each room or hallway and a number of sheets for the exterior areas. Information is provided in the following sections on what to look for in each area of your home.

As you do your own survey, remember the following:

(a) Use a pencil to complete the form (to allow for corrections).

(b) Identify the room or area in the top left-hand corner.

(c) Complete worksheets for each room or area.

(d) Identify the renovations that are needed in that room or area.

(e) Divide the renovations into steps.

(f) Assign estimated hours to each step of the renovation.

(g) Include time needed for choosing, purchasing, and transporting material.

(h) If you are hiring other people to do the work, include the costs of that labor in the costs column.

(i) Determine what materials will be needed for the renovation.

(j) List the estimated costs.

(k) Total the estimated labor hours and costs *for each renovation.*

(l) Add the total cost for each renovation to the running total in the accumulated costs column. If you use more than one sheet for a room, remember to carry the accumulated total costs over to the second sheet.

(m) Assign an order to the renovations based on the logical progression of work.

b. GUEST BEDROOMS

The bedroom is the most important room to your guests because it will be their only private space within your B & B. You should, therefore, pay special attention to the facilities that you provide in the bedrooms. Keep in mind the type of customers you have decided to target, look around the room, and decide what needs to be done to properly service those customers. You should survey the room as if you were going to pay for a night's lodging. Use the following guidelines as you survey the room.

1. General

(a) Check the ceilings and walls for cracks, peeling paint, or faded wallpaper.

(b) Examine the condition of the electrical wiring, switches, and outlets.

(c) Assess the overall color scheme and atmosphere. Compare this to your customer's expectations.

(d) Check the condition and color of the rugs. Do they fit in with the overall effect you are trying to create for your customers?

(e) Are the lighting fixtures suitable for your customers? Consider installing high efficiency fixtures or light bulbs.

(f) Check the room ventilation and air circulation. Are ceiling fans required? Air conditioning?

2. Beds

(a) Do you need to purchase new beds? Double beds are acceptable to most couples, but there are a minority who insist on either king or queen-sized beds. If you don't already own these larger beds, they may not be worth the expense.

(b) If you are providing more than one bedroom to guests, do you have a variety of bed arrangements? It is worthwhile having at least one room with twin beds, as they provide flexibility when accommodating children, pairs of women or men travelers, or couples who prefer twin beds.

(c) Do you have single beds or roll-out cots that can be rolled out on an as-needed basis? These are very useful, particularly if you are catering to children, and they provide additional flexibility when accommodating more than two adults to a room.

(d) Can you provide extras like a crib if you accept small children?

3. Other furniture

(a) Does the style of the furniture complement the style of the house? Modern furniture in an historic house is not what your customers will expect, for example, if you advertise the house as being historic. Try to anticipate the expectations of your guests. Consider the ambience that you are trying to create. Remember too, that your customers want to feel "at home" so you should furnish the rooms like a home, not like a hotel or motel.

(b) Consider if additional clothes racks are required. Is there adequate shelf space? A chest of drawers should also be available to store smaller articles.

(c) Do you have bedside tables in your guest rooms? Are lamps provided? Remember that your guests will be sleeping in an unfamiliar room, and they will need an easily accessible light if they need to get up during the night.

(d) If you have room, can you provide a corner for a private sitting area in each bedroom? Most guests will spend some time during the day in their bedroom, writing letters or resting and they will appreciate an area within their room where they can relax in comfort. You should provide several comfortable chairs for this purpose and a small desk or table if possible.

(e) Do you have a bookcase or shelf where you can display travel brochures, local information, your

house rules, etc.? In addition, it is good public relations to have a selection of books and magazines available for your customers in their rooms.

4. Accessories

There are a number of bedroom accessories needed for the comfort and convenience of your guests:

(a) The color and style of drapes should complement the rest of the room decoration, particularly the bedspread. In addition, there must be some provision for privacy. Make sure that the drapes can be closed tightly or provide separate window blinds.

(b) Your visitors will need a large mirror, preferably full length.

(c) If you don't provide an alarm clock, your guests will probably ask you for a wake-up call. An illuminated digital clock is the easiest to read, especially at night.

(d) You should provide a waste basket in each guest bedroom. Most customers will make an effort to keep their room clean if you provide a receptacle for their trash. It is also a good idea to use waterproof liners in these baskets to avoid leakage and to make it easier to empty.

(e) Locks on the doors will be appreciated by most guests for both privacy and security.

(f) If you allow smoking in the bedrooms, don't forget to provide an ashtray and an air purifier. It is also wise to install individual smoke detectors in each of the rooms. If you don't allow smoking in the bedrooms, a smoke detector in the common hallway may be adequate. (**Note:** Check your local fire codes for the correct placement of these smoke detectors and for local code requirements. You may be required to provide smoke detectors in every room.)

(g) Consider whether you want to provide a radio or television in each guest bedroom. Alternatively, you may want to have a television in the common guest sitting area only, or not at all. If you do provide televisions, remember that you may need extra wiring. You also risk disturbing next-door guests if you provide televisions. Do televisions fit in with your target customers' needs and your overall plan?

(h) Not many B & Bs provide telephones in guest bedrooms because it is difficult to control misuse. You will need to guard against unauthorized long distance telephone calls, so you should maintain reasonably tight control over your telephones.

(i) Note any other accessories you would like to include in your guest bedrooms. Remember to choose your accessories to please your target customers and to reinforce the "home" aspect of your accommodation. Small touches like a vase of fresh or dried flowers or family photographs on the walls can make a room more appealing.

c. GUEST BATHROOMS

The state of bathrooms is very important to most people. You should make extra efforts to see that the bathrooms are nicely decorated, clean, and safe. In addition, some municipalities may require you to provide guest bathroom facilities on the same floor as the guest bedrooms. If your home layout does not allow this, check with your municipality to see if the bylaws allow some other arrangements. Otherwise, you will be faced with major home renovations.

1. General

Check the condition of the ceilings, walls, and floor. Is the plaster, tile, and paint in good order? Is there mildew on the tile grout? Examine the bathtub, shower stall, toilet bowl, and sink surfaces for discolorations, cracks, or water stains. Check the finish on the taps and faucets for pitting or peeling. Will the color and decoration fit in with your customer's expectations?

Here is a suggested checklist for possible renovations:

(a) Additional lighting fixtures for better light levels. Use energy-efficient fixtures or light bulbs.

(b) Replace cracked or badly stained porcelain fixtures or have them refinished.

(c) Install a new toilet seat and cover.

(d) Paint the ceilings and walls with flat-finish paint to add softness to the surface finish.

(e) Use vinyl wallpaper to add decorating interest.

(f) Consider an increase in mirror size to make the room seem larger and visually more interesting.

(g) If there is a window in the bathroom, consider a window treatment that is both pleasing to the eye and that provides a good level of privacy.

(h) Install ground fault interrupter (GFI) electrical outlets for safety.

(i) Install grab bars inside tubs and near toilets.

(j) Install non-skid strips on floors of tubs and showers.

(k) Install sliding shower doors to replace shower curtains. (Doors are less likely to cause water spills onto the bathroom floor).

(l) Install a bathroom exhaust fan that activates with the light switch.

(m) If the bathroom is not en suite, install a door lock that is approved for bathrooms. (These locks can be opened from the outside with a special key in an emergency).

(n) Consider installing energy-efficient shower heads and toilets to conserve water. Water-saving shower heads are available at most hardware stores and they are easy to install. If you have standard toilets, a good solution is to place several masonry bricks inside the toilet tank. This will save a considerable quantity of water each time the toilet is flushed.

2. Accessories

Your guests will require certain accessories in their bathrooms. The style of the accessories will depend somewhat on the ambience you are trying to create. Here is a suggested list:

(a) Terrytowel bath mat.

(b) Foot-operated covered waste basket with waterproof liner.

(c) Bathroom-sized paper cups in a dispenser.

(d) Box of facial tissue.

(e) Extra roll of toilet paper.

(f) Tub and tile cleaner and paper towel (for people who choose to clean the toilet seat or sink before using).

(g) An air freshener.

(h) A few small bars of soap. Individually wrapped bars can be purchased in large quantities at reasonable prices from wholesale suppliers. Any bars of soap larger than the one-ounce size results in excessive waste. Alternatively, you can provide a liquid-soap dispenser in each bathroom.

d. GUEST HALLWAYS AND STAIRWAYS

Any hall used by your customers is a "guest hallway" and stairways are included in this category. It is important to pay special attention to any hall or stairs used by your customers because these passageways represent a fire escape route. They should provide a safe and quick means of exit. Halls and stairs should be in a good state of repair and have adequate light levels.

1. General

Here are some renovation factors you should consider for your guest hallways and stairways:

(a) Check the ceilings and walls for cracks, loose surface material, and protruding hazards.

(b) Check the floor surface for wear and hazards.

(c) Examine the condition of the electrical wiring, switches, outlets, and fixtures.

(d) Assess the overall color scheme and atmosphere. Compare this to your customers' expectations.

(e) Check stair treads and handrails for damage or looseness.

(f) Consider increasing the light levels and using energy-efficient fixtures or light bulbs.

(g) Provide 24-hour lighting, and use rechargeable battery-operated night lights in case of a power failure. You must not leave your guests in total darkness during a power failure.

(h) Check for adequate air circulation, and consider installing ceiling fans or air conditioning.

2. Accessories

(a) Install smoke detectors on every floor of your home; hallways are convenient locations. Since many home fires originate in the electrical panel, thus knocking out the lights immediately, we recommend battery-operated detectors that have a built-in spotlight. The light can be aimed to illuminate the stairway. Check your local fire codes before you purchase or install any fire-safety equipment.

(b) Install fire extinguishers on every floor and near each exit door. Again, check your local fire codes before purchasing as there are many types of extinguishers.

(c) Remove any furniture that could be an obstruction during a fire escape. Try to keep passageways as clear as possible while still retaining a home-like atmosphere.

(d) Provide suitable racks for umbrellas and overcoats and a waterproof mat for wet or muddy shoes and boots.

e. COMMON SITTING AREA

We previously suggested that you provide a small sitting area in each of the guest bedrooms. It is also necessary to have a common sitting area where the guests can spend time socializing. If you do not provide guests with a common sitting area, you will find them gravitating to private rooms that you consider to be "off limits."

Travelers don't always want to be out late at night or confined to their rooms; they will appreciate having access to a common area where they can relax, play some cards, or chat. It doesn't have to be a large area, but it should be readily accessible. Consider using a spare bedroom, screened-in porch, or unused family room. Some older homes have very large upper halls, and a section can be divided off and furnished as a guest lounge.

Here are some factors to consider when you are planning a common sitting area for your guests:

(a) Consider the overall style and ambience, and try to provide the type of sitting area that your customers would want. Most guests will be attracted to an area that reminds them of home.

(b) Furnish the room with upholstered chairs and rugs to help reduce noise. Arrange the furniture so that guests can talk to each other easily.

(c) Decide if you are going to provide a television set in this area. Remember that you are the one who sets the house rules. If television is an option, you will need to wire the area accordingly. A radio, record or disk player, or piano are other options you could consider.

(d) If you are thinking of installing a telephone, be prepared to deal with unauthorized long-distance calls. It might be better to provide a phone jack in the area, and then supply a telephone on request. If the call is not local, ask your guest to fill out a long-distance telephone slip (see chapter 9).

(e) Consider a table at which guests can write letters or play cards.

(f) Soft lighting should be installed. Use floor or table lamps to create a quiet lighting effect.

(g) Books, magazines, and a copy of the local daily newspaper will be appreciated by your guests.

(h) If you allow smoking, an exhaust fan that comes on with the lights would be a good idea. Also have ashtrays available and consider installing an air purifier.

(i) A coffee- or tea-maker could be included, but be careful of potential spills onto your furniture. A small bar refrigerator or ice-maker is a nice touch, too, but you should guard against turning your sitting area into a snack bar.

(j) A waste basket should be provided for trash.

f. GUEST EATING AREAS

You will want to do a renovations survey for your guest eating area as well, but the facilities provided there are specific to your food services provided, and so are discussed separately in chapter 7. Keep a blank copy of the renovations survey worksheet for use later.

g. EXTERIOR GUEST AREAS

Exterior areas, such as patios, gardens, pools, play areas, and parking, should also be considered during your renovations survey. In some jurisdictions, you will be guided by the bylaws, and in others you will be free to make your own choices. Here are some factors to consider:

(a) Off-street parking is very desirable and often mandatory. Decide how you can accommodate extra car parking.

(b) A porch or patio is a desirable feature to offer to your guests, particularly in good weather. If summer insects are a problem in your area, try to provide some protection by screening the area.

(c) A swimming pool can attract customers. If you already own a swimming pool, whirlpool, or sauna, you should advertise the fact. Make sure that these areas are fenced to avoid accidents with small children and non-swimmers.

(d) If you are targeting families with small children for your business, consider some type of safe play area for them. A section of the backyard could be set aside and furnished with swings, slides, etc.

(e) If you encourage pet owners to visit your B & B, consider building a fenced area where pets can run. Don't forget to provide a pooper scooper and disposal area or waste can so that pet owners can pick up after their pets.

(f) Gardens can be a great attraction for almost all visitors. If you are a gardening enthusiast, encourage your guests to visit your garden. Most people who are not in a hurry will appreciate the opportunity to enjoy a leisurely stroll through your garden.

(g) Signage is an important part of your B & B exterior. If you are allowed a sign, make sure it conforms to all municipal guidelines. If signs are not allowed, see that your house number is clearly visible from the road. Also make sure that the number is illuminated after dark so late arrivers can find you easily.

h. PRIVATE FAMILY AREAS

Now it is time to look at all the areas of your home that you want off-limits to guests. These areas will not be used by your guests, but there may be some work required to make them private.

1. Privacy versus inaccessibility

As a B & B host, you will be sharing your home with your paying guests and this will inevitably result in many demands on your time as you go about your "hosting" duties. At the end of a busy day, you will be ready to relax and enjoy some privacy. Set aside some rooms of the house that you can designate as private or family areas. Your guests should be made aware that these are family areas, but they should be encouraged to knock on the door if they require help. In other words, you should seek privacy but not inaccessibility.

If you plan to use an existing living room or family room as one of your private areas, consider installing doors if they don't already exist. Doors provide a psychological as well as a physical barrier that tends to stop people from wandering into a room. Doors with glass panels are useful because they send a "private" signal to your guests without implying that you are inaccessible.

If you run your business efficiently and you have anticipated the needs of your customers, you should not be disturbed very often.

Here are some factors to consider:

(a) Can you easily hear both the telephone and the doorbell when you are in any of your designated family areas?

(b) Are you accessible during the night in case of emergency? Consider how your guests will locate you, and how they can awaken you. You should let all your guests know which room is yours, and encourage them to knock on your door if they require help during the night.

(c) What bathroom facilities will your family use? Most bylaws stipulate that several guest rooms can share one bathroom, but the host family must have a bathroom to itself. The host bathroom does not need to be on the same floor as the host bedroom, so many families use a washroom located on the main floor or in the basement. If you do not have a second bathroom, check with your municipality. You may be required to install another facility.

2. Children

If you have small children, they probably have a play room inside the house. It is important not to impose too many restrictions on your children because of your business. They should realize, however, that some restraint is required with regard to noise inside the house. You might want to soundproof the play area so that both children and guests can coexist.

The extent of soundproofing will depend on the location of the play room. A suspended ceiling of acoustic tiles is very effective for noise reduction. The floor could be covered with inexpensive carpeting, and the doors could be lined on the inside with sound absorbing material. When the children are older, they will probably listen to the current version of "heavy metal" music, so your investment in soundproofing will pay off in spades!

3. Your office

You will need a space where you keep your files and do your paperwork. You might set aside a corner of an existing room or a separate room. The office should be a private and quiet place where you can attend to business matters undisturbed. Consider any labor, materials, or accessories needed to establish your office area.

This area can be treated as a business expense and the costs of maintaining it can be deducted on your income tax return. However, regulations concerning the definition of "office space" and the latest deductions should be confirmed by your accountant.

4. Exterior family areas

You may wish to spend some of your private time outside. If you are digging in the garden, you probably wouldn't mind the company of a guest or two, but if you are relaxing with a barbecue or a good book, it is another story.

Everyone is entitled to their own private space and you should consider what exterior areas you can set aside for family use. A rear deck, patio, or porch could be considered as possible options. If the area has limited access, it will be easier to maintain your privacy. Access from a master bedroom or kitchen is ideal for this purpose. Again, you want to have privacy, but not be inaccessible. Let your guests know which areas are for family only, but encourage them to call you if they need assistance.

i. DOCUMENT YOUR COSTS

Cost Sheet #3 in Appendix 4 has been provided to allow you to collect all the estimated costs for guest facilities. The cost sheet is divided into the various areas of the house. You should collect all your renovation survey sheets (Worksheet H) and make a one-line entry for each. Enter the name of the room surveyed and the estimated total renovation costs for that room. (This is the figure at the bottom of your "Accumulated Costs" column.) Don't total the cost sheet at this time because there are additional entries to be made later.

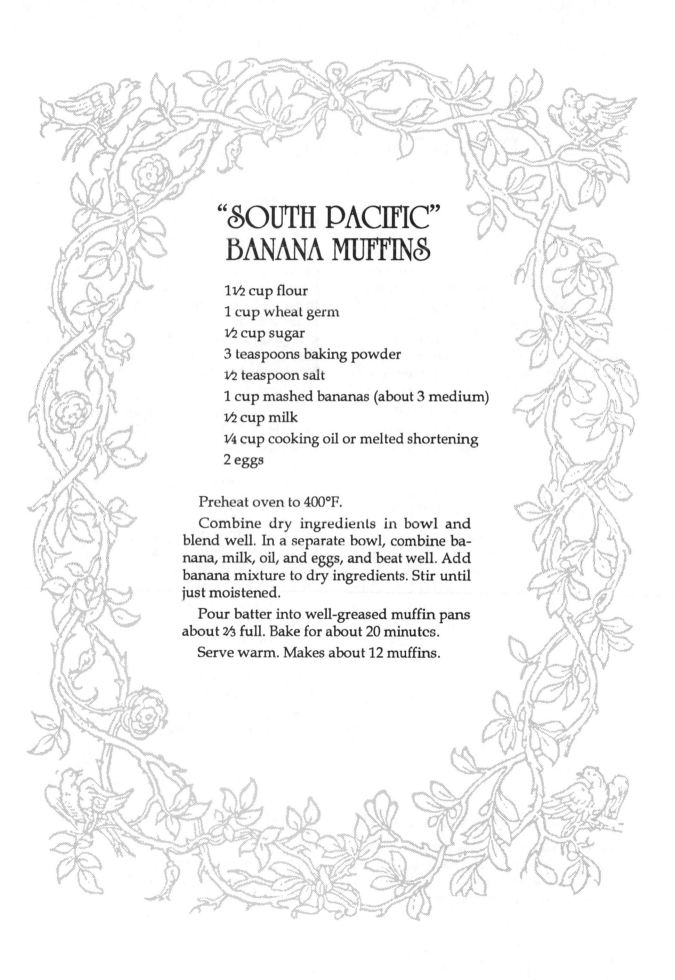

"SOUTH PACIFIC" BANANA MUFFINS

1½ cup flour

1 cup wheat germ

½ cup sugar

3 teaspoons baking powder

½ teaspoon salt

1 cup mashed bananas (about 3 medium)

½ cup milk

¼ cup cooking oil or melted shortening

2 eggs

Preheat oven to 400°F.

Combine dry ingredients in bowl and blend well. In a separate bowl, combine banana, milk, oil, and eggs, and beat well. Add banana mixture to dry ingredients. Stir until just moistened.

Pour batter into well-greased muffin pans about ⅔ full. Bake for about 20 minutes.

Serve warm. Makes about 12 muffins.

7

PLANNING YOUR FOOD SERVICES

In this chapter, you will decide on the range of food services that you will provide to your customers. Bed and breakfast implies that you will be serving some type of breakfast, but there are a number of additional food services that could also be offered. We discuss breakfasts, extra meals, packed lunches, and a variety of guest refreshments. You will make your selections, and choose your menus. In addition, you will establish your house rules concerning guest anniversaries and social events.

The issue of food handling is also discussed as well as methods of calculating food costs.

a. A GOOD BREAKFAST — A GOOD START TO THE DAY

It is true that the shortest way to a person's heart is through his stomach. We have found that a good breakfast gives the finishing touch to the stay at a B & B and that guests leave with a feeling of satisfaction at good value received. Many of our visitors say that they had forgotten the joys of a good breakfast, and they vow to continue the practice when they return home.

A good breakfast is one that is —

(a) served at a convenient time,

(b) provided in a suitable style,

(c) uses inviting food, and

(d) provides a pleasant atmosphere.

b. "WHAT TIME IS BREAKFAST?"

You must discourage guests from drifting down to breakfast any time during the morning. You will have a tight working schedule to follow, particularly in the morning: dealing with departing guests, welcoming new guests, cooking and serving breakfast, changing bed linen, and cleaning bedrooms and bathrooms. To keep yourself on schedule, breakfast must be served and eaten within a reasonable time frame. At the same time you shouldn't give your guests the impression that you are rushing them out of the house. Remember that most of them are on holidays, and they have all the time in the world.

The best solution is to set a time slot when breakfast will be available. Calculate when your check-out time will be, and then establish your breakfast hours. A common check-out time is 11 a.m., so a reasonable time slot for breakfast would be between 8 a.m. and 10 a.m. Remember that some guests will interpret your hours to mean they can *start* breakfast as late as 10 a.m., which means they may not be able to enjoy an unhurried breakfast, pack their belongings, and check out by 11 a.m. To solve this problem, tell your customers to come for breakfast anytime between 8 a.m. and 9 a.m., which will allow them plenty of time.

Many of your guests will appreciate an 8 a.m. start time because they will be anxious to get on the road for their next destination. For business travelers, you may be asked for an earlier breakfast — usually no earlier than 7:30 a.m. You should be prepared to accommodate these requests.

c. "WHAT KIND OF BREAKFAST DO YOU SERVE?"

There are many different styles of breakfast you might offer to your customers. Your choice might be influenced by the style of

B & B you run (e.g., family-oriented versus romantic and intimate), the number of rooms you have (it's easier to plan breakfast in bed for one guest room than for five), or other factors. Ask yourself who your targeted customers are and what style breakfast would most appeal to them.

These are some of the most popular breakfast styles:

(a) Continental

(b) Hot or cold buffet

(c) Full or cooked

(d) Cook-your-own

(e) Breakfast in bed

1. Continental

In North America, a continental breakfast can mean many different things. Traditionally, it implies coffee and croissants, but nowadays it usually means coffee or tea, perhaps fruit juices or fruit, and croissants, muffins, toast, bagels, etc.

A continental breakfast is always self-serve. It provides a minimum variety of food and it requires no participation of the host during the meal.

If most of your guests are business travelers, the continental style is a good choice. Generally, business travelers prefer an early start, and they don't want to linger too long over breakfast. These days, with more people being health conscious, most people have abandoned the "coffee and cigarette" routine and are attracted to healthy foods. A continental breakfast would be quite acceptable for business customers as long as you offered more than just coffee and croissants.

2. Hot or cold buffet

A buffet breakfast offers a wider selection of food than the continental style. It may be "hot" or "cold," which hints at the range of foods you might expect to find. A buffet breakfast implies that it will be self-serve, although the hosts are usually available to provide assistance.

A cold buffet generally includes tea or coffee, fruit and/or fruit juices, and a selection of cold foods similar to the continental style, but also including a selection of cold cereals, cold meats, etc.

A hot buffet features, in addition, a selection of hot foods such as hot cereals, eggs, bacon, sausages, etc.

A buffet breakfast provides a good variety of food and it can be provided with relatively little host participation during the meal.

3. Full or cooked

A full or cooked breakfast means the host cooks and serves breakfast to the guests. There is sometimes a menu available, or the host will offer a range of suggestions. Special requests can often be accommodated if advance notice is given.

A full or cooked breakfast provides a good variety of food, but it requires a high level of host participation during the meal. It is well suited to B & Bs that attract many holiday travelers who have more time to spend over breakfast. Our experience has shown that one to two hours is normally spent at the breakfast table. These guests will look forward to a substantial meal and the chance to sit around the breakfast table and socialize.

If you run a farm B & B, you might take the opportunity to offer fresh produce from the property. Homemade preserves, fresh fruits from the orchard, honey, and fresh eggs can tempt the palates of most guests. Visitors to a farm B & B will certainly anticipate a substantial breakfast.

4. Cook-your-own

Some establishments provide kitchen facilities to their customers, either as part of the guest rooms or in a common part of the house. An assortment of breakfast food can be left for the guests to prepare for themselves.

Cook-your-own breakfast is often the preferred style when the B & B is a self-contained apartment. This type of breakfast provides a limited variety of food, and it requires no host participation during the meal.

5. Breakfast in bed

Some B & Bs offer a breakfast-in-bed service as a regular option. Others may deliver a tray to the room by special request only. This can be a very nice service, especially if you promote your B & B as a "romantic get-away."

However, you may prefer no food to be consumed in the bedrooms because it can mean extra cleaning. You should be guided by the types of customers you are targeting and what their expectations might be and then determine your own house rules.

d. "WHAT'S FOR BREAKFAST?"

1. Offer a variety

You will want to offer a wide variety of food in your breakfasts to interest your customers. If you favor a self-serve style of breakfast, you can provide this variety by increasing the number of items that you offer. If you offer a full breakfast which you prepare and serve, variety can be offered by preparing the same food in different ways. For example, eggs can be prepared in a number of ways without increasing your workload substantially.

You must guard against offering too sophisticated a menu, or you will find yourself swamped with multiple breakfast orders, all requiring different preparation times, kitchen utensils, and cooking techniques. We have seen a number of hosts who have literally burned themselves out trying to be all things to all people. Don't fall into the trap of becoming too exotic. Your customers are staying in a home, and they expect a home-style breakfast.

Variety should also be considered for guests that are staying more than two nights. Even with a buffet selection, the third morning will find your guests running out of choices. Introduce some new items into your menu when you have long-term guests, and rotate those items in and out of your menu. Fresh fruit, ethnic foods, and "specials of the day" could all be rotated into your menu to give it more variety.

2. Special diets and allergies

From time to time, you may be asked by guests to provide or avoid certain foods. Vegetarians, some religious groups, or guests with food allergies fall into this category. If you can accommodate special diets without overburdening yourself, it will be appreciated.

Most guests following very strict medical or alternative diets will bring their special food with them, and they will probably ask you to provide some assistance in preparation. Most people can be accommodated easily if you provide a sufficient variety of food so that they can make their own selections. For this reason, self-serve or buffet breakfasts accommodate special diets more easily.

Generally, people with special needs have learned to take care of themselves. Your job is to respect their needs and do what you can to help — without creating too much work for yourself. For example, a guest with an allergy to peanuts will want to ensure you haven't used peanut oil in your cooking.

You can use a food services bulletin to remind guests to tell you about any special dietary needs. Sample #9 shows a food services bulletin for Carol and Bob's B & B. They place this bulletin in each guest bedroom to provide advance information about the range of food services available.

3. Developing your menu

Note on Sample #9 that Carol and Bob have remembered to state the time breakfast will be served and the type of breakfast (hot

SAMPLE #9
FOOD SERVICES BULLETIN

WE ARE PLEASED TO OFFER THE FOLLOWING FOOD SERVICES FOR YOUR ENJOYMENT

BREAKFAST   Each morning between 8 a.m. and 9 a.m. we offer a hot buffet breakfast in our Victorian dining room, including the following selections:

Chilled orange or grapefruit juice
A choice of individual cereals
Canadian back bacon
Scrambled or soft-boiled eggs (or low-cholesterol egg substitute)
Fruit of the day
Brown or white toast, homemade muffins
Marmalade, jam, and honey
Tea or coffee (Decaffinated is available)
Milk (2%)

Our muffins are baked fresh every morning. The marmalade, jam, and honey is locally produced.

SPECIAL DIETS
AND
ALLERGIES   If you have special dietary needs, we will provide assistance.
We can heat food if requested.
Please let us know if you have any food allergies.

EXTRA MEALS
License bylaws allow us to serve you breakfast only. However, we would be pleased to pack you a tasty picnic lunch for a small additional charge.

Please contact us for further details.

REFRESHMENTS
An after-theatre tray has been placed in your room.
We would be pleased to provide tea or coffee if requested.

Ice cubes are also available on request.

Fire regulations do not permit cooking in your room. We appreciate your cooperation.

buffet). A good variety of food is offered and an item is rotated into the menu each day (fruit). Dietary options are offered (decaffeinated beverages and an egg substitute), and a reminder about special diets and allergies is included directly below the breakfast menu. (Extra meals and refreshments are discussed later in this chapter).

You can use Worksheet I in Appendix 3 to list food services that are suitable for your targeted customers. Add any cautionary notes concerning special diets and allergies. (Leave the sections on extra meals and refreshments blank for now.) You might want to think of creative names for your menu items to "personalize" your breakfast. As you can see in this book, the recipes we offer between chapters have playful theatrical names, often relating to the works of George Bernard Shaw, because our B & B accommodates many visitors to the nearby Shaw theater festival.

4. Serving hints

Here are some suggestions that suit any style of service:

(a) Use clear acrylic jugs with lids to hold milk and fruit juices. Your guests will be able to identify the contents on sight, and they will appreciate the protection of the lids.

(b) Provide manufactured cereals in single-serving packages.

(c) Bulk cereals should be presented in clear glass or acrylic containers with lids and scoops. Each container should be clearly labeled.

(d) Put breads, muffins, croissants, and other breads in cloth-lined baskets. Imitating the techniques from finer restaurants will give the message to your guests that you know what you are doing.

(e) Keep coffee and tea hot on the stove or in insulated containers with lids. Merely warm coffee or tea is unacceptable.

(f) If you are offering self-serve foods, keep them in covered dishes. Have serving spoons, forks, or tongs close to each covered dish.

(g) If you are serving expensive fresh fruit such as berries, offer them in individual, single-serving bowls to ensure more equitable — and economical — distribution among your guests.

(h) Use warming trays to keep food hot.

(i) Use ice or refrigerated containers to keep food cold.

When your guests enter your breakfast area, they should receive all the right signals. The area should be scrupulously clean and the decorations should be pleasing to the eye. The table should be neatly set with complementary tableware and in colors and textures that are visually attractive. The food should be properly displayed and protected, and the quality and variety should be excellent. If you are offering a buffet or cooked breakfast, you should personally welcome each guest to the dining area and remain available to attend to their needs.

e. "IS THIS THE BREAKFAST ROOM?"

1. Location

Where will you offer breakfast? An existing dining room? An eat-in kitchen area? A common sitting area or lounge? Do you have enough room in your eating area to accommodate all of your guests?

If your house provides a good view or if the weather is usually fine, a sunroom, solarium, porch, or patio (preferably screened) can be made into a very pleasant eating area.

If you plan to offer breakfast in bed, you will still need to think about an eating area as not all guests will want to eat in their bedroom every morning.

Consider what changes you have to make to the chosen area to provide a pleasant and safe breakfast area. Will you need to upgrade any electrical wiring? Hot plates, toasters, coffee- and tea-makers may overload existing circuits. Consider any additional lighting required and don't forget supplies and decorations for this special area. What additional chairs or tables are required? What other furniture would be helpful in displaying or serving the food? Note any decorations needed to meet the expectations of your guests and to establish the right atmosphere.

Use a copy of the renovations worksheet from Appendix 3 to outline what renovations are needed (Worksheet H). (This is the same worksheet you used in chapter 6 and which is shown as Sample #8.) Complete it following the instructions given in chapter 6 and the guidelines given here.

2. Accessories

Accessories for the eating area will probably include —

(a) dishes and glassware,

(b) cutlery,

(c) serving dishes, and

(d) linens.

It is better to have completely different sets of dishes, cutlery, and linens for the guests; it is simpler to sort a different pattern than your own after washing and you won't have to worry about your own family using items you had cleaned and planned for your guests. The quality and pattern of all accessories should reflect the overall ambience you are creating for your customers.

You will need extra drinking glasses in case a guest wants more than one beverage. If you are catering to families with small children, you might want to have a few decorative plastic glasses or less-expensive glassware for the children.

You must anticipate whatever serving dishes and utensils will be needed to present your breakfasts and remember that some foods require special cutlery (e.g., grapefruit spoons). Check your menu, and supply the correct serving dishes and cutlery.

Don't forget the milk and juice containers and the coffee and tea flasks. You will also need warming trays and covered containers to keep food hot. Food can be kept cold using insulated or pre-chilled covered containers.

Condiments can be served in small containers that match your china or complement it. Sugar, cream, salt, pepper, jam, and honey all require their own special containers. As you want to promote a home atmosphere around your breakfast table, avoid institutional-looking containers that you often see in restaurants.

The table linen you choose can make or break your decor. Plastic tablecloths and paper napkins say "cheap and tacky" to your guests. Invest in several good quality tablecloths in a pattern and texture that enhances your china and cutlery. Choose matching sets of cloth napkins.

Purchase three complete sets of table linen so you can have one set in use, one set being washed, and one set in reserve.

3. Atmosphere

Regardless of the location that you choose to serve your breakfast, you should make every attempt to create a favorable impression with your customers. Some or all of your guests will be departing after breakfast, so this is your last opportunity to turn them into satisfied customers. If you can satisfy the majority of your guests, you will reap the rewards through many customer referrals.

The total atmosphere you create around your breakfast is almost as important as the food you serve. A mediocre cup of coffee may be more acceptable if the surroundings are delightful. On the other hand, excellent food becomes inedible in dirty surroundings. You should strive to make the food and surroundings as good as possible.

Some guests are quite happy sharing cereal boxes, pouring milk or juice from a communal jug, and pulling slices of bread from the cellophane wrapper. They will consider this as just being "part of the family." The majority of your guests, however, will expect to receive a higher level of service, and you need to find a style that will suit both your needs and theirs. Whether it is warm rolls and fragrant tea steaming in bone china on a white-linen-clad table delicately patterned with sunlight peering through lace cafe curtains, or thick hot chocolate in pottery mugs alongside pancakes smothered in maple syrup, all on a table decked in red gingham, it is the *atmosphere* of your breakfast that guests will remember and comment on for years afterward.

f. OTHER FOOD SERVICES

You may want to consider offering other food services as part of your B & B operation. Providing extra meals or extra touches to celebrate special occasions, offering to pack a picnic lunch, or leaving a tea or coffee tray in the guest bedrooms are some options you might explore.

1. Extra meals

First, ask yourself if you *want* to offer any extra meals to your guests. At some time, you will probably be asked by guests if you do provide other meals, so you should be prepared to deal with this issue. There are four considerations:

(a) Is it legal? B&Bs may only serve breakfast in many municipalities. The health and safety regulations are less stringent on B & Bs because they are not viewed as full-service restaurants. If you want to offer other meals, you may run into licensing problems. Check your local bylaws before you proceed.

(b) Is it physically possible? Do you have the cooking and preparation facilities to handle many varieties of food? More to the point, do you have the physical stamina? You will find your hosting duties quite labor intensive; if you add the responsibility of preparing and serving extra meals, you may find it too much.

(c) Is it worth it? What could you charge for extra meals? What would your net profit be? Consider *all* expenses including utilities, food, preparation, serving and cleanup costs, etc.

(d) Can you be competitive? What do local restaurant or hotels charge for a comparable meal? Determine if you can compete with their prices.

The planning, preparation, and serving of full meals will put you almost in the same category as a restaurant and that is a complex business. This is not our field of expertise and rather than cover this in an inadequate fashion, we refer you for more information to *Start and Run a Profitable Restaurant*, another title in the Self-Counsel Series.

2. Lunch packs

Some customers will appreciate the opportunity to purchase a packed lunch from you before they set out on their day. Long-term guests and travelers heading for another destination are both candidates for this service. Generally, bylaws do not restrict this kind of service because it is impossible to enforce.

If you are thinking about offering this service, here are some points to consider:

(a) Have several different lunch menus prepared ahead of time and ask your customers to pick one of them. Include the price on the menus. The lunches can be different prices depending on their content and complexity.

(b) Choose foods that are easy to prepare. Keep it simple.

(c) Choose foods that do not spoil easily. Cheese, fruit, breads, rolls, muffins, and crackers are good choices.

(d) Choose foods that are easy to eat. Avoid runny foods or foods that need a lot of preparation in the field. For example, use cherry tomatoes in place of large ones, rolls or crackers instead of an unsliced loaf of bread.

(e) Include single-serving cartons of fruit juice for the beverage. Milk does not keep well.

(f) Don't forget straws and napkins.

(g) Pack each lunch separately in a paper bag.

(h) Always charge extra for this service.

(i) Make sure your guests know that you need advance notice to provide this service. Asking you to "throw something together" fifteen minutes before their departure is unrealistic. Ask guests to choose their menu and inform you of their needs the day or, at very least, the night before.

(j) Suggest a pleasant area where your guests can eat their picnic lunch if they prefer to stay close to home.

3. Room refreshments

Providing room refreshments may be a simple way to add a special touch, but you must first decide whether you want any food or drink consumed in the guest rooms.

Many travelers prefer to have a picnic-style midday meal. These guests may ask to use your patio or they may eat the lunch in their rooms. Some may bring their own portable tea- or coffee-makers; others may heat soup in a portable hotpot. If you haven't stipulated that you do not want any food or drink in the guest bedrooms, you must be prepared for guests to use their rooms for other meals.

Keep in mind that if you do allow food in the rooms, some guests may abuse the privilege. Cooking odors could be a problem to guests next door. Food odors linger in bedding, drapes, and rugs. Spillage could damage carpets or furniture and careless use of electrical outlets could present a fire hazard. Your insurance policy may not permit this activity.

Alternatively, if you provide a coffee or tea service to the guest rooms, you will remain in control and discourage cooking in the room. For an added touch, you could include a few cookies or a fruit bowl. The additional cost of this service is minimal and it is excellent public relations.

Most of your guests will not abuse this service, but you will need to guard against the few individuals who might expect to receive a continuous supply of coffee throughout the day. To avoid this you could charge for the service, but that would turn an act of hospitality into a money-making scheme. A better solution would be to offer the service as only an "afternoon tea tray" or an "after-theater tray."

If your bedrooms are equipped with kitchenettes, as some are, then you may decide to allow cooking in the rooms. In this case, make sure the kitchenettes meet all building codes, are equipped with automatic ventilating fans, and that your insurance policy allows them.

If you do provide a food service in the rooms, remember to provide napkins and line your waste baskets with waterproof liners to minimize your clean-up.

There are a number of other room refreshments that you may want to consider for the comfort of your clientele:

(a) Provide two drinking glasses in each guest bedroom. Many customers also appreciate a small, covered, water jug that they can put on their bedside table. Sit the glasses and jug on a tray or cloth to avoid water marks on your furniture.

(b) Some hosts provide a few mints or candies in each guest room. This is an extra sign of hospitality and the cost is minimal. Choose hard candies that keep well in warm weather. The candies should be individually wrapped and placed in a small dish.

(c) Many of your visitors will ask for ice cubes. You can supply these on request from your kitchen refrigerator or, if your rooms have kitchenettes, you might consider small individual refrigerators in each.

4. Special services

When your guests arrive, they have probably been traveling for many hours. Most likely, they will be tired and thirsty, and would appreciate the friendly gesture of being offered some refreshment such as a glass of chilled fruit juice or a cup of tea or coffee. You might also include a few cookies.

If your guests tell you that they are celebrating an anniversary, birthday, or other special day during their stay, you may wish to do something extra. Here are a few options:

(a) Leave a congratulations card in their room. Keep a stock of generic cards on hand to use for any happy occasion.

(b) Put cut flowers from your garden in their room. A small, attached card could contain an appropriate "best wishes" message.

(c) Leave a half-bottle of wine or champagne and two wine glasses in their room. Tie a few multi-colored ribbons to the neck, and attach a small card.

You will need to decide if you are going to advertise the fact that you provide something special for anniversaries, or whether you are going to leave it as a surprise. We leave it as a surprise, but if a prospective customer or their booking agent specifically asks about our policy, we tell them.

If a group of people stays at your home, one or more of them may wish to sponsor a social event such as a cocktail hour on the patio or a surprise gift presentation for one of the group. You may be asked to supply additional food, ice, supplies etc. You must exercise your own judgment as to how involved you want to become, or even if you are going to allow it. Remember that this is your home, and you set the rules.

Generally, we recommend that you co-operate in helping your guests with a social event, provided that it appears to be in good taste, and it does not violate any of your house rules. There may be extra expense involved, and you should be reimbursed for those expenses. If you do not wish to get involved or even allow the event to happen, then you must find some diplomatic way to deny the request. Always be courteous and sympathetic.

Now refer back to Sample #9 earlier in this chapter and the accompanying worksheet. Complete the lower two sections which show the extra meals and refreshments you plan to offer. Notice the references to licenses and regulations. If you want to impose restrictions, it is always easier — and better from a public relations point of view — to place the responsibility for your decision on the authorities.

g. HANDLING FOOD

1. Purchasing

Generally speaking, there are three levels of food pricing: manufacturer's price, wholesale price, and retail price. You probably won't be able to buy at the manufacturer's price unless you have better connections than we do. You can, however, buy at the wholesale level because you are a business.

Find a wholesale grocery outlet in your area, and make an appointment to register with them. They will probably require you to fill out an application form and supply them with some proof that you are actually in business. A business card or business license is usually all that is required.

Although you will be purchasing a reasonable quantity of food supplies, you will not require supermarket quantities, so it is better to deal with a "cash-and-carry" type of wholesale outlet, rather than a bulk-delivery, warehouse facility. Cash-and-carry outlets generally offer ½ or ¼ cases of items, which are much more suitable for a B & B.

Food prices are very competitive, so you should constantly be on the lookout for the best prices. Buying items at a wholesale outlet does not guarantee a best price. Special deals at retail or discount outlets can often beat the wholesale price. Keep your eyes open for these bargains, and take advantage of them.

You will require fairly large quantities of paper products and cleaning supplies. These items are sometimes available at drug stores, department stores, and variety stores. Don't overlook these outlets as possible sources of lower-priced supplies.

2. Storage and spoilage

You will soon discover that you will need additional storage space to handle the guest food and supplies for your B & B. Paper products should be stored in a dry location to avoid deterioration. Cleaning supplies must be stored securely where children cannot gain access.

Non-perishable food products should be stored in a clean, cool, and dry location. An existing pantry or food cupboard could be used with a section set aside for guest food products.

Perishable foods require refrigeration for proper storage, so you will need to reserve a few shelves in your refrigerator for guest supplies. If you happen to own a second refrigerator, consider designating one of them for guest food. For safe storage of these products, keep the refrigerator temperature between 42°F (5.6°C) and 45°F (7.2 °C).

Check all perishable foods daily for freshness. Be sure to check the expiry dates on perishable foods when you purchase them. Remember that warm weather will accelerate the spoilage of perishable foods. Check all fresh fruit for soft spots, and all bread products for dryness or mold. Samples of fruit juice and milk should be tasted daily. Follow the rule: *When in doubt, throw it out.* The reputation of your B & B is worth more than a slice of stale bread or a glass of sour milk.

3. Preparation

The level of activity in the kitchen when preparing breakfast for your B & B guests is about the same as for a typical dinner party. If you cast your mind back to your last family reunion or dinner gathering, you will probably recall the inevitable confusion in the kitchen. As much as possible, you will want to streamline your kitchen routines.

Using your breakfast menu as a guide, prepare and serve each of the menu choices. Make sure you have enough utensils to prepare each menu item without using anything more than once. This will ensure that the entire breakfast can be prepared without having to stop your preparations to wash dishes. Keep track of how long it takes to prepare each dish and decide how best to coordinate preparation steps. For example, if two items each require baking in the oven, how best can you handle that? Which one should go first, or could the recipes be altered slightly to allow both in the oven at the same time?

4. Hygiene

Your personal hygiene and the state of your kitchen is important both for health reasons and for overall presentation of your breakfast. If your planned eating area for guests is the kitchen, you must keep it attractively decorated and clean and tidy at all times. Even if your guest eating area is elsewhere, guests often find their way into the kitchen. Your customers will be reassured by the appearance of a clean kitchen.

Your personal hygiene is also very important when you serve food to the general public. For health reasons, it is imperative that your hands be scrupulously clean, and you should avoid touching the food with your hands if at all possible. Wash your hands before you begin preparations, and be ready to wash them each and every time you think they have been contaminated again. Antiseptic hand soaps are available in drug stores, and we recommend their use in the kitchen.

Clean hands are only one aspect of personal hygiene and your total personal appearance must reflect cleanliness. Your guests will be very uncomfortable if you appear in creased, stained, or worn clothing. Make sure your hair is clean and well groomed, and check under your fingernails. If you have long hair, you may want to tie it back, both for hygienic and convenient reasons. Don't smoke when you are cooking or serving the guest food because ashes may fall into the food. If you are a pet owner, keep pets out of the kitchen, particularly when preparing guest food.

5. Disposal

It is important to have efficient food disposal facilities in place. If you already have a garbage disposal unit attached to your sink, you are fortunate. If not, you might want to consider adding one in your renovation plans. At the least, put a small covered garbage receptacle in the kitchen for food scraps. Use odor-free removable liners and empty the receptacle at least once per day.

Between garbage collection days, you should store your food garbage in large outside containers secure from animals. These containers should be out of sight of any areas that you have set aside for the use of your guests.

6. Plan for renovations

Using copies of the renovation survey (Worksheet H), determine what renovations are required in your home to establish food-handling facilities including storage, preparation, and disposal areas. Complete a separate worksheet for each of the three areas following the same format as shown in Sample #8.

h. DOCUMENT YOUR COSTS

Cost Sheet #3 shown in Appendix 4 has been provided to allow you to collect all the estimated costs for guest food facilities. (Remember, this is the cost sheet that you began to complete in chapter 6.) You should now collect all the renovations worksheets that you completed in this chapter, and make a one-line entry for each room.

On Cost Sheet #3, enter the room name and the estimated total costs for that room. (This is the figure at the bottom of your "Accumulated Costs" column.) The estimated hours are not recorded here, but they are used later in chapter 15. Don't total the cost sheet yet.

i. CALCULATING GUEST FOOD COSTS

There is a large cost to providing food to guests and it is important that you know how much you are spending on guest food. Without these details, you may find you are subsidizing every meal you serve and not taking full advantage of the costs as legitimate business expenses.

For example, a simple breakfast could consist of cereal with toast and coffee. You could calculate the cost of the three items on the menu, but you have to remember the milk and sugar poured on the cereal, the butter and jam for the toast, and the cream and sugar for the coffee.

1. Item-by-item vs. average method

There are two methods of calculating your total food costs: the item-by-item method and the average method. (How to calculate indirect costs of food services, such as the cost of food storage and preparation costs, is discussed in chapter 11.)

The item-by-item method is used by commercial establishments that deal in large quantities of food and have sophisticated bookkeeping. They obtain receipts for each food shipment and then enter these receipts as separate business expenses.

You could do this for your B & B, but you may find it too unwieldy. First, you will have to purchase and store business food and family food separately. As well, you must be sure to get a receipt for every purchase and then enter each as an expense. Finally, if you are ever audited by the tax department, you will have to justify your total food purchases against your total customer count. All in all, this might be too much bookkeeping for you.

With the average method, you calculate your cost of providing food to an average customer by doing a food-cost analysis (see below). You then claim this cost as a business expense for every customer you service during the season.

The advantages of using this method are that it is not necessary to separate business and family food and receipts are not required. If you are ever audited, you don't need to justify every food purchase against your total customer count; however, you would still need to show that your calculations were based on realistic food quantities and accurate prices.

2. The food-cost analysis

Sample #10 shows a food-cost analysis for a typical B & B breakfast menu (the breakfast shown in Sample #9) using the average method of calculating food costs. A food-cost analysis worksheet is provided in Appendix 3 for your use (Worksheet J). Two copies are provided, but you should make as many photocopies as you will need. You will want to fill out one sheet for each different menu you offer. You should also update your food-cost analysis from time to time to monitor increasing costs.

As you complete this worksheet, keep these points in mind:

(a) Always note the date; food costs change and you will want to use the date as a reference point.

(b) For each food item, decide on the most efficient size to purchase. Mark down the product, purchase size (e.g., 454 grams, 4 dozen, etc.), and price.

(c) Establish how many "units" that package contains. A "unit" will vary with the specific product. For pre-portioned items like eggs or tea bags, a unit is obvious. For items like jam, coffee, or cereals, you will probably resort to good old-fashioned cups, teaspoons, or other measures. Choose units that are in proportion to the servings you expect guests to require. For example, you wouldn't choose cups for your jam unit, as it is highly unlikely that anyone will want a cup of jam on their toast! Similarly, using teaspoons for your cereal unit would be time-consuming. For products that are not pre-portioned, open each package and actually count the number of units you can obtain from that size of package. Since you are making a record of these numbers, you won't have to repeat this procedure next year.

(d) Under "Units per Serving," write down your best estimate of how many units your average customer might consume for breakfast. For example, you might guess that a guest will eat 2 egg units (eggs or egg substitutes), 3 bacon units (slices), 1 juice unit (glass), 3 topping units (teaspoons), etc. As you gain experience in your business, you will be able to improve the accuracy of your estimates. We have found that people on holidays tend to consume rather large breakfasts, followed by lighter lunches. Also you will encounter some food spoilage, which will require you to discard a small percentage of the food.

(e) Now, you can use the formula of:

(Purchase price ÷ # of Units in Package) x Units per Serving = Price per Serving

This will give you the "Price per Serving" to enter in the last column.

(f) Finally, total the "Price per Serving" column to get the total cost of providing one average customer with this breakfast. In Sample #10, we show that it would cost about $4.89 to provide each customer with one breakfast from the menu shown in Sample #8.

You should do a cost analysis for any alternative food services you plan to offer your guests such as packed lunches and room refreshments.

The total of your cost analysis worksheets can be claimed as a business expense in proportion to all your B&B customers. If some of your extra food services are provided to only some of your customers, those costs must be proportioned properly — not applied to every customer.

Do a new food-cost analysis at least once every year and more frequently if food costs seem to be escalating. Make sure you date all your analysis sheets, and retain them for your tax records.

SAMPLE #10
FOOD COST ANALYSIS

FOOD SERVICE _Breakfast_   DATE _Jan. 15, 199–_

DESCRIPTION	SIZE	PURCHASE PRICE	# OF UNITS IN PACKAGE	UNITS PER SERVING	PRICE PER SERVING
Orange juice	48oz	2.79	6 glasses		
Grapefruit juice	48oz	2.99	6 glasses		
AVG. JUICE		5.78	12 glasses	1 glass	0.4816
Dry cereal	Pkg	3.59	10 cups		
Muslix cereal	350gr	3.49	10 cups		
AVG. CEREAL		7.08	20 cups	1 cup	0.3540
Milk for cereal	2 qts	2.69	8 cups	1 cup	0.3362
Cdn. back bacon	1 lb.	4.50	14 slices	3 slices	0.9642
Large white eggs	1 doz.	1.75	12 eggs		
Egg substitute	6 pack	1.98	6 "eggs"		
AVG. EGG		3.73	18 eggs	2 eggs	0.4144
Bananas	1 lb.	0.75	4 bananas		
Oranges	1 doz.	4.49	12 oranges		
Pears	each	0.39	1 pears		
Peaches	each	0.40	1 peaches		
AVG. FRUIT		6.03	18 fruit	1 fruit	0.3350
White bread	675g.	0.99	20 slices		
W.W. bread	675g	0.99	18 slices		
AVG. BREAD		1.98	38 slices	2 slices	0.1042
Muffins	1 doz	2.95	12 muffins	2 muffins	0.4916
Marmalade	750ml	4.19	30 tsp		
Strawberry jam	500ml	3.39	20 tsp		
Raspberry jam	500ml	3.69	20 tsp		
Honey	750g	3.89	20 tsp		
AVG. TOPPING		15.16	90 tsp	3 tsp.	0.5053
Tea	72 bags	3.19	72 cups		
Coffee	300 gr	2.99	28 cups		
Milk	2qt.	2.69	8 cups		
AVG. BEVERAGE		8.87	108 cups	2 cups	0.1642
Brown sugar	1 kg	1.49	50 tsp		
White sugar	1 kg	1.33	50 tsp		
Sugar substitute	100 gr	2.69	100 tsp		
Cream	500ml	1.96	10 tsp		
AVG. ADDITIVES		7.47	210 tsp	6 tsp	0.2134
H.P. Sauce	250 ml	2.09	2 tsp	2 tsp.	0.1990
Salt & Pepper					0.1000
Butter	454gr	2.75	48 tsp	4 tsp.	0.2291

AVERAGE INDIVIDUAL SERVING COST _4.8922_

"OKLAHOMA" OATMEAL BREAD

1¼ cups all-purpose flour

1 cup rolled oats

1 teaspoon baking powder

1 teaspoon baking soda

1 teaspoon salt

½ teaspoon cinnamon

¼ teaspoon nutmeg

⅔ cup brown sugar

1 egg

⅓ cup vegetable oil

1 cup thick applesauce

1 tart apple, peeled, cored, and diced

½ cup chopped nuts (optional)

½ cup raisins (optional)

Preheat oven to 350° F.

Combine flour, rolled oats, baking powder, baking soda, salt, cinnamon, nutmeg, and brown sugar in a large bowl.

In a separate bowl, beat the egg, oil, and applesauce together. Add apple, nuts, and raisins, and stir only until ingredients are just moistened.

Pour into a greased 9½ x 4½ loaf pan. Bake for 1 hour 15 minutes or until center is cooked.

Slice and serve warm with butter.

8

SETTING YOUR HOUSEKEEPING STANDARDS

Housekeeping is one area that can make or break your B & B reputation. People are very particular when they sleep in strange bedrooms or use unfamiliar bathrooms. They are equally concerned about the level of hygiene maintained in the cooking and eating facilities and the overall level of cleanliness in the common areas designated for their use. Your customers will scrutinize the cleanliness of all these areas very carefully, and on the basis of their inspections, they will form an opinion of your entire operation. If your rooms are spotless, your guests can forgive almost any other shortcoming, so you must clean your guest areas to a much higher standard than normally found in good housekeeping practices. Your rooms must not only be clean, they must *appear* to be clean. In other words, you must leave evidence that you have cleaned the rooms recently.

In this chapter, we describe the methods and products used to achieve a high standard of housekeeping, and we point out the areas that are often overlooked in normal cleaning routines. We also provide some tips on signalling to your guests that you have recently cleaned their rooms.

a. BEDROOMS

First, you must provide the right quality and quantity of bedding for your customers. For each guest bed, purchase three complete sets of bedding which include a bottom sheet, a top sheet, and pillow cases. Three sets are required so you can have one set in use, one set being washed, and one set in reserve. For each bed you will also need at least one blanket,

one waterproof mattress cover, one bedspread, and at least one spare pillow (many visitors ask for an additional pillow). Floral or patterned sheets are better than plain colors, as they show creases less. Purchase the best linen you can afford because the quality of your bedding will be scrutinized by your customers.

Some hosts provide bathrobes to their customers. These are very appropriate for homes that do not have en suite bathrooms.

In maintaining a bedroom, remember that a bedroom that looks and smells clean will put your guests at ease, so your worst enemies are dust, stains, finger marks, and residual odors.

Dust, stains, and finger marks can be easily removed with good housekeeping. Minor residual odors caused by stale air and poor ventilation can be corrected by allowing fresh air in and by using an air freshener. Tobacco or food odors are more difficult to deal with because they tend to settle into drapes, rugs, and bed linens.

The best advice is to attack the problem at the source. Instituting "no smoking" and "no cooking" rules for your guest bedrooms is probably the best solution. If you do allow smoking and/or cooking in the bedrooms, provide ventilating fans and air purifiers so that the level of the odors is reduced. You will also need to wash the drapes and bedspreads and shampoo the rugs frequently to control odors.

Guest bedrooms will require cleaning after each guest has checked out. Here is a typical daily cleaning routine that you can follow. It takes about 20 to 25 minutes for each guest bedroom.

(a) Remove the top sheet and spread it out on the floor.

(b) Remove the bottom sheet and pillow cases and pile them in the middle of the top sheet.

(c) Remove all towels, facecloths, bathrobes, etc., and place them in the middle of the top bed sheet. Assume that all linens are soiled, whether they appear to be used or not.

(d) Gather up the four corners of the sheet and, using it as a carrier, take it immediately into the laundry room. Don't leave it in the hallway because it is unsightly to guests and presents a hazard.

(e) Remake the bed using clean linen. Place fresh towels, facecloths, bathrobes, etc. in the room.

(f) Replace the water glasses, water jug, and other room-refreshment equipment. (We place the water glasses upside down and put a new paper doily under each glass to signal to our guests that the glasses have been changed. Paper doilies are very inexpensive when purchased in boxes of 1,000 at a wholesaler.)

(g) Using a feather duster, dust all furniture surfaces, lamps, pictures, bookcases, etc. A feather duster removes dust efficiently and won't scratch the furniture.

(h) Using a furniture cleaner and soft cloth, clean all surfaces including headboards, table tops, chairs, and door surfaces. Look for finger marks.

(i) Using a window cleaner and paper towels, clean all mirrors and glass surfaces. Look for finger marks on all smooth surfaces including glass lamp shades. It is easier to spot finger marks if you turn the room lights off and look across the surfaces at an angle. Dispose of used paper towels in the waste basket.

(j) Empty the waste basket by removing the liner and its contents; install a new liner.

(k) Replenish any bedroom supplies such as facial tissue, soap, candies, fruit, flowers, information brochures, etc.

(l) Vacuum the floor. Also check for dust or cobwebs on the ceiling, lighting fixtures, door or window trim, ventilating grilles, and drapes. The vacuum cleaner is the best device to tackle these dust and cobweb problems.

(m) Air out the room by turning on the air conditioner or ceiling fan or by opening a window. In addition, you can use an air freshener.

(n) If you have individual bedroom door locks, make sure that the lock is operational and that the room key is in place.

(o) Check the room to make sure you have not overlooked anything. If you are working as a team, it is a good idea to have your partner do the check.

b. BATHROOMS

A clean bathroom is one that is free of stains, splash marks, mildew, and odors. Stains and splash marks can be controlled through good housekeeping. Air circulation is very important in controlling mildew and odors, and we highly recommend the use of mechanical ventilation such as an exhaust fan that is activated by the bathroom light switch. Some municipal governments have made these fans mandatory for B & Bs.

If you do not install mechanical ventilation, you will have to be extra vigilant for the appearance of mildew. Odors will need to be controlled by ventilation and air fresheners.

You will need to provide towels and facecloths for each of your customers. A good combination is one hand towel, one bath towel, and one facecloth. As with bed linen, you should have three sets for every customer that you can accommodate in any one night. You will also need bath mats; three per room should be adequate. Again, buy the best quality towels you can afford; when people are wiping their faces in something, they do notice the quality. If your guests use a shared bathroom, you may choose to hang their towels and facecloths in their bedrooms.

The guest bathrooms will get much heavier use than a normal family situation and require a much higher standard, so you will need to clean them every day. The cleaning won't take long if you establish an efficient routine. For hygienic reasons, wear rubber gloves and use throw-away paper towels.

Here is a typical daily bathroom cleaning routine that takes one person about 15 to 20 minutes to complete and results in a clean, sparkling, and odor-free bathroom. Your guests will appreciate all the extra effort you put into your bathroom housekeeping standards.

(a) Remove loose articles from the bathroom (facial tissue, extra toilet paper roll, soaps, potpourri, floor rug, etc.). This makes it easier to clean the bathroom. Remove the waste basket lid, but not the waste basket. Keep the used bath mat for step (b).

(b) Remove water residue from shower doors, walls, bathtub, etc., using the bath mat as a mop. Don't forget to check the bathtub drain strainer for hair or other dirt accumulated.

(c) Using a tub and tile cleaner and paper towel, clean all the surfaces of the shower walls, shower fixtures, bathtub, and tap fixtures. If mildew is showing in the tile grout or corners, you will need to use a mildew cleaner to remove the dark spots. If

mildew is a continuing problem, try to increase the amount of ventilation in the bathroom. Daily applications of tub and tile cleaner will also help retard mildew growth.

(d) Using a window-cleaning solution and paper towel, clean both sides of the shower doors, all mirrors, and windows. If the shower doors are coated with a soap or lime scum, you will need to use an acid-based product to remove the coating (e.g., vinegar or a manufactured product). Daily applications of the window-cleaning solution will eliminate the problem.

(e) Using a toilet-bowl cleaner and a brush, clean the toilet bowl. We recommend using a cleaner that tints the water a light blue. If you leave a little cleaner in the bowl, it will be a visible sign to your guests that the bathroom has been cleaned recently. If you use a non-tinted toilet bowl cleaner, you might also want to use one of the products that you hang inside the toilet tank and which "cleans with every flush." This will enhance the freshness of the bathroom.

(f) Using tub and tile cleaner and paper towel, clean all exterior surfaces of the toilet bowl, both sides of the toilet seat and lid, and the toilet tank. It is important to clean the bottom of the toilet seat and also the floor area around the toilet.

(g) Using tub and tile cleaner and paper towel, clean the vanity top surface, vanity sink, and tap fixtures. Remove any finger marks from doors or door hardware.

(h) Vacuum the bathroom floor. Also check the exhaust fan grille and lighting fixtures for accumulated dust. You will need to wash the bathroom floor, if it is not carpeted, at least once per week. We recommend selecting a product that is wax free because it is important to maintain a safe, non-slip surface on the bathroom floor.

(i) Discard all used paper towels in the waste basket and empty the waste basket by removing the liner and its contents. Put a new liner into the waste basket and replace the lid.

(j) Replace all the loose articles previously removed. Check that there is an adequate supply of soap, paper cups, facial tissue, toilet paper, potpourri, etc. Make sure there is an extra roll of toilet paper easily accessible.

(k) Hang a new bath mat onto the towel rail. We keep a variety of different colored bath mats in stock, and we change the color every day. Any guests that are staying for more than one night will be reassured by the sight of an obviously different (and clean) bath mat.

(l) Ventilate the room for at least half an hour by running the exhaust fan or opening the bathroom window.

(m) Check the room to make sure you have not overlooked anything. If you are working as a team, get your partner to do the check. A tip: sit down on the toilet seat and look for splash marks or finger marks on walls or mirrors. You will often see additional marks that are not visible when you are standing up.

c. EATING AREA

It is essential that the eating area be kept clean at all times. You must be diligent wherever food is prepared or stored. Following is a typical daily cleaning routine which should be performed after your guests have finished their breakfast. Quite often you can perform some of this cleaning during the time that your guests are packing their bags prior to check-out. This procedure takes about 20 to 25 minutes.

(a) Remove all food to storage areas.

(b) Remove all dishes and serving equipment in preparation for washing.

(c) Remove all tablecloths and napkins for laundering.

(d) If you provide a toaster for your guests, empty the crumb tray at least once per week.

(e) Using a feather duster, dust all areas above the food-serving surfaces. Dust all picture frames, door and window frames, and furniture.

(f) Wipe all eating and serving surfaces with a cloth dampened with a mild antiseptic solution, then wipe dry.

(g) Using a furniture cleaner and soft cloth, clean all surfaces including table tops, chairs, and door surfaces. Look for finger marks and food stains.

(h) Using a window cleaner and paper towel, clean all glass, plastic, marble, or chrome surfaces. Look for finger marks.

(i) Vacuum the floor and check for dust or cobwebs on ceilings and light fixtures. Vacuum the drapes.

(j) Tidy the area and either set the table with clean linen or decorate the table with a bowl of fruit or flowers.

(k) Check your work. If you are working as a team, get your partner to do the check. Pay particular attention to finger marks and stains.

(l) Ventilate the room for at least one hour.

d. COMMON SITTING AREA

A common sitting area offers your guests a chance to relax and socialize. Because they will be spending more than just a few minutes in the sitting area, they will have ample time to assess your housekeeping skills. It is important, therefore, to maintain a high standard of cleanliness in this area. Use the same level of care that you took in the guest bedrooms. If you allow food in these areas, apply the same housekeeping standards as in the main eating area. Fresh flowers used as decoration will signal to your guests that this area has received recent housekeeping attention.

e. GUEST HALLWAYS AND STAIRWAYS

The hallways and stairways used by your guests require the same level of housekeeping as would be expected in the average household, except that cleaning will need to be done daily. Your guests will be coming and going regularly and they will bring in dirt and dust from the outside, particularly in bad weather. You should provide places to hang wet overcoats, muddy shoes, and wet umbrellas. In addition, a daily dusting and vacuuming will be required. Pay particular attention to dust and cobwebs on ceilings, lighting fixtures, doorways, etc.

f. FOOD PREPARATION AREAS

If your guests eat in the main kitchen, or if they use a guest kitchenette, they will be very aware of the cleanliness of the food preparation area. If your guests eat in a separate dining area, they might be curious about the level of hygiene used in the kitchen. Don't be surprised if your guests "accidently" wander into your kitchen to make their own quick assessment.

B & Bs are not subjected to the same rigorous inspections as full-service restaurants, so the public is not protected to the same degree. The rest of your home will signal the level of hygiene that you maintain in your kitchen. If the rest of your home is spotless, your guests will be reassured about your kitchen.

In chapter 7 we discussed some of the precautions needed to maintain good kitchen cleanliness; these points are repeated in the following list. Your greatest cleaning challenge will be the control of germs, residual grease, dust, and odors. Here are some points to consider:

(a) Prior to food preparation, wipe all surfaces with a mild antiseptic solution, then wipe dry.

(b) Prior to food preparation, wash your hands with an antiseptic hand soap.

(c) Avoid touching the food with your hands if at all possible. Wash your hands each time you think they have become contaminated.

(d) Don't use cracked or chipped food storage containers, or stained, cracked, or rusted food preparation containers or utensils.

(e) Keep the kitchen sink scrupulously clean, as well as the sink strainer and drain.

(f) Throw away all kitchen scraps in a covered container, and empty the container after each kitchen clean-up.

(g) Using a kitchen cleaner, remove all grease from around the cooking area. Clean the exhaust fan and filter at least once per week.

(h) Vacuum the floor daily and check for dust on ceilings and lighting fixtures.

(i) Clean the kitchen floor at least once per week with a no-slip floor cleaner.

(j) Maintain kitchen ventilation during cooking, and at least one hour after cooking. The breakfast odors that appealed to your departing guests in the morning, will not be appreciated by your arriving guests in the afternoon.

The above procedures will ensure that your food preparation areas are free of germs, residual grease, dust and odors. If you always prepare your food in a clean and hygienic environment, you will put your guests at ease, and more important, you will help to avoid accidental food poisoning.

g. WASHING DISHES

When you wash the dishes, your overriding concern must be to destroy germs, but you should also ensure that there are no residual food deposits, stains, and water marks. Here are some points to consider:

(a) Use the hottest water possible, to destroy germs and to dissolve food residue. If you are using an automatic dishwasher, make sure that the water temperature is set high enough to clean well and kill germs. Some machines have a "sani-dry" setting that dries the dishes with very hot air, which may also help to kill germs. However, be warned that it can also melt plastic dishes! Refer to your manufacturer's brochure.

(b) Use a good quality dish detergent. Inferior products may cost less but will not clean the dishes well. Add a water spot remover.

(c) If you wash by hand, wash the glasses first (with the cleanest water). Follow with the cutlery, dishes, and then the pots and pans.

(d) Dry glasses with a lint-free cloth.

(e) Check all cleaned dishes for food residue, stains, and water marks. Pay particular attention to fork prongs and the backs of spoons. Rewash any items that are unacceptable.

(f) Examine all dishes and glasses for cracks or chips. Discard any that show such signs of wear.

h. LAUNDRY

You will need to do laundry daily to keep an adequate supply of clean bedding in store. Here are some helpful hints:

(a) Select a detergent that will work effectively at lower, energy-saving temperatures (warm wash, cold rinse). Some products leave a residue if the water is not hot.

(b) Use a "static control" product, either in the wash or the drying cycles. These products help prevent wrinkles.

(c) Remove the laundry from the drying cycle before it is bone dry. If you fold the no-iron sheets and pillow cases at this stage, they will have fewer wrinkles. The articles will still be warm, and they will continue to dry even though they are folded.

(d) Store bathrobes on plastic or wooden coat hangers. Steel hangers can rust and mark the bathrobes.

i. ORDER OF CLEANING

The check-out and check-in times you establish must leave you enough time to clean the rooms in preparation for the next guests. Occasionally, you will be faced with a guest that leaves later than the check-out time and some new guest may arrive early. Obviously, if this occurs, you have less time to clean the house.

It is important therefore, to establish an order of cleaning that will present the least disruption to the arriving customer. The following is the order of cleaning that we established for our B & B and that has worked well for us.

(a) Clear the dining table. Dirty dishes are not attractive to arriving guests and it takes only a few minutes to clear this area.

(b) Do a quick tidy-up of the common sitting area. If new guests arrive immediately, we ask them to relax in the sitting area until their rooms are ready. We always apologize for being behind on our schedule (even if it is not our fault). Most people are very understanding.

(c) Clean the bedrooms.

(d) Clean the bathrooms.

(e) Clean the hallways and stairways.

(f) Complete the cleaning of the eating area.

(g) Complete the cleaning of the common sitting areas.

(h) Clean the kitchen and wash the dishes. In our house, the guests rarely enter the kitchen, so they aren't affected by a late clean-up of this area.

(i) Do the guest laundry. Our guests do not have access to our laundry area, so they will not be affected by this activity.

Your home will have a different layout than ours, so you will need to develop your own order of cleaning. En suite bathrooms, en suite kitchenettes, and eating areas that are combined with kitchens or sitting areas, will all influence your order of cleaning. Some careful planning now will avoid confusion and chaos in the future. Take the time now to document an order of cleaning that will present the least disruption to your arriving guests.

j. EXTERIOR HOUSEKEEPING

It is important to maintain a tidy look to the exterior of your B & B. Our customers tell us that they judge the quality of a B & B from the appearance of the house exterior and that they would refuse to book into homes that look untidy. Prospective guests will be discouraged if they see uncut grass, cluttered driveways, weed-filled flower beds, or piles of trash. They may assume that the inside of the house will be in the same untidy state. Remember, in the world of business and advertising, first impressions can make or break a sale.

Use the following checklist from time to time to view your house exterior through the eyes of your guests and keep it clean and safe:

(a) Check for paint that is faded or peeling.

(b) Check for damaged window glass, screens, and shutters.

(c) Check all exterior doors and door hardware for damage or faulty operation.

(d) Look for loose eaves troughs and downpipes.

(e) Check porch and patio floorboards, railings, and steps for safety.

(f) Check for loose chimney bricks or missing mortar.

(g) Check the condition of all your walkways for any safety hazards. Look for loose or cracked cement slabs, stones, or bricks. Look for holes or other tripping hazards in gravel pathways.

(h) Trim any tree branches or bushes that block the walkways.

(i) Keep the grass cut and neatly edged and flower beds weeded and tidy.

(j) Fences and gates should be in good repair.

(k) Garden furniture must be comfortable and safe.

(l) Driveways should be in good repair and free from oil or grease.

(m) Try to eliminate obvious garden hazards such as thorn bushes, poisonous plants, bee nests, etc.

(n) If you have a dog, it is a good idea to provide a separate fenced dog run. Not all guests are comfortable with pets.

(o) Protect small children from swimming pools and fish ponds by restricting access to these areas with appropriate fencing.

(p) Hide any garbage or trash out of sight of your exterior guest areas. Place garbage in covered containers that are odor-free and resistant to animals.

(q) In some climates, there is a heavy morning dew that needs to be removed from patio furniture prior to use. It is wise to remove this dew first thing in the morning in case your guests wish to sit outside after breakfast.

k. PEDESTRIAN AND VEHICLE ACCESS

You must ensure that your customers always have access to the house, regardless of the time of day or the prevailing weather. Here are some points to consider:

(a) If your local bylaws allow you to hang a sign outside your B & B, place it so that it is easily visible from a passing vehicle. If you expect guests to arrive after dark, have some method to illuminate the sign.

(b) Make sure your house number is visible from the road. Trim any bushes or tree limbs that might obscure the numbers, and illuminate the house numbers after dark.

(c) Make certain that the driveway and parking places are clearly visible. After dark, provide good lighting to this area.

(d) Provide a clearly visible and safe walkway to the entrance to your home. Access should be from both the front sidewalk and the parking area. After dark, the walkway should be well lit. Remove all obstacles from the walkways including overhanging bushes and tree limbs.

(e) The entrance door to the house should be well identified, and a clearly marked and illuminated door bell button should be available. After dark, provide the front door area with good lighting.

(f) Walkways and driveways should be kept free of snow, ice, wet leaves, or any other hazards.

l. EQUIPMENT AND SUPPLIES

Use Worksheet K in Appendix 3 to plan for any housekeeping equipment and supplies you need to purchase. You can use a copy for your B & B's interior and a copy for the exterior. Sample #11 shows how Carol and Bob Morris completed this worksheet for their interior supplies. Use the checklists given in this chapter when planning out the different supplies you will need. Estimates should be quoted to the nearest dollar. Don't forget to estimate the hours it will take to purchase the items and transport them to your home.

When you plan your purchases, you might want to consider purchasing products that are less harmful to the environment — or "green" products. These days, we have all become more aware of the harmful effects of many cleaning products on the environment. Most of us have also made an attempt to reduce the amount of household garbage we create and to increase the use of reusable or biodegradable materials.

We encourage you to seek out those products that produce good results and have the least-harmful effect on the environment. Most environmentally friendly products will do a good job, but as with any other consumer product, the selection of an effective brand name is largely an exercise in trial and error. Here are some suggestions for your cleaning products and supplies:

(a) For waste basket liners, use waxed paper bags in place of plastic bags.

(b) Use cleaning liquids in pump-operated containers, rather than spray cans.

(c) Buy your cleaning liquids in bulk, and refill a pump-operated container, rather than buying a new container each time.

(d) Use paper products made of recycled paper (e.g., paper towels, toilet paper, facial tissue, picnic napkins, etc.).

(e) If you use colored paper products, choose a manufacturer that uses environmentally friendly dyes.

SAMPLE #11
START-UP EQUIPMENT AND SUPPLIES

AREA __INTERIOR HOUSEKEEPING__   SHEET # ____1____

ITEM #	EQUIPMENT AND SUPPLIES	EST. COST	EST. HOURS
1	Folding step stool	$10	
2	2 feather dusters	3	
3	2 furniture polishing clothes	2	
4	2 pair rubber gloves	4	
5	2 lint-free towels	4	
6	waxed paper wastebasket liners	5	
7	paper doilies	13	
8	window cleaner	4	
9	paper towels	3	
10	furniture polish	4	
11	mildew remover	3	
12	tub & tile cleaner	5	
13	shower door cleaner	3	
14	toilet bowl cleaner	3	
15	antiseptic handsoap	4	
16	household disinfectant	3	
17	laundry soap	7	
18	static control liquid	3	
19	dishwashing soap	4	
20	3 sets of bedding - single bedroom	90	
21	3 sets of bedding - double bedroom	120	
22	3 sets of bedding - twin bedroom	180	
23	3 sets of bedding — roll-out cot	90	
24	18 facecloths	72	
25	18 handtowels	126	
26	18 bath towels	180	
	Purchasing time		
			8
	TOTAL	945	8

71

(f) For air fresheners, use herbs and pot-pourris.

(g) For window cleaner, try vinegar and water.

(h) Compost your kitchen scraps and garden clippings.

(i) Use biodegradable bags for your disposable garbage.

m. DOCUMENT YOUR COSTS

You can now make the first entries on Cost Sheet #4 in Appendix 4. Take your total estimated costs from your start-up supplies worksheet and enter them in Cost Sheet #4. Enter the area of the house (i.e., interior or exterior) and the estimated cost for equipment and supplies. Do not total the cost sheet at this time because there are additional entries to be made later.

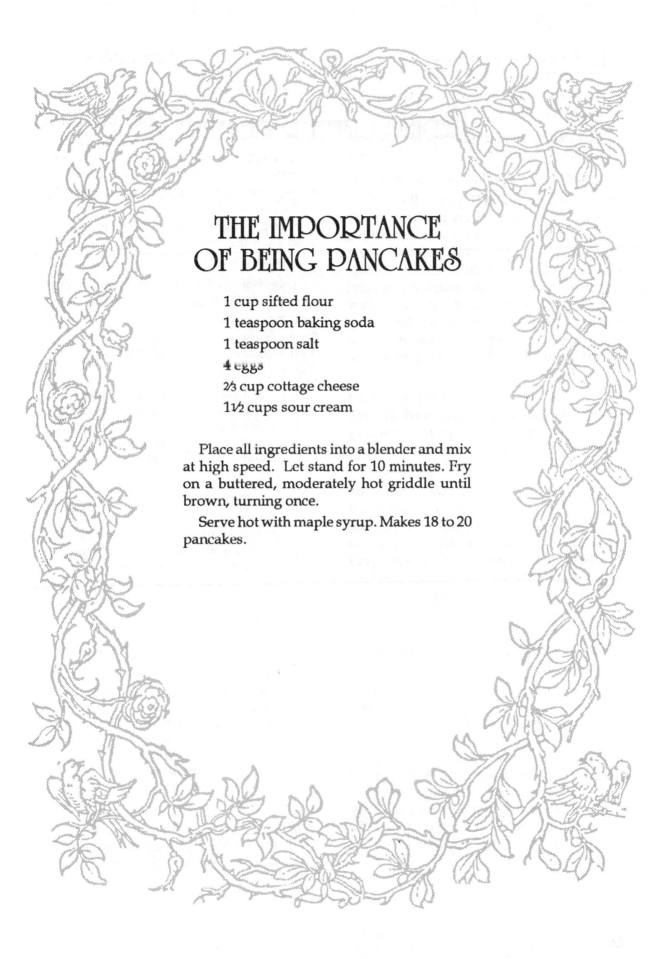

THE IMPORTANCE
OF BEING PANCAKES

1 cup sifted flour
1 teaspoon baking soda
1 teaspoon salt
4 eggs
⅔ cup cottage cheese
1½ cups sour cream

Place all ingredients into a blender and mix at high speed. Let stand for 10 minutes. Fry on a buttered, moderately hot griddle until brown, turning once.

Serve hot with maple syrup. Makes 18 to 20 pancakes.

9

KEEPING CLIENT RECORDS

As you run your B & B, you will deal with many different customers and their needs every day. Guests arriving will be checking in; guests departing will be paying and checking out. You will need to calculate amounts owing, make out receipts, and answer any questions your guests may have. At the same time, you will be dealing with ongoing telephone calls inquiring about your B & B and with mail and paperwork.

To bring order to this chaos, you need to establish client records procedures that are easy to use and readily understood by anyone in your family involved in hosting.

This chapter describes the various records that are necessary to collect client information and, at the same time, provide a means of capturing statistical data that can be used to monitor and improve your business. Sample client forms are provided that you can copy and modify to suit your specific needs.

a. USE TECHNOLOGY WISELY

Today, we are surrounded by an array of electronic gadgets that promise us everything from greater levels of enjoyment to greater levels of profit. You may have bought one or two of these technological devices only to discover that 80% of the features are seldom used. However, now that you are running a business, you may find useful applications for all the "bells and whistles" on telephones, fax machines, and other devices.

1. Telephones

Nothing is more important to your business than the telephone. It is your link to potential customers.

Telephones offer many features that can make your business more efficient. Before you buy and install a new phone, review these features and choose the telephone that will serve you best. Think about the following options:

(a) Push-button phones are easier to use than dial phones, and they are considerably faster when you dial a number. Time can be important in the middle of a busy day.

(b) An automatic dialing (memory button) feature can be a big time-saver. You can store the numbers of local restaurants, airport reservation desks, and a taxi service, as well as emergency numbers. We are often asked to make dinner reservations for our guests and it is much easier to press one button for each restaurant rather than looking up the number and dialing each time.

(c) A portable phone will let you clean the rooms or stroll in the garden with your guests without worrying about missing an important call. (If you do choose a conventional phone, then place one on each floor of the house; it is inconvenient and dangerous to run up or downstairs to answer the phone.)

(d) Consider a telephone with a "hold" button. That way, if you answer a call upstairs, you can put a customer on hold while you move downstairs to get to the reservation book. After you have completed the call on the downstairs phone, you needn't worry about running back upstairs to hang up the first phone, as you would have to with a conventional extension setup.

(e) An intercom is a useful feature if you and your spouse are running your B & B together or if you have an employee. You can quickly locate someone else without physically searching for them. Intercoms are found on better-quality portable telephones.

(f) A system with speaker-phone capability is convenient because it leaves your hands free. You can carry on a conversation while you take down a customer reservation, for example.

(g) Custom-calling services are offered by many of the local telephone companies. These optional services usually require a one-time administration fee plus an additional monthly fee. Contact your local telephone company and ask for a list of optional calling services available to you. Some of the more common services are the following:

(i) Call waiting: Allows you to answer one call and hold another call. This feature helps avoid missing important business calls.

(ii) Call forwarding: Lets you transfer your calls to another telephone number. You could use this service to transfer calls to a message service or to a car phone.

(iii) Call identification: Gives you two telephone numbers on the same telephone line, each with a different ring. You could use this feature to let you distinguish between personal and business calls.

(iv) Three-way calling: Allows conference calls among three different telephone numbers.

2. Answering machine

When you are running a business, it is important not to "abandon" the telephone. In other words, your telephone should be answered 24 hours a day every day of the year. Obviously, you cannot be there to answer every call, but an answering machine can do the job for you.

If you do use an answering machine, record a message that is short, courteous, and professional — about 20 seconds long. Some customers, if they are calling long distance, will resent getting an answering machine, so be sure to offer to return the call in your message.

You should have a selection of recorded tapes with different messages to cover a variety of circumstances. For example, if you are out for a few hours only, your message could say: "Hello, this is the Morris Bed and Breakfast. We are unable to come to the phone right now, but if you leave your name and phone number after the beep, we will return your call as soon as possible. Thank you for calling the Morris Bed and Breakfast."

If you have left town for a vacation, your message could be: "Hello, this is the Morris Bed and Breakfast. We are closed for a few weeks, but if you wish to make future reservations, please call Anne White at 555-1234. She will be happy to assist you. If you would rather leave a message, please wait for the beep. Thank you for calling the Morris Bed and Breakfast."

Set the answering machine to pick up after about four rings. If it picks up sooner than that, you will find that you miss some calls when you are at home because the machine got the call before you did. If you leave more than four rings, many people will hang up before the answering machine clicks on.

3. Facsimile machine

If your clientele is composed of many business travelers, you might consider acquiring a facsimile (fax) machine. A fax machine will send or receive printed pages using an ordinary telephone line. Your use of a fax machine will be limited, so cost them carefully if you decide to purchase. You might find a good used machine at a substantially reduced price, or you might investigate a leasing arrangement with an option to buy.

Investigate the possibility of sharing a fax machine with another B & B or small business. This can help save in the purchase and maintenance costs. If your customers want to use your fax for outgoing messages, you may want to implement a per-copy charge. Check what other businesses charge and price yourself accordingly.

Some fax machines are built for home businesses and work on the same telephone line as your regular telephone. This is a good choice if you aren't going to use a fax often, but there are drawbacks. If the fax is in use, your telephone is out of service and vice versa. For higher-volume usage, it is better to install a separate telephone line for the fax. Of course, this is an additional cost.

4. Typewriter

Most offices have abandoned their typewriters for computers, so there are good buys to be found in the used-typewriter market. If you have no intention of buying a computer, or if you think you will wait a few years before buying, consider buying a good used typewriter to write your business letters and design your business forms.

5. Personal computer

A computer is not a necessity to the efficient running of a B & B, but there are many advantages to using one especially in creating and maintaining proper client records. With a variety of software, you can do your own word processing, make charts and graphs, establish a filing system, and do your own bookkeeping.

With word-processing software, you can create and store all the forms needed for your B & B, create standard business letters, and create your advertising pieces. Other software packages that include graphics and artwork can add an additional level of sophistication to your documents and customize your business forms. You can also easily analyze the business statistics you gather over the years using spreadsheets, charts, and graphs.

One of the best applications of a personal computer is filing. The computer can scan all the records in any particular file and select only those that you specify for a certain purpose. You can produce year-end reports, Christmas-card labels, and any other listings from a computerized filing system. Client names, addresses, and phone numbers can all be kept on a computerized file system.

If you are already familiar with computers, you may decide to purchase a computer and/or some software and charge it to your business. Make sure you can afford this additional expense during this critical start-up time. More important, can you spend the time necessary to learn how to use the computer effectively? If you are not currently familiar with computers, we advise you to delay purchase for at least one year. You are going to be very busy establishing your B & B and you should concentrate on the myriad details of starting up before getting involved in something new.

b. TYPES OF BOOKINGS

You will deal with two types of bookings in your business: advance and same-day. Each requires particular procedures to be followed and records to be kept.

1. Advance bookings

Obviously, advance bookings are preferable because they allow you to plan ahead and project customer needs and your business cash flow for the season. As your business grows and people come to know about your B & B, you will receive an increasing number of advance bookings. Some customers may want to book, for example, a regular time every year, and so you will need to have a bookings record book prepared for one year ahead.

You will have to establish a system of deposits to guarantee advance bookings. You can mail a receipt and confirmation slip to your guests, and remind them of your policy regarding non-returnable deposits if they fail to show up or inform you of changed plans after a certain date.

If you find that many of your customers book one week or less in advance, we strongly recommend that you accept credit cards for deposit payment because customers won't have time to mail you a check and receive their confirmation.

When you take advance bookings, keep these points in mind:

(a) During the telephone conversation, try to assess if the customer is acceptable. Remember that you have no obligation to accept unsuitable or rude customers.

(b) Briefly outline any important house rules (e.g., no pets or no smoking) to avoid misunderstandings.

(c) Be clear about your reservation deposit policy. Insisting on a deposit is a strong incentive for a customer to honor the reservation.

(d) Take the customer's name and address to mail a confirmation to him or her. It is important to properly identify your customer for security reasons. (Security is discussed in more detail in chapter 10.)

2. Same-day bookings

Same-day bookings can be less certain. Many people arrive in town without a place to stay and begin calling a number of establishments without committing to a reservation. To avoid being left with an empty room for the night because a same-day reservation doesn't show up, ask a caller for advance payment on a credit card. If the caller is reluctant, refuse the booking. Sincere customers with good intentions will agree to pay in advance.

You will have less time to assess the suitability of customers if they call at the last minute. Always ask if they have been referred by a fellow B & B operator or by one of your booking agencies; if that is the case, you know that some screening has already taken place. If they have not been referred, take the time to describe the accommodations and your house rules. Base your decision on the reaction to your rules. Remember, you don't have to accept anyone you are uncomfortable with.

If the customer is a "walk-in" (i.e., a customer that knocks on the door and asks for a room), then you must make your own quick assessment. If you have any reason to feel uncomfortable, simply tell the person that your rooms are booked.

c. BOOKING PROCEDURES AND FORMS

You will need to record each client from initial reservation to final check-out. At any time, you will have customers who are in various stages of the booking process, and efficiently designed forms will help you keep your records straight.

We have developed the following procedures and forms that have proven effective for keeping accurate client information and for tracking the booking procedure. They are described below using our hosts, Carol and Bob Morris, and two guests, Marjory and Bill Smith.

1. Reservation book

Every B & B needs some type of reservation book. It should be in calendar format and, beside each day of the year, there should be one space for each room that you rent. If you rent only one room, you can use a regular household calendar. If you rent two rooms, you will easily find one of a variety of business calendars in book form with enough room. If you have three or more rooms, you will probably need to purchase a reservation book specifically designed for the hotel/motel/B & B industry. These books can be ordered from stationery supply stores. (Remember to keep your receipts for any stationery purchases to claim as business expenses on your income tax.)

Keep your reservation book close to the telephone so you can easily consult it whenever anyone calls. The reservation book is your primary document and, therefore, it *must* be kept up to date at all times.

When you book a room for a customer on a specific date, be sure to mark the person's last name in the correct space in the book. We recommend that you enter the last name only, and we suggest that all other client information be noted on a separate reservation slip. Make all your entries in pencil so that they can be erased if customers call to change or cancel plans. Sample #12 shows one page from a typical reservation book. Note the following as you review Sample #12:

(a) Carol and Bob have identified each room they rent by the beds available in each. If you have multiple rooms with the same type of bed, you will have to find some other way to identify each room. You might use numbers, color schemes (e.g., blue room), etc.

(b) The sample shows that Smith has booked for the two nights of Wednesday, August 12 and Thursday, August 13; he will not check out until the morning of Friday, August 14. Jones has booked for the one night of August 12, and Brown has booked for one night on August 13.

(c) The "hold" on Friday, August 14 is drawn through Friday, August 14 because Carol and Bob want to attend a business seminar that afternoon and won't be available for guests that night. Note that if the seminar they are attending were to begin in the morning, they would have to put a hold on the previous day because they will be preparing and serving breakfast to their guests on the morning of August 14 before those guests check out.

This reservation book style provides Bob and Carol with a "week-at-a-glance." At the beginning of the week, they can look at the upcoming guest schedule and estimate the amount of food and other supplies needed. They can also refer to the book daily to determine their working schedule for each day. For example, on the morning of August 12, they note that they should be available to greet both Jones and Smith sometime in the afternoon. On the morning of August 13, they must prepare and serve breakfast to Jones and Smith, take care of Jones checking out, clean his room, and prepare for Brown to arrive.

2. Reservation slips

Reservation slips are used to document the names and addresses of all your customers and to track the status of each booking from initial customer contact to the completed transaction. Sample #13 is an example of a reservation slip showing all the entries that should be made during the initial telephone call. As you make each entry, you should read it back to the caller to ensure accuracy.

Note the following features:

(a) "Call date" shows the date the reservation was made, either by telephone or mail.

SAMPLE #12
RESERVATION BOOK

DATE	SINGLE BED	TWIN BEDS	DOUBLE BED
MONDAY AUGUST 10			
TUESDAY AUGUST 11			
WEDNESDAY AUGUST 12		JONES	SMITH
THURSDAY AUGUST 13	BROWN		↓
FRIDAY AUGUST 14	←	HOLD	→
SATURDAY AUGUST 15			
SUNDAY AUGUST 16			

SAMPLE #13
RESERVATION SLIP

_____July 4/92_____   _____August 12/92_____
CALL DATE   SINGLE BED _____   DATE OF ARRIVAL

_____D_____ _____   _____Wednesday_____
CALLER   NOTIFY   TWIN BEDS _____   DAY OF ARRIVAL

                                              _____2 p.m._____
                          DOUBLE BED _X_   TIME OF ARRIVAL

_____$160_____   __2____ __2____
TOTAL TARIFF   ROLL-OUT COT____   NIGHTS PERSONS

_____$80_____   _____CARD   Visa # 1234567890123   REMIND_____
DEPOSIT   _____CHECK _____CASH   DATE__11/93 CONFIRM_____

_____$80_____   _____CARD   _____#_____   _____ADDRESS BOOK
BALANCE   _____CHECK _____CASH   DATE_____ _____LEDGER ENTRY

_____Smith, Marjory and Bill_____
NAME
_____235 Address Avenue_____ Apt. 301_____
STREET   BOX / APT.NO.
_____Village_____ Vermont_____
CITY   STATE / PROVINCE
_____12345_____ (890)_____ 123 4567_____
ZIP CODE / POSTAL CODE   AREA CODE   PHONE NUMBER

DETAILS : Celebrating their 5th wedding anniversary._____

_____

_____

(b) "Caller" shows the *type* of client that made the reservation, that is, the source of the client. You will find it useful to keep statistics on these sources. In Sample #13, Bob and Carol have assigned a code for each of their customer sources: A = local attraction brochure (advertisement); B = B & B association (booking agent); C = chamber of commerce (booking agent); D = direct customer (repeat or referred).

(c) The slip also shows the total tariff for the room, the amount paid on deposit and the method of payment, and the balance owing. The method of payment for the balance is not filled in until Smith pays at check-in or check out. In the example, Smith put an $80 deposit on the reservation giving his credit card number over the telephone. If the customer wants to mail you the deposit, you should develop a policy about how long you will hold the reservation; two weeks should be sufficient.

(d) Arrival time is important to record accurately. Note the date *and* day of the week to avoid misunderstanding. For example, over the phone you might mis-hear the second of August as the seventh of August. We have also encountered quite a few customers who were looking at the wrong month of their calendars when making reservations, and it was only when we mentioned the day of their reservation that they discovered their mistake. You should also note the estimated time of arrival and the number of nights the guest is staying.

(e) Note the number of persons staying under each reservation. In Sample #13, the reservation slip shows two people staying. You will need this information to calculate the amount of food for breakfast.

(f) Take down the full name, address, and telephone number of each customer as well as any other details that will help you. In Sample #13, the Smiths mentioned that they would be celebrating their fifth wedding anniversary, which the Morris' chose to acknowledge with a congratulations card and a half-bottle of wine in their room. Other details you might include in this section are things such as dietary requirements, special interests, requests for early breakfast, etc.

Keep your completed reservation slips by your reservation book in order of dates of arrival. You should review them weekly to check for any outstanding room deposits.

You will also want to notify any booking agencies you use so they can keep their records up to date. In the example, the reservation was made by direct call so Bob and Carol will have to call their B & B association and the chamber of commerce. Once they have done so, they will enter B&C on the "Notify" line on their reservation slip.

Notifying booking agents is a very important step. It is very important to keep booking agents informed of reservations you receive from other sources. Booking agents cannot act in your best interests if their records are out of date. Also, frequent calls to update their records will keep your name front and foremost in their minds. They will soon learn that they can rely on your records to be accurate and up to date and they will be more inclined to send business your way.

If you do not receive a room deposit in the mail after two weeks, send out a deposit reminder slip (see section **4.** below) and check off the "Remind" section of the reservation slip.

Confirm all reservations with your customers by sending out a booking confirmation slip (see Sample #15 and section

5. below). Then check off the "Confirm" section of the reservation slip.

Finally, once the customer has come and gone, use the reservation slip to record the customers' names and addresses in your client address book and note the transaction in your financial records. Boxes to note that these tasks have been completed are shown on the sample reservation slip.

3. Canceled reservations

If a reservation is canceled, you must remove the reservation slip from the stack and erase the entry in your reservation book. Be sure to telephone the booking agencies to update their records. If your house procedures allow, send the appropriate deposit refund.

If any amount of the deposit is kept by you, enter the amount into your revenue ledger, check off the appropriate box on the reservation slip, and write in the retained amount under the total tariff.

If you think the customer might be a future client, enter his or her name in your address book. Also, make a note of the reason for cancellation — you may find the information useful in the future.

4. Deposit reminder slips

Use a deposit reminder slip when you have not received a promised room deposit in the mail. If two weeks have passed, mail the reminder slip specifically asking for a reply. If another two weeks go by with no reply, cancel the reservation. (If you accept credit cards for deposit payment, you will not need to use the reminders.) Sample #14 shows a deposit reminder slip.

Include a thank-you and always strive to be courteous. Your customer will probably respond to the reminder and there may be a legitimate reason why the deposit did not arrive.

If you cultivate a loyal following of repeat customers, you will find that some will book with you as far as a year in advance. We are reluctant to accept a deposit from these customers so far in advance, so in these cases we use a deposit reminder slip a few months before the intended visit asking the guests to confirm their intentions and to send their deposit.

5. Booking confirmation slips

With the exception of reservations made on very short notice, all reservations should be confirmed by mail after you receive a deposit. Sample #15 shows a booking confirmation slip used by Carol and Bob Morris.

A booking confirmation slip should document the details of the booking including the name of the customer, the date and day of arrival, the number of nights accommodation booked, and the type of room booked. The slip can also serve as a receipt for the deposit payment and a reminder of how much is owing on the room.

The slip shown in Sample #15 also outlines the cancellation policy and check-in times. It will also be helpful if you mail with the confirmation slip a map of your immediate area with your B & B's location clearly identified. You might use this opportunity to send a complete package with your business card and/or brochure.

We encourage you to copy and modify the slips shown in Samples #13, #14, and #15 to suit your own B & B.

6. Client address book

Before you file your completed reservation slips, you should transfer the customer's name, address, phone number, and any detailed comments into a client address book. Use a looseleaf business-sized telephone book with alphabetical index tabs (available at business stationery stores).

If you keep your address book close to your reservation book, you can quickly refer to it when repeat customers call. Use the information to personalize the call: call the client by his or her first name and mention details that will tell the customer you remember previous visits. These details

SAMPLE #14
DEPOSIT REMINDER SLIP

NAME: _____Smith, Marjory and Bill_____

DAY & DATE OF ARRIVAL:_Wednesday, August 12, 1992_____ NO. OF NIGHTS: _Two_____

ROOM(S):   _____SINGLE BED   __X___DOUBLE BED

                  _____TWIN BEDS   _____ROLLOUT COT

THE ABOVE BOOKING WAS REQUESTED ON THE DATE :___July 4, 1992_____

BY: __X__PHONE   _____IN PERSON

         _____FAX   _____VIA AGENCY

         _____MAIL   _____REFERRAL

Our 1992 rates are $ 80   per room per night, double occupancy. (Includes a full breakfast for two) To retain this booking, please send a ___$80___deposit to the address below by return mail. (Make check payable to R. Morris.) On receipt of the deposit, we will send you a confirmation, along with a map and brochure. Thank you for choosing our home.

Carol and Bob
Carol and Bob Morris
Box 500, 132 State Lane
Anywhere, New York, 14411
phone or fax (123) 4567890

SAMPLE #15
BOOKING CONFIRMATION SLIP

NAME:_____Smith, Marjory and Bill_____

DAY & DATE OF ARRIVAL: _Wednesday, August 12, 1992_____NO. OF NIGHTS: _Two_____

ROOM(S):   _____Single bed   __X___Double bed

                  _____Twin beds   _____Rollout cot

Please check that the above room(s) and date(s) are correct. We acknowledge receipt of a deposit on the above rooms of $___80___. The balance will be $___80___

Our cancellation policy permits a 50% rebate of the deposit, only if more than 7 days' notice is given. You may check into your room after 1:00 p.m. Please let us know if you plan to arrive after 6:00 p.m. Please feel free to contact us if we can be of further service. We look forward to your visit.

Sincerely,

Carol and Bob
Carol and Bob Morris
Box 500, 132 State Lane
Anywhere, New York, 14411
phone or fax (123) 4567890

will tell your customers that they are important to you and you will benefit by using this simple customer relations tool.

7. Long-distance telephone slips

You will often get requests from your customers to use your telephone. As long as these requests are reasonable and do not tie up your phone for too long, you should allow them.

From time to time, guests may also want to make long-distance calls and these should also be allowed on the understanding that guests will pay for the calls and complete a long-distance telephone slip. Of course, you will have to monitor guests for possible abuse. If a telephone call turns into an over-long conversation, don't hesitate to interrupt and politely ask the customer to finish the conversation. Most customers will appreciate that your telephone needs to be available for business purposes.

Use long-distance telephone slips to keep track of all long-distance calls originating from your telephone. Customers should note that they charged the call to their home number or called direct. If they call direct, you can ask the operator to calculate the cost of the call. When calls appear on your next phone bill, you can use the long distance telephone slips to trace each call.

Sample #16 shows a long distance telephone slip. You can buy a supply of slips from a stationery store or modify Sample #16 to suit your own needs. Note that the sample slip clearly spells out the house rules concerning telephone calls. You can leave one of these slips in each room.

8. Guest book

It is good practice to keep a guest book on a table near your front door. You will find that most customers will be eager to enter their names along with a few comments when they are checking out. If you have provided an excellent breakfast, they will be in a very receptive mood to praise your establishment. Many of the entries in our guest book are humorous, and our guests have fun reading through them.

You can purchase a guest book from most stationery suppliers. Be sure to select a large book because some of your guests will write a lot.

You should also keep a supply of business cards and/or brochures next to the guest book and encourage guests to take a few to hand out to their friends. (Business cards and brochures are discussed in chapter 12.)

d. DOCUMENT YOUR COSTS

Using a copy of the start-up supplies worksheet (Worksheet K), make a record of all your client recordkeeping costs. Enter any purchases or costs discussed in this chapter: telephones, answering machines, reservation book, etc. Estimates should be quoted to the nearest dollar and hour.

Now return to Cost Sheet #4 in Appendix 4 and complete the portion marked client recordkeeping. Make a one-line entry of your estimated total costs.

LONG DISTANCE TELEPHONE SLIP

Guests wishing to place a local or long distance telephone call are requested to notify the hosts prior to the call.

We ask you to make your call as brief as possible because our telephone is needed for business purposes on a continuous basis.

If your call is long distance, please complete this form and give it to the hosts.

Thank you for your cooperation.

Carol & Bob Morris

GUEST NAME: <u>Marjory Smith</u>

CALL DATE: <u>August 12, 1992</u>

NUMBER CALLED: <u>(890) 123 4567</u>

ESTIMATED LENGTH OF CALL <u>3</u> MINS.

METHOD OF PAYMENT:

        _____CHARGE CARD

        _____CASH PAYMENT OF $

        __X__CHARGED TO <u>(890) 123 4567</u>

THE MORRIS HOUSE
BOX 500, 132 STATE LANE
ANYWHERE, NEW YORK, 14411
PHONE OR FAX (123) 4567890

CRITICS' CHOICE
CRANBERRY RELISH

2 medium oranges
1 lb. fresh cranberries
2 cups sugar

Cut unpeeled oranges into 5 or 6 pieces. Remove the seeds and chop coarsely in a blender. Pour into a 3-quart casserole.

Add cranberries and sugar and stir until well mixed.

Cover and cook 15 minutes until cranberries are soft, stirring every 5 minutes.

Pour into sterilized jars.

Makes four 6-oz. jars. Great with any egg dish.

10
CUSTOMER SERVICE OPTIONS

No two B & Bs are exactly alike. Each has its own unique mix of location, ambience, accommodations, and services. Each one will have its own methods of operating to effectively cater to its customers.

In this chapter, we discuss various operating options. You should consider each option carefully, and then select the procedures that best meet the needs of your specific business.

a. CHECK-IN PROCEDURES

When new customers arrive, you have the opportunity to make your first personal meeting a memorable and pleasant one. How organized, efficient, and friendly you are will set the tone for the rest of the customers' stay. Your customers will have talked to you over the phone or corresponded with you by mail, so they have formed a preliminary opinion of you. If you have been courteous and efficient in your reservation procedures, you will have created a favorable impression. Now you have an opportunity to reinforce that good opinion by making your customers feel welcome and putting them at ease.

1. Check-in times

How you implement and enforce your check-in policy is the start to efficient and respected organization. You will want your guests to be clear on your policy when they make their reservations, and you must enforce that policy once the guests arrive.

Hotels are becoming stricter in enforcing their check-in times because their profits were being hurt by unacceptable numbers of "no shows." Most hotels now require a credit card number when accepting a reservation or will only hold the room until about 6:00 p.m. As a B & B operator, you should follow their lead.

When you take a reservation over the telephone, tell your customer what your check-in time is, and be sure to put this information on your booking confirmation slip. Your check-in time should be two to three hours after your check-out time to give you adequate opportunity to clean the rooms and prepare for the new arrivals.

Your check-in time should extend to no later than about 6:00 p.m. This will allow you to prepare and enjoy your own dinner undisturbed and will let you plan your "after dinner" family activities. Always tell your customers to telephone you if they will be later than 6:00 p.m. to avoid the necessity of waiting all afternoon in vain. If you know they are going to be late, you can make use of the free time in the afternoon.

2. Put your customers at ease

When your customers arrive at the door, you should strive to put them at ease. The B & B is a young industry in North America, and many of your guests will be "first-timers." They may feel uneasy about approaching a private residence and apprehensive about the type of reception they will receive.

When you greet your guests at the door, your first action should be to smile. Body language is very powerful, and a smile is recognized as "friendly" by everyone. A smile will signal to your customers that they are welcome visitors.

Introduce yourselves and welcome them to your home. A typical greeting would be "Hello, my name is Bob, and this is my wife Carol. Welcome to the Morris Bed and Breakfast Home. Please come in." With this greeting, you have personally introduced yourselves, and then invited them into your home — good first steps to putting your guests at ease.

It will help to establish a first-name relationship with your guests. If they do not respond to your lead, ask them for their names. A typical approach would be, "I believe you are the Smiths. Is that correct? And you must be...? (Customer says Marjory). Hello Marjory. And you must be ...? (Customer says Bill). Hello Bill." Some customers are very shy, and you will have to break the ice. Others are very gregarious and will initiate their own introductions.

Get into the habit of remembering their first names. Write their names on their reservation slip (if they are not already entered). If you forget their names, you can recheck the slip.

Offer to help with the luggage. Most people will have at least one suitcase, and one hang-up suit/dress carrier. A few extra hands are appreciated by your arriving customers. It also indicates to them that you are sincere in your desire to be hospitable.

3. Orient your customers

Your new guests will be entering a totally unfamiliar world. They will be unsure about the layout of your home and about your house rules. Also, they may want to ask you questions about local attractions, restaurants, transportation, etc. As soon as you have completed the initial check-in, you should orient your customers to your B & B.

Start by conducting a quick tour of your facilities. Show the guests the areas that they can use both inside and outside the home. Don't just tell them about the areas, actually show them. Include the common sitting area, dining area, porches and patios, and, of course, their own bedroom and bathroom. If you take the time to show them the guest areas, they will be more likely to confine their activities to those areas. Also they will be more at ease using these facilities because you have specifically given them permission to do so.

Next, inform them about your house rules. When you are conducting your tour of the guest areas, you can mention some of your more important house rules as they apply to the specific areas you are showing. For example, when you are touring the dining room, you can mention the hours that breakfast will be available. You can ask the customer if that is acceptable or if they prefer an earlier breakfast? (Notice that you don't offer a later breakfast because that would disrupt your schedule.) Similarly, when you tour the common sitting area you could mention your "no smoking" rules, and then offer them the use of an outside area for smoking. When you tour their bedroom, you could mention room keys, room refreshments, and private telephone calls. You could also point out the complete set of written house rules that you provide in each guest room.

The complete tour should take no more than five minutes. The tour provides a diplomatic way to emphasize some of your more important house rules. Most of your guests will not bother to read printed house rules, but they are willing to go on a quick tour of the home. The tour also gives your guests a chance to get to know you, and visa versa.

After the tour, inform your guests about your food services. A printed food services bulletin similar to Sample #9 in chapter 7 should be available in each room. You should point out the bulletin to your guests during the house tour. They will probably take the time to read this particular bulletin because it involves food, and everyone is interested in food.

Finally, tell your guests that you would be happy to answer any questions about the local area, shopping, restaurants, etc. Some customers will be reluctant to "bother" you, so you should encourage them to ask questions. It is also reassuring to tell your guests to knock on your bedroom door if they have an emergency situation during the night. A good host is always ready to give advice and assistance to guests — day or night.

b. SAFETY AND SECURITY

Naturally, you will be concerned about your own safety and security when you invite total strangers into your home. How safe are you, and how secure are your possessions? These are normal concerns, but if you have chosen your target customers using the criteria in chapters 3 and 4, you should have arrived at types of customers that are acceptable to you and compatible with each other. You will have selected customers that you feel comfortable about, and, therefore, you should feel safe in your own home.

Your first year of operation will give you the most concern because you are inexperienced and the majority of your guests will be strangers. Each successive year will prove to be easier, as more guests are repeat customers and you feel more at ease in running your business. As you establish policies and procedures, they will become part of your overall customer service plan. Your guests will appreciate the professionalism and organization of your rules that protect not only you and your possessions, but theirs as well.

In our years of operating a B & B business, we have hosted over 1,800 people, and we have not had one single problem with safety or security. We chose our target customers carefully, and we take the time

to properly screen and identify each new customer. We also follow commonsense precautions concerning household valuables. The following tips will help you to identify your customers and lessen your apprehension about safety and security.

1. Customer identification

It is important to properly identify the people staying at your home. Aside from the question of security, you may wish to contact your customers to inform them about some aspect of their booking. If you didn't take the time to properly identify guests, you may not have sufficient information to be able to reach them.

Here are some ways you can verify the identification of your guests:

(a) Whether you are taking a booking over the telephone, by mail, or in person, take the time to completely fill out a proper reservation slip (see Sample #13). By using a reservation slip, you will remember to ask all the questions necessary to properly identify the customer.

(b) If the customer pays for the deposit by credit card, you will have one more piece of identification that can be traced to the customer through the credit card company, if necessary.

(c) If the customer pays for the deposit by personalized check, the name and address will appear on the check. Make sure it agrees with the information you received when you were making out the reservation slip. If not, telephone the customer so that he or she can explain the discrepancy. When you phone the customer you will also be verifying their phone number. You can use the same checking procedure if you accept personalized check payments for the balance of the tariff.

(d) When you mail a booking confirmation slip, you will be verifying the customer's address. If the letter is not returned, you can be fairly certain that the address is correct.

(e) If the customer arrives by automobile, make a point of entering his or her license plate number on the reservation slip. Try to do this discreetly to avoid upsetting the customer. Even if your guest is using a rental car, the license plate number can be traced back to the person who rented the car, if necessary.

2. House security

(a) Door locks

Because most of your guests will be vacationers, they will be staying out fairly late in the evening. You must decide what your policy will be about handing out keys or locking doors. You have three options:

(a) Announce a curfew, then lock the door at the appointed hour. This choice is unenforceable and it will only make your customers angry. They are adults and they expect to be treated as adults. You cannot accept money from your guests and then lock them out of their accommodations.

(b) Stay up until every guest has returned, then lock the door. When we first opened for business we used this method, but found ourselves exhausted the next day. You will be getting up fairly early in the morning, and, therefore, you should not try to stay up late in the evening. If you have a member of the family or an employee on the afternoon shift, this option might work. Otherwise, we don't recommend it.

(c) Issue front door keys to customers as they check-in. We have found that this option works quite well. We issue front door keys on unmarked key tags, so if the customer loses the key, there is no way to trace it back to the house. We also have a second keyed lock on the front door which

we use when we take a day off or go on vacation etc. Even if a dishonest customer copies a key, he or she wouldn't be able to open your front door when you are away, because the door would be secured with the second lock.

You can also install locks on the doors to your private family areas for your own security. Install locks on all areas where you wish to control access. Have all the family locks keyed the same, so that one key opens all the private doors. This will allow you to carry one key rather than a ring of keys.

(b) Bedroom security

You should give your customers the option of locking their bedroom doors. Your guests probably will trust you as their host, but they will be somewhat unsure of the other guests in the house. When you issue the guests with their own room key, make sure that the room key tag is different than the front door key tag. If you don't do this, your customers will try to open the front door with their room key and vice versa. Also, choose key tags that are relatively large so that they will be easily found in a pocket or purse.

(c) Valuables

Valuables should be treated with a measure of common sense. An antique dining room suite is very unlikely to be stolen by a guest. On the other hand, if you display Uncle Harry's gold pocket watch in the common sitting area, you are placing too much temptation in front of your guests.

You needn't be paranoid about your valuables, but a little common sense will ensure that your most treasured possessions will be secure. Our house is full of antiques and interesting bric-a-brac, but we have had no thefts. We display our antiques freely, but we choose the items for the guest areas with some discretion.

(d) Alarm systems

An alarm system can be incorporated into a B & B if you feel it is necessary. We installed an alarm system that can be used to protect the whole house or, optionally, it can be switched to protect only the non-guest areas of the house. However, we only use the alarm system if we take a day off or go on vacation. We feel that the potential embarrassment caused by accidentally tripping the alarm would be too traumatic for our customers, so we have decided to leave the alarm system off when we have guests in the house. You will have to evaluate your own security situation, and act accordingly.

(e) Exterior

The exterior areas should not be overlooked for security protection. You may wish to control access to a garage, swimming pool, or tool shed by installing locks on the entrances. You may also want exterior flood lights to illuminate the front and back yards after dark. These lights can be turned on with a switch located inside the house, or by an automatic device that senses motion.

c. TARIFF PAYMENT

Room tariffs are usually paid in two installments. The first is the deposit, which demonstrates the good intentions of the customer. We recommend that you always ask for a deposit. In our first year of operation, we had quite a few customers who did not show up for their reservations. We tightened our deposit requirements, and have had no trouble since.

The second installment of the tariff is the balance payment, which is usually paid when customers arrive at the B & B or just before they depart. You must decide when you will ask for the balance of the tariff. If you are unsure of your customers, you should ask for the payment when they arrive. If you have repeat customers, you will probably feel comfortable waiting until they depart. We usually collect the tariff balance just before our guests depart. We find that they are in a good frame of mind after a hearty breakfast. Experience will tell you when to ask for the tariff payment from your specific customers. If in doubt, ask for it when they arrive.

Below are brief discussions on different methods of payment you may encounter.

1. Cash

Cash is a common means of paying for accommodations at a B & B. Because the tariff is generally lower than hotels, customers often have sufficient cash to pay for the tariff. Our older clientele seem to be moving away from credit card use, while the younger customers still prefer to pay with plastic. You should keep a supply of smaller bills available in your office so that you can provide change to cash-paying customers.

2. Foreign currency

Because of the good relationship between Canada and the United States, there are large numbers of Canadians and Americans traveling across the border. You will find that it is good business to accept the other country's currency at a fair rate of exchange.

It is important that you not use the rate of exchange as a means of making additional profits because your customers will become annoyed. Monitor the rate of exchange at the bank, and charge accordingly.

Convert your rates to the other currency ahead of time, so that you can quote your rates in either currency if requested. We make up a conversion table using the current rate of exchange plus one or two percentage points above and below the current rate. If the exchange rate changes during the operating season, our conversion table can still be used.

When you take the foreign currency to the bank for deposit, you usually have to go through a conversion procedure before the bank can credit your account. This procedure takes extra time that can be annoying in the middle of a busy day. To receive a speedier deposit, open a "foreign currency" account at your bank. You can use that account to deposit cash, personal checks, or money orders in the foreign currency. You can also issue checks from this account, which can be useful if you are refunding a deposit to a foreign customer.

A few of your customers will want to pay in currency other than Canadian or U.S. dollars. When this happens we contact the bank and accept the currency at the official rate of exchange. Due to the low number of these customers, we feel the good customer relations are worth the delay of the conversion procedure at the bank when we deposit these funds.

3. Postal money orders

Some of your customers may want to pay their deposit using a postal money order. This usually occurs when the customer is from another country. Money orders should be made out in the currency of your country, and then they can be easily cashed at your local post office.

4. Bank drafts

Some overseas customers will use bank drafts if they are mailing you a deposit. The bank draft may be made out in the currency of the originating country, or your country. Check with your bank to determine the redeemable value of the draft and to see if a service charge will be applied. Credit your customer only with the actual dollars that are deposited into your account so that you do not absorb any service charges.

5. Travelers' checks

You should be prepared to accept all the major travelers' checks in either Canadian or U.S. funds. For travelers' checks from other countries, check with your bank. Your guest should make the check payable to your B & B, date it and sign it. Make sure

that the signature of your guest is the same as the sample signature already on the check. If the check is issued by an institution you are not familiar with, take the time to phone your bank before you accept it.

6. Personal checks

Your decision to accept personal checks will depend largely on the type of clientele you have targeted. If you have cashed a customer's personal check for his or her deposit payment, there is a good chance that their check for the tariff balance will be okay. But if the deposit check is returned to you marked NSF (not sufficient funds), you should contact the customer immediately. Add the bank penalty payment (if any) onto the tariff payment, and resubmit a new invoice. You should not absorb any bank charges that result from customer error.

In our operation, we targeted mature customers who attend live theater and/or appreciate historic homes. About 80% of our customers pay by personal check and we have had no problems. You must assess your own customers and act accordingly. If you decide to accept personal checks, make sure you have properly identified your customer (see the section on customer identification above). If the customer is unknown to you, ask for his or her driver's license and check identification. Mark the license number on the back of the check (just in case).

7. Credit cards

In this day and age, credit cards are a very popular means of tariff payment. Today's travelers don't want to carry too much cash with them when they are on the road, so they use their credit cards whenever possible. Most successful B & Bs accept credit cards; the most popular cards seem to be Visa or MasterCard.

Credit cards are a safe way to guarantee deposit payment, particularly for same-day reservations. If you take a credit card number over the telephone, you are guaranteed to receive the amount, even if the customer turns out to be a "no-show."

If you decide to accept credit card payments, you must apply at a bank to open a merchant account which is specifically used for deposits from one particular credit card. (There may be a sign-up fee involved.) If you wish to accept two or more different credit cards, you may have to open merchant accounts at several banks because most banks only handle one specific credit card.

When you open the merchant account, you will be asked to sign some type of merchant agreement, which will detail the rules that you agree to follow concerning the acceptance of credit cards and the depositing of the sales drafts at the bank. You will be charged for one imprint machine and one imprint plate, which will be valid for all the different credit cards you have applied for. You will also be charged a fee for each transaction. The fee can vary depending on your monthly volume of credit card business and the average amount of each sale. The fee usually ranges from 2% to 5%.

You can receive a better rate if you join as part of a larger group of B & B businesses. Check with your B & B association for their policy regarding credit card group memberships.

Most merchant agreements will not allow you to pass the transaction fee on to the customer. In other words, you may not be able to charge a higher tariff fee for credit card users, which means that your profit is less for a credit card customer. If you anticipate that most of your customers will pay by credit card, you should consider raising your tariff structure across the board to cover this extra cost.

After you have signed the merchant agreement, you will receive a visit from the credit card company representative who will explain the operation of their system, and will answer any questions. You will be given a floor limit (i.e., the maximum amount you can accept from one customer without getting additional authorization over the telephone), which is set to agree with the normal tariff amount received from your average customer.

d. CHECK-OUT PROCEDURES

We have discussed the necessity of having an efficient and friendly check-in procedure in order to put your arriving customers at ease. It is equally important to treat your departing customers with the same care and attention. Check-out time is the last opportunity to demonstrate your expertise and hospitality. You have just served them a wonderful breakfast, so they should be in a good frame of mind.

1. Check-out time

Establish a check-out time and make sure your customers are aware of it. The best way to do that is to include your check-out time in your printed house rules.

Your check-out time should occur a few hours after breakfast. Allow your guests plenty of time to enjoy their meal because a leisurely breakfast is the essence of a good B & B.

Your check-out time should also be two or three hours prior to your check-in time so that you have ample opportunity to clean the house and prepare for the arriving customers. A very popular check-out time is 11:00 a.m.

2. Keys

As discussed earlier, most bed and breakfast businesses issue guest room keys to their customers and many also issue front door keys. You should make a point of reminding your departing guests about any keys that have been issued to them.

We have found that about 40% of our customers hand us their keys when they come down to breakfast on their departing day. Another 40% tell us they have left the keys in their room, and the remaining 20% produce the keys from their pockets or purses when we ask for them. The few customers that take their keys by mistake have always sent them back by mail within a week or two. You should keep one or two extra sets of keys in case a set does go missing.

3. Guest book

As discussed in chapter 9, we recommend keeping a large guest book near the front door. Most of your guests will appreciate the chance to write their names into your guest book when they are departing. It also presents an opportunity for them to leave a permanent thank-you for the hospitality and friendliness that you have provided during their stay. The comments in your guest book will reflect the level of success of your business. If the guests' comments are terse or non-existent, then you should assume you are doing something wrong.

4. Tariff collection

As host, it is your responsibility to ensure that the balance of the tariff has been paid by the departing guest. Below is how we handle tariff collection in our B & B; you can follow suit:

(a) Make a quick check of your departing guest's reservation slip to check whether the balance of the tariff has been paid. Do this discreetly to avoid the appearance of being too mercenary. If the guest does owe you money, make a mental note of the amount, and put the reservation slip in your pocket.

(b) Some guests like to load up their car, and then as the final act, they will come back and pay the tariff. This can create the impression that they are leaving without paying, so don't overreact to this scenario! To protect ourselves, we always tell departing guests "When you are ready to leave, let us know. We would like to say goodbye." This friendly gesture of

hospitality will favorably impress the guests and they will inevitably come back to say their goodbyes. If they have remembered the tariff balance, they will pay it, and if they have forgotten, you can retrieve the reservation slip from your pocket and diplomatically ask them "How would you prefer to pay the tariff balance?" The customer is thereby saved from a potentially embarrassing situation.

5. Tariff receipts

Some of your customers will ask you for a receipt for the tariff payment. This request will most likely come from guests who are on business, or attending a business-related function. You can purchase a book of duplicate receipts from a stationery supply store. Make sure you date the receipt, and include the words "For ____ night(s) bed and breakfast." Also be sure to sign the receipt. Give the customer the top copy, and keep the bottom copy for your records.

In our B & B, we also ordered a self-inking stamp with our business name, address, and telephone number. We mark all our receipts with this stamp. It saves the necessity of handwriting all that information each time we make out a receipt.

6. Articles left behind

A cardinal rule in the hotel trade is never to notify guests about articles left behind. The reason for this rule is that a guest may not have stayed at the hotel with his or her spouse, so any reminder notice could cause a great deal of domestic trouble! As the host of a B & B you should follow the same rule.

If an article is left behind in our B & B, we put the guest's name and date on a tag, and store the article in our office. Then we leave it up to the customer to contact us. Our experience has shown that customers will enquire about valuable articles only. We mail the articles back to the guest only if requested and ask the customer to pay the postage.

7. Tips

A tip is a gift of money given for a service performed. Originally, it meant "to insure promptness," but now a tip is used to reward a whole range of customer services. Generally, it is a token of appreciation from a satisfied customer.

However, as a general rule, the public does not tip proprietors or managers. Therefore, as a B & B host, you should not expect to receive tips. In our years of business we have received tips from only three customers. Our guests always appreciate our high level of service, but they don't consider us as service employees to be tipped. Instead, they thank us personally and occasionally will present us with small gifts, flowers, or thank-you cards. And, best of all, they become loyal return customers.

e. CUSTOMER SERVICES

Because each B & B is different, you will need to select a range of services that best meets the needs of your target customers. B & Bs offer a wide range of individual services to their guests, and it would be an impossible task to mention every one, but here is a list of some of the more popular services being offered. Study each service carefully and decide if you will offer that service to your customers. We are certain that you will be able to think of other useful services you can provide to your guests based on the needs of your customers.

1. Babysitting

If you plan to welcome families with children of all ages at your B & B, you might consider providing babysitting services in the evenings. You may wish to provide these services personally, or you could hire outside help. It would be wise to screen a few candidates ahead of time, so that you have several sources of help available.

You should always charge extra for babysitting services. If the guests were in their own home, they would have to pay for the service, so they should not expect you to provide it free of charge. If you are hiring outside help, you will be screening the candidates, making all the arrangements, and paying the sitter on behalf of the customer. For all this effort, you should charge a percentage of the sitting costs.

You will need to provide some additional equipment to assist in the care of children. Families traveling with young children are usually well-equipped with the paraphernalia needed to care for young children, but if you can offer cribs, baby monitoring devices, high chairs, and a lot of child-oriented games, your efforts will be appreciated.

2. Pet care

If you allow pets to accompany your B & B guests, you might offer pet-sitting or dog-walking services. As with babysitting services, your guests should expect to pay an added fee for this special service. If you are willing to pet sit while guests are elsewhere, you will need to consider how you will accommodate the animal. You will not want to simply lock it up in the guest bedroom — a bored animal could cause chaos in your carefully decorated room. And remember, even a fully fenced yard is not secure enough for some escape-artist dogs. A quiet, minimally furnished room in your home, perhaps a laundry room, equipped with a warm sleeping place, a dish of water, and a few safe dog toys might be the best solution for accommodating a pet.

3. Laundry services

Some B & Bs will wash and iron guests' laundry if requested. Personally, we find ourselves busy enough without this extra chore, so we direct our customers to the local laundromat. If we are asked, we lend our customers an iron and an ironing board, which we set up in the laundry room. Often customers do ask to borrow an iron and ironing board, and we do not charge for this service.

4. Pick-up and drop-off service

If you live in an area that is not serviced by good public transportation, you may wish to offer a pick-up and drop-off service. You could offer to provide taxi service to the local train station, bus depot, or airport. It would be wise to provide this as a part of your total hospitality package, rather than charging separately for the service. If you charge people to ride in your automobile, your legal liability is affected. Your insurance company should be consulted if you intend to charge your guests for this service.

5. Information services

You should be fully familiar with your local area and should be able to provide information on a wide range of services. Make sure you know the operating hours of local attractions, museums, shops, druggists, libraries, etc. Keep a list of useful local telephone numbers available in each of the guest rooms. Be able to direct the customers to your local barber, hairdresser, shoe repair shop, laundromat, car repair shop, telegraph office, bank, restaurant, taxi, bus, train, etc.

6. Reservation services

Some B & Bs provide their guests with reservation services. When a customer books a room, they may ask the host to reserve a table at a restaurant on their behalf, or book theater tickets for them. This type of request usually comes from a customer who is calling long distance and who wants to make all the arrangements with just one telephone call.

We suggest that you try to cooperate with these requests if at all possible. Restaurant reservations should be no problem because no money changes hands. Other reservations such as theater tickets require prepayment, so you will need the customer's credit card number and expiry date. Never use your own money to pay for a customer's reservations.

7. Medical aid

You may be asked from time to time for minor medical assistance or simple first aid. We keep a stock of supplies for the use of our customers that includes the following items:

(a) A good selection of adhesive strips in various sizes

(b) Gauze pads and adhesive tape

(c) Antiseptic cream

(d) Sunburn lotion

(e) Buffered aspirin

(f) Antacid tablets

(g) Upset stomach medicine

(h) Tweezers to remove splinters

(i) Scissors to cut tape and bandages

If you don't want to build your own first aid kit, you can purchase completely assembled kits from your local safety supply dealer or drugstore. You should notify your guests that you have a first aid kit by mentioning it in your house rules.

More serious medical problems should always get professional attention. You should keep a complete list of emergency numbers at each telephone location in the house, so that you can quickly summon assistance. The following list of telephone numbers is suggested as a minimum:

(a) Emergency 911 (if available in your area)

(b) Ambulance

(c) Dentist

(d) Doctor

(e) Fire

(f) Hospital

(g) Pharmacy

(h) Poison Control

(i) Police

8. Tax rebates

Most provincial and state governments levy a sales tax on items bought at the retail level within their jurisdictions. Some of those governments allow visitors to claim refunds of those taxes if the goods are removed from their jurisdictions within a specific time limit. Each state and province has its own rules, so you should check with your own government.

If your state or province does allow your customers to claim a tax refund, you should provide a copy of the rules and an application form in each guest room. Also, you should make yourself familiar with the rules so that you can provide refund advice to your customers.

In Canada, the federal government imposes a tax on most goods and services. If your customers are not residents of Canada, they are entitled to claim a GST refund, subject to certain restrictions. If you are operating a B & B in Canada, you should put copies of the booklet *GST Rebate for Visitors* in each guest room. This booklet is available from chambers of commerce, Tourist Information Centres, or directly from Revenue Canada. The booklet explains how to claim the refund and also contains an application form.

For more information you can call 1-800-66-VISIT from inside Canada, or (613) 991-3346 from outside Canada. Alternatively, you can write Revenue Canada, Customs and Excise, Visitors' Rebate Program, Ottawa, Canada, K1A 1J5.

9. Other customer services

There are many other possibilities of extra services you could provide to your customers to make your B & B just a little special. If your B & B is close to water, you may wish to provide fishing guide services, pleasure boat rides, or boat rentals. If you are near woodlands or open spaces, you may decide to provide organized trail walks, or bicycle rentals. If you are close to an historic area, you could provide guided tours to the more interesting places.

The variety of services you provide is limited only by the time you have available and your physical stamina. We suggest that you start slowly, by offering only one extra service. As you become more relaxed in the day-to-day operation of your B & B, you can decide if you want to offer more services. Whether you charge for these extras or include them in your total package price is up to you. Your market research has told you what your competition is doing, so you should price your extra services accordingly.

f. PROBLEM CUSTOMERS

If you have selected your customer types carefully and properly identified them, you should encounter a minimum of problem customers. If you do run into problems from time to time, you should create a D.N.B. list. D.N.B. stands for "Do Not Book." A D.N.B. list contains the names and addresses of problem customers that you do not wish to book again. Customers have to display pretty awful behavior to make it onto a D.N.B. list, so the list should be short. Most B & B hosts will gladly share their D.N.B. lists with other operators.

Keep the D.N.B. list at the back of your reservation book. When you get a call for a booking and the customer's name is unknown to you, you can quickly check the D.N.B. list. You can avoid disruptive customers by stating that all your rooms are taken.

We have never encountered a customer who we would classify as a serious problem. A few guests could be considered as "rather odd," but none of them created a major problem.

The first step in knowing how to handle problem customers is to establish and stick to a set of clearly defined house rules. Whatever rules you decide to make, it is important to inform all your customers so that they will be aware of the do's and don'ts. The best way to do this is to leave a copy of the rules in each guest room. They can be left in a conspicuous place along with the food services bulletin and the list of local telephone numbers. Sample #17 shows the house rules for the Morris Bed and Breakfast. Keep your house rules short (no more than one page). If you present your customers with a lengthy document, they won't bother to read it.

Here are some problem situations that could develop during the running of your B & B along with our suggestions for handling the situation.

1. Early arrivals

If your customers arrive before your stated check-in time, remind them of your normal check-in time and tell them when their room will be ready. You might suggest that if they wish to go shopping or have lunch, you would be happy to store their suitcases in your office until their room is ready. Alternatively, you can seat them in the common sitting room to relax until their room is ready.

2. Late arrivals

If your customers arrive after your stated check-in time, consider yourself lucky that they turned up at all. No good will come of chastising your customer, so assess how you feel about them after they have completed their stay. If they apologize for arriving late, and there are no further problems, forget about the incident. If their late arrival proves to be the beginning of a long series of problems, then put them on your D.N.B. list.

In the middle of a busy holiday season, some customers are bound to arrive late due to unforeseen circumstances. If you have collected a room deposit from the customer, they will have a greater incentive to telephone you about their delay. Always stay in close proximity to your telephone, either by carrying a portable phone

or by checking your answering machine regularly.

3. Late cancellations

If a customer calls you on the arrival date and declares that he or she cannot honor the reservation (for whatever reason), you should invoke your deposit refund rule, which will be printed on your booking confirmation slips. Because you confirm all your reservations, your customers will already be aware of your deposit refund rule, and they will be less likely to complain. If they do object, you could reassure them that their deposit will be returned less a $10 handling fee if you are successful in finding another customer for their room. This is a very fair policy, and is more forgiving than commercial hotel policies.

4. Late check-out

If a guest is still on the premises 15 minutes after your check-out time, ask him or her if you could please start cleaning the room because your new guests will be arriving in a few hours. Most guests will get the hint.

If customers say they want to go shopping and then come back and check out, remind them of the stated check-out time, and tell them they are welcome to store their luggage in your office until they are ready to leave, but that you must start cleaning the bedroom in preparation for arriving guests.

5. Breaking your house rules

If a customer breaks a house rule, tactfully point out the problem. Try to stay cheerful and apologetic. For example, you might say, "Excuse me, Mr. Smith, but our insurance policy doesn't allow smoking in the house. You are most welcome to smoke on the back patio." If at all possible, try to place the blame on government, insurance companies, or town councils. Everyone can relate to regulations coming from these sources. Also, make sure you follow all the house rules yourself.

THE MORRIS BED AND BREAKFAST — HOUSE RULES

SMOKING	Insurance Regulations do not permit smoking inside the house. Please use the outside patio area.
SMOKE ALARMS	For your safety we have installed smoke detectors on each floor of the house. If you hear the smoke alarm, please exit your room promptly, and proceed down the stairs to the front door. We will advise you immediately of the situation.
FACILITIES	In addition to your private room, we encourage you to use the screened front porch, and the patio area.
FOOD SERVICES	Please see our separate Food Services Bulletin for a list of available meals and refreshments.
INFORMATION	If you require information about the local area, please do not hesitate to contact the hosts. They are always available to assist you.
MEDICAL AID	For minor problems we have a first aid kit available. We can also direct you to medical professionals. Please contact the hosts day or night for assistance.
TELEPHONE	Guests wishing to place a local or long distance telephone call should contact the hosts. If the call is long distance, please fill out a "long distance telephone slip" and hand it to the hosts. We ask you to make your call as brief as possible because our telephone is used for business purposes.
LOCAL NUMBERS	For useful local telephone numbers, please consult the separate listing.
CHECK OUT/IN	To help you plan your day, and to help us prepare for other guests, please observe the following:

        Check-out time: 11:00 a.m.

        Check-in time: 1:00 p.m. to 6:00 p.m.

DOOR KEYS	The colored key will open the door to your private guest room. We encourage you to lock your door if you are leaving any valuables in your room. The silver key will open the front door of the house. The hosts will lock the front door each time they leave the premises, and after dark. We suggest that you carry your keys with you at all times. When you are checking out, please return the keys to the hosts.
TARIFF PAYMENT	We accept:

1. All foreign currencies at prevailing bank rates.
2. Visa and MasterCard.
3. Travelers' Checks
4. Personal Checks (with I.D.)

6. Disruptive behavior

You have no obligation to put up with disruptive behavior. You should ask the offending person to stop immediately or you will call the police. Don't hesitate to follow through with the call if a guest continues to be disruptive.

Don't give the person a second or third chance because it simply isn't worth the aggravation. Put a stop to the behavior immediately. Don't attempt to physically remove the offender yourself. The police are trained to handle these situations in a professional manner.

When the police arrive, return the deposit to the customer and ask the police to escort the person off the property. Give the police the name, address, and telephone number of the person, put the customer on your D.N.B. list, and consider the matter closed. If necessary, apologize to your other customers, and assure them that the offender is now in the hands of the police.

We have not heard of any B & B operator who had to resort to this procedure, but it is worthwhile to have a plan of action prepared ahead of time, just in case.

g. DOCUMENT YOUR COSTS

Using a copy of the Start-up Supplies Worksheet (Worksheet K), list any equipment and supplies needed to establish your chosen operating options discussed in this chapter. Anything from extra locks on doors for security to buying a highchair for a family with young children. Price only the items you will need to purchase.

Now turn to Cost Sheet #4 in Appendix 4. Using the section labeled "Operating Options," make a one-line entry for your worksheet. Do not total the cost sheet at this time because there are additional entries to be made later.

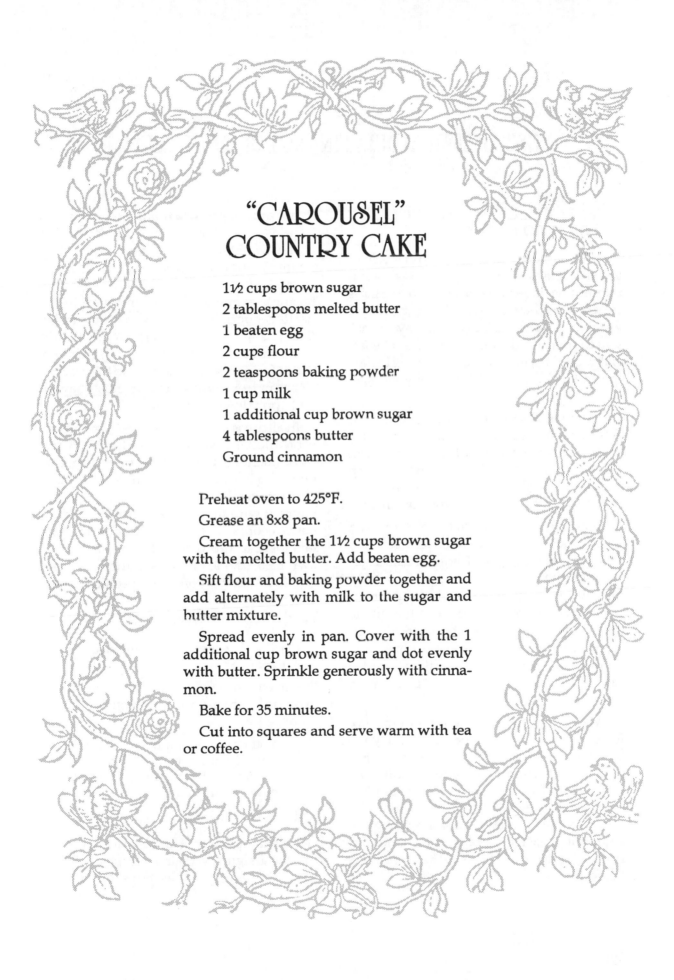

"CAROUSEL" COUNTRY CAKE

1½ cups brown sugar

2 tablespoons melted butter

1 beaten egg

2 cups flour

2 teaspoons baking powder

1 cup milk

1 additional cup brown sugar

4 tablespoons butter

Ground cinnamon

Preheat oven to 425°F.

Grease an 8x8 pan.

Cream together the 1½ cups brown sugar with the melted butter. Add beaten egg.

Sift flour and baking powder together and add alternately with milk to the sugar and butter mixture.

Spread evenly in pan. Cover with the 1 additional cup brown sugar and dot evenly with butter. Sprinkle generously with cinnamon.

Bake for 35 minutes.

Cut into squares and serve warm with tea or coffee.

11

ESTABLISH YOUR FINANCIAL RECORDS

a. WHAT RECORDS DO YOU NEED TO KEEP?

When you run a B & B, various levels of government will require you to keep accurate financial records of all your business expenses and revenues. If the government wishes to audit your business, they will ask you to produce these records. These financial records will also be used to calculate the annual income tax return for your business.

As a B & B owner, you will be able to claim a variety of business expenses, which should lessen your total tax payable. Therefore, it is in your best interest to keep accurate records of all your expenses and revenues as they apply to your business.

Generally, the financial records for an average-size B & B are much simpler than for many other types of home businesses. You will be receiving revenue from only one source (your customers) and your expenses will be confined to providing goods and services to those customers. If you were running an import/export business, or operating an international mail-order catalogue, you would need to maintain more sophisticated records.

When you complete your income tax forms, you will be asked to report your business expenses and revenues in a specific format under a number of different categories. To make the process simpler, you should keep your own business expense records under these same categories so that it is easier to transfer the amounts from your expense sheets to the preprinted tax forms.

In Canada, you will report your business expenses and revenues on Revenue Canada's "Statement Of Income And Expenses From A Business" (Form T2124 E). In the United States, you will report your business expenses and revenues on Internal Revenue Service's "Profit Or Loss From Business — Sole Proprietorship" (Schedule C, Form 1040). The Canadian and United States forms are very similar, so the discussions and examples used in this chapter will apply to both countries.

In all areas of finance, it is prudent to get professional assistance. In chapter 5 we recommended the services of an accountant who has other B & B clients. We suggest you read this chapter and familiarize yourself with the sample expense and revenue records. Then, consult your accountant for final approval on the layout of your own records. He or she is in the best position to advise you on your specific needs.

b. BUSINESS EXPENSES

1. What is a legitimate business expense?

For an expense to be a legitimate business expense, it should meet the following criteria:

(a) You have spent money to earn business income or you have spent money in the hope of earning business income, and

(b) the expenses are reasonable.

For example, Carol and Bob Morris purchased a sign for their front lawn. They spent the money in the hope of earning business income from customers who see their sign. This is a legitimate business expense unless the cost of the sign is unreasonable. A computerized sign that costs $10,000 would not be a reasonable expense for a small B & B.

Business expenses can be classified into one of three categories: direct, capital, and prorated.

(a) Direct expenses

Any money spent strictly on the business is a direct business expense. An example are the three ice buckets (one for each guest room) that Carol and Bob bought. They would not have bought the buckets if they were not running their B & B, so the total cost of the three ice buckets should be charged directly to the business in the year that they were purchased.

Other examples of direct expenses are business loan interest, insurance to cover your paying guests, office expenses, booking agents' fees, accountant's fees, guest supplies, and guest food.

(b) Capital expenses

Large business expenses may have to be treated as capital expenses. Generally, these are the more expensive items, where the business will derive a benefit over an extended period of time. Capital expenses are charged to the business over a number of years, rather than charging the whole amount in the year of the purchase.

For example, the purchase of a new bed for one of the guest rooms would be a capital expense. The business would derive the benefit of the bed over an extended period. Therefore, the cost of the bed would be charged to the business over a number of years. A depreciation rate (charge rate) would be specified by the tax department, and this rate would be applied each year until the total cost of the bed has been charged to the business.

Different items are assigned different depreciation rates. Also, if you use the item partly for business and partly for personal use, you will be allowed to depreciate only the business portion.

Your accountant can provide details for major purchases. A good rule of thumb is to ask about any item that exceeds $200 in value.

(c) Prorated expenses

A prorated expense is one that can be proportionally assigned to your business. Prorated expenses generally relate to house expenses such as property taxes, mortgage interest, utilities, home repairs, and house insurance. Because you operate a business from your home, you may be allowed to proportionally charge (prorate) these expenses to your business. Always check with your accountant, as rules about what can be prorated, how much, and under what conditions can be complicated.

If you are thinking about deducting a portion of your car expenses to your B & B, again, check with your accountant first. You may need to keep accurate records of dates, mileage, purpose of each trip, as well as receipts for all gas, oil, and repairs. Vehicle depreciation may also be involved in the calculations, so get professional assistance before you begin.

2. Calculating the business portion of your house

There are two ways that you can calculate the business portion of your house expenses: the room method and the square-foot method.

In the room method you count the number of rooms that you use for B & B and divide this number by the total number of rooms in the house. The Morris Bed and Breakfast has twelve rooms (halls and stairways count as one room). Six rooms are used exclusively for the B & B business (three bedrooms, a bathroom, the office, and the sitting room) and a proportion of the dining room, kitchen, halls and stairways are used by the business. Sample #18 shows how Carol and Bob would calculate the portion of the home used for business purposes using the room method.

In the square-foot method, you total the square footage of your home used for your B & B and divide this number by the total square footage of your house. Sample #19 shows how a B & B would calculate the portion of the home used for business purposes using the square-foot method.

In these examples, both the room method and the square-foot method produced almost the same results. This may not be true for your house, so you should calculate your business portion using both methods, then let your accountant choose the most appropriate figure to work with. In some cases, your accountant may suggest a lower figure than your calculated percentages in order to bring your prorated house expenses within the acceptable limits of the tax rules.

3. Converting personal items to business use

When you convert your home to a B & B, you probably will use some of your existing furniture and fixtures. In other words, you will be using items that are now "personal" for "business." You should take advantage of this situation by selling your furniture to your business. Here are the general steps to do this:

(a) Make a list of all items to be converted to business use.

(b) Assign a fair market value to each item. The fair market value is the cost of the item in the same condition on the open market (check used furniture stores, want ads, garage sales, auctions, etc.).

(c) Treat the total value as a capital business expense. The business will buy these items from you, and the cost of the items will be part of the total start-up costs for the B & B.

The cost of these capital items will then be depreciated over a number of years. We advise you to seek the guidance of your accountant when you have assembled your list. He or she will be familiar with the different depreciation rates to be assigned to the various items.

4. Guest food costs

In chapter 7 we listed the various costs that arise from providing food for your guests. Now you need to categorize these expenses as direct, capital, or prorated.

Food storage space can be included in your square-foot method of calculating the business portion of your house expenses.

Minor equipment purchases for food preparation and serving (e.g., linen and dishes, utensils) could be a direct expense, but more expensive equipment (e.g., tables, chairs, appliances) may need to be capitalized (ask your accountant about any item over $200).

Utilities are prorated based on your business portion calculations.

Hired labor is a direct expense.

Food products and ingredients are a direct business expense.

You will sometimes use your automobile to travel to various food suppliers to buy food supplies. This portion of the automobile expenses should be prorated to the business.

c. EXPENSE RECORD FORMS

1. Keep your receipts

For every entry on your monthly expense record, you will have an individual invoice, or receipt. The only exceptions would be property taxes, mortgage interest, and any food that is calculated using the average method. In these cases, it is perfectly acceptable to make a monthly entry as long as you have the documentation to back them up. Retain your yearly property tax bill, the computer printout of your mortgage interest payments, and your food calculations in case they are required for the auditor.

SAMPLE #18
CALCULATING BUSINESS PORTION OF A HOME
(ROOM METHOD)

No.	Room Description	Business Use
1.	Guest Bedroom	1.0
2.	Guest Bedroom	1.0
3.	Guest Bedroom	1.0
4.	Guest bathroom	1.0
5.	Host bedroom	0
6.	Host bathroom	0
7.	Office	1.0
8.	Guest sitting area	1.0
9.	Dining room	0.3
10.	Kitchen	0.3
11.	Family room	0
12.	Halls and stairways	0.5

Total rooms in the house = 12

Total rooms used for business purposes = 7.1

Business portion of house = 7.1 divided by 12 X 100 = 59%

SAMPLE #19
CALCULATING BUSINESS PORTION OF HOME
(SQUARE FOOT METHOD)

No.	Room Description	Total Ft^2	Business Ft^2
1.	Guest bedroom	150	150
2.	Guest bedroom	200	200
3.	Guest bedroom	250	250
4.	Guest bathroom	50	50
5.	Host bedroom	150	0
6.	Host bathroom	40	0
7.	Office	120	120
8.	Guest sitting area	110	110
9.	Dining room	225	175
10.	Kitchen	120	75
11.	Family room	250	0
12.	Halls and stairways	300	15

Total square footage of house = 1,965

Square footage for business purposes = 1,145

Business portion of house = 1,145 divided by 1,965 X 100 = 58%

All the receipts for one month should be placed in an envelope and marked with the month and year. When you start a new month, start a new envelope. At the end of the year place an elastic band around the 12 envelopes, and store them in a safe location. These receipts will be required if your records are audited by the tax department.

2. Monthly expense record

Sample #20 shows a monthly expense record for the Morris B & B. The expenses are listed using standard 13-column ledger sheets, and the column headings represent the most common categories of expenses found in a typical B & B. The entry numbers are preprinted on the ledger pages and they appear on the left and right edges of each sheet. Since these sheets are 17 inches wide, the entry numbers help you follow each entry across the sheet.

You can use this kind of ledger for your own expense record. Enter each invoice by date and vendor, and any brief description of the item if necessary. All items are entered under "Total" (column 1), and then again under the appropriate columns 2 to 13. Most invoices would be entered into only one of the columns, but you may encounter an invoice that should be split into several columns. Make sure that for any one entry, the total of columns 2 to 13 equals column 1.

Refering to Sample #20, here is an explanation of each column.

"Utility" refers to all household utilities including telephone, electricity, gas, water, sewer, cable television, etc. You may want to separate your telephone invoice into "business long distance" and "regular service." These two categories will often have different calculations for business expense deduction. Do not prorate any of these entries at this time; you will prorate the yearly totals.

"Property taxes" are the full amount of the monthly property taxes of the building used for your B & B.

"Mortgage interest" should reflect the monthly mortgage interest you pay on the B & B building. Do not include any mortgage principal.

"Repairs" includes all repairs and maintenance costs associated with the B & B building such as painting, decorating, house repairs, and maintenance costs.

"Bank charges" include bank service charges, voucher return fees, credit card fees, check charges, etc.

"Office expenses" include postage, stationery, office supplies, non-capitalized equipment, etc.

"Accounting and legal" expenses include accounting fees, legal fees, and professional consultations associated with the business.

"B & B fees" includes booking agents' fees, listing fees, licenses, B & B inspection fees, etc.

"B & B supplies" are all non-food items needed to supply and service your guests such as paper towels, toilet paper, facial tissue, soap, cleaning supplies, non-capitalized guest room equipment, etc.

"Food" includes all food purchased for guest use. If you are using the item-by-item method for calculating food costs, you will have many entries in this column. If you are using the average method, you will make one entry at the end of the month. If you are serving extra meals, make a separate entry for the cost of this food.

"Capital items" includes any items that your accountant has advised you to capitalize. The items in this column will be summarized at the end of the year and entered onto the relevant tax documents.

"Other" is used to collect any other expenses not specifically covered in the other columns. Typical entries would be insurance,

SAMPLE #20
MONTHLY EXPENSE RECORD

MORRIS BED AND BREAKFAST EXPENSE RECORD

FOR THE MONTH OF AUGUST 1992

Page 1 of 1

ENTRY NO.	DATE	EXPENSE INVOICE	1 ENTRY TOTAL	2 UTILITY	3 PRCP. TAXES	4 MRTG. INT.	5 REPAIRS	6 BANK CHARGE	7 OFFICE	8 ACCOUNT & LEGAL	9 B.&B. FEES	10 B.&B. SUPPLY	11 B.&B. FOOD	12 CAPITAL ITEMS	13 OTHER	ENTRY NO.
1	Aug.3	Post Office - Stamps	4.00						4.00							1
2	Aug.3	Mr. Lumber - Fencing	32.50				32.50									2
3	Aug.5	Foodmart - Paper Towel	12.80									12.80				3
4	Aug.7	Hardware Store - Nails	5.78				5.78									4
5	Aug.9	Accountant - Fee	150.00							150.00						5
6	Aug.10	Foodmart - Detergent	7.99									7.99				6
7	Aug.13	Bargain City - Bedding	39.50									39.50				7
8	Aug.14	Carpetland - Cleaning	75.00				75.00									8
9	Aug.14	Office Store - Pens	7.99						7.99							9
10	Aug.15	Town Bank - Fees	20.50					20.50								10
11	Aug.17	Bargain City - Chairs	240.50											240.50		11
12	Aug.20	Electricity Company	89.01	89.01												12
13	Aug.20	Business Insurance	150.00												150.00	13
14	Aug.22	Mr. Lumber - Lawnmower	350.00											350.00		14
15	Aug.24	Natural Gas Company	110.00	110.00												15
16	Aug.24	Telephone Company	80.50	80.50												16
17	Aug.27	Quickprint - Brochures	100.00												100.00	17
18	Aug.29	Cable T.V. Company	20.00	20.00												18
19	Aug.31	Property Taxes	216.80		216.80											19
20	Aug.31	Mortgage Interest	80.56			80.56										20
21	Aug.31	B.& B. Assoc'n. - Fees	90.00								90.00					21
22	Aug.31	Chamb./Commerce - Fees	60.00								60.00					22
23	Aug.31	Food - 99 meals @ $6	594.00										594.00			23
24	Aug.31	Extra Meal Supplies	31.00										31.00			24
25																25
26																26
		Total For August -->	2568.43	299.51	216.80	80.56	113.28	20.50	11.99	150.00	150.00	60.29	625.00	590.50	250.00	

advertising, equipment rental, car expenses, wages, etc. The items in this column will be summarized at the end of the year and entered into the appropriate spaces on the tax forms.

These headings are what we use in our expense records, but they are not written in stone. You or your accountant may wish to record business expenses using other headings. For example, if you are collecting the GST or any other taxes, you may want to use separate columns to record them.

If you need more than one page to record your monthly expenses, total page 1 at the bottom and enter that amount as your first entry on page 2. Continue with as many pages as you need, but be sure to number your pages consecutively. For each entry line and for all page totals, column 1 must equal the sum of columns 2 to 13. This is how you check the accuracy of your entries on your monthly expense records.

Take the time to study Sample #20 to get an overall picture of how a small B & B can record its business expenses using standard, 13-column ledger sheets.

3. Expense summary form

At the end of your business year, fill in a summary sheet showing each month's totals from your monthly expense records. Sample #21 shows the expense summary form for the business year of the Morris Bed and Breakfast. The headings of the 13 columns are identical to the monthly sheets, and the totals of each monthly sheet have been transferred onto the summary form.

The 12 monthly figures have been added to get the yearly totals for each column. To check the accuracy of the totals, make sure that the sum of columns 2 to 13 equals column 1.

On Line 16, the prorated amounts of columns 2 to 5 are shown. The totals of columns 8, 12, and 13 have been split into subtotals for clarification. Carol and Bob

have prepared a summary and done these extra calculations and subtotals to make it as easy as possible for their accountant to make out their business income tax form.

Keep in mind that accountants charge by the hour, so it makes sense to present them with neat, accurate, detailed, and easily understood financial records. Also, if your business is subjected to an audit by the tax authorities, they will be favorably impressed by your well-organized and detailed records.

Stack all your monthly expense records in order, then place the expense summary form on top. Staple all these expense sheets together in the upper left-hand corner. This stapled package plus the 12 envelopes containing the monthly receipts represents your total expense records for one business year.

d. REVENUE RECORD FORMS

1. Keep your reservation slips

For every entry on your monthly revenue record, you will have a reservation slip. As with your expense receipts, all reservation slips for one month should be placed in an envelope and marked with the month and year. At the end of the business year, wrap them with an elastic band and store them in a safe place.

2. Monthly revenue record

Sample #22 shows a monthly revenue record for one month at the Morris Bed and Breakfast. Again, Carol and Bob have used a standard 13-column ledger sheet to record their business revenues. They have customized the column headings to record essential revenue totals and to collect useful statistics that will be used to monitor their business. Here is an explanation of each column.

"Entry number" is the preprinted number that appears on the left and right edges of each sheet.

SAMPLE #21
EXPENSE SUMMARY

MORRIS BED AND BREAKFAST EXPENSE SUMMARY

FOR THE YEAR 1992

ENTRY NO.	MONTH	1 ENTRY TOTAL	2 UTILITY	3 PROP. TAXES	4 MORTG. INT.	5 REPAIRS	6 BANK CHARGES	7 OFFICE	8 ACCOUNT & LEGAL	9 B.&B. FEES	10 B.&B. SUPPLY	11 B.&B. FOOD	12 CAPITAL ITEMS	13 OTHER	ENTRY NO.
1	January	881.87	279.25	216.80	82.52	35.79	17.10	50.40		200.00	0.00	0.00			1
2	February	844.20	342.57	216.80	82.24	50.19	12.10	7.80			96.50	36.00			2
3	March	833.15	241.85	216.80	81.96	80.49	9.90	12.35		25.00	50.80	114.00			3
4	April	1414.64	326.94	216.80	81.68	200.63	11.55	12.29	180.00	5.00	71.75	108.00		200.00	4
5	May	1065.98	310.40	216.80	81.40	208.79	10.69	9.50		15.00	59.40	154.00			5
6	June	1471.41	301.18	216.80	81.12	284.01	12.10	29.71		75.00	73.50	398.00			6
7	July	1401.69	287.33	216.80	80.84	225.33	15.95	40.69		85.00	43.85	406.00			7
8	August	2568.43	239.51	216.80	80.56	113.28	20.50	11.99	150.00	150.00	60.29	625.00	590.50	250.00	8
9	September	1353.58	332.38	216.80	80.28	81.53	9.90	21.10		90.00	70.59	451.00			9
10	October	1014.30	325.01	216.80	80.00	28.52	7.70	35.58		60.00	40.69	220.00			10
11	November	1156.85	288.73	216.80	79.72	20.98	17.10	27.42			20.10	36.00	450.00		11
12	December	746.42	305.83	216.80	79.44	21.43	14.42	87.50			15.00	6.00			12
13															13
14	Total For 1992	14752.53	3640.99	2601.60	971.76	1350.97	159.01	346.23	330.00	705.00	602.47	2554.00	1040.50	450.00	14
15															15
16	Expenses Prorated at 50% --->		1820.49	1300.80	485.88	675.48									16
17															17
18								Income Tax Return = $180 <-	Guest Chairs = $240.50 <-						18
19								Consultation = $150 <-	Lawn Mower = $350 <-						19
20									Dining Table = $450 <-						20
21															21
22															22
23														House Insurance = $200 <-	23
24														Business Insurance = $150 <-	24
25														Advertising = $100 <-	25
26															26

SAMPLE #22
MONTHLY REVENUE RECORD

REVENUE RECORD FOR AUGUST 199

ENTRY NO.	DATE	CLIENT NAME	AGENCY A (1)	AGENCY B (2)	AGENCY C (3)	AGENCY D (4)	MEALS INCL. (5)	ROOM TARIFF (6)	EXTRA MEALS (7)	EXTRA SERVICE (8)	DEPOSIT HELD (9)	BOOKING FEE (10)	BOOKING FEE (11)	DEPOSIT RECV'D (12)	BALANCE RECV'D (13)	ENTRY NO.
			<--- ROOM/DAYS BOOKED --->					<--- REVENUE --->			B. & B.	B. & B. ASSOC.	C of C	OFFICE USE		
1	Aug.1	Able	2				4	170						85	85	1
2	Aug.1	Best				2	4	160				5		80	80	2
3	Aug.1	Charles		1			2	85	6		35				56	3
4	Aug.2	Dirk				1	2	80						40	40	4
5	Aug.4	Edwards			3		6	255					15	85	170	5
6	Aug.4	France	1				2	85						85		6
7	Aug.7	Greece		3			6	255			35	15			220	7
8	Aug.8	Hart				2	4	160						80	80	8
9	Aug.8	Income			2		4	170					10	70	100	9
10	Aug.12	Jones		1			2	85	6		35				56	10
11	Aug.12	Smith				2	4	160				5		80	80	11
12	Aug.13	Brown			1		2	85					5	35	50	12
13	Aug.18	Caller		9			18	765			35	45			730	13
14	Aug.21	Douglas	2				4	170						85	85	14
15	Aug.21	Entry				2	4	160						80	80	15
16	Aug.21	Forbes		2			4	170			35	10			135	16
17	Aug.25	Green			2		4	170					10	85	85	17
18	Aug.27	Hunt	3				6	255						85	170	18
19	Aug.28	Interest				3	3	240	9					80	169	19
20	Aug.28	Jack		2			4	170			35	10			135	20
21	Aug.31	King			2		4	170					10	85	85	21
22	Aug.31	Long			2		4	170					10	170		22
23	Aug.31	Major	1				2	85						35	50	23
24																24
25																25
26																26
			9	18	12	12	99	4275	21		210	90	60	1345	2741	

110

"Date" reflects the date of the booking. If the booking was for more than one night, the first night's date is put here.

"Client name" is the guest's last name.

"Room/Days Booked" reflects that the Morris B & B gets clients from four major sources (advertising, B & B association, chamber of commerce, and direct bookings), so they have used four columns to record these sources. Under each, the number of room/days that the client booked are recorded. Room/days are calculated by multiplying the number of rooms booked by the number of days stayed. If you have more than four sources of clients, you will need more than four columns to record them.

"Meals Included" records the number of meals included in the room tariff rate and consumed by the client(s) during their stay. In a standard B & B, this column would record the number of breakfasts consumed. This column is particularly significant if you are using the average method of food costs.

"Room Tariff" records the fee charged for that booking. Figures should be entered in your currency. If you accept foreign currency, convert it before you make your column entries. Note that Carol and Bob charge $80 per room for people who book directly with them, and $85 per room for bookings from the three other sources. The two booking agencies charge $5 per day for each room booked, and the brochure advertising costs $200 per season. The hosts decided to offset these extra costs by charging $5 extra to these clients.

"Extra meals" records the revenue obtained by supplying food other than breakfast. These meals are not included in the room tariff, so they should be recorded separately. The hosts have decided to offer a packed picnic lunch for their clients, priced at $3 each.

"Extra services" records the revenue obtained by supplying extra services.

"B & B Association" is a booking agency that collects a room deposit on behalf of the hosts. They also charge the hosts a $5 booking fee per room per night. The two columns are used to record the deposit held on behalf of the hosts and the booking fee being charged.

"Chamber of Commerce" is a booking agency that does not collect room deposits, and so Carol and Bob must collect their own. The chamber does charge the hosts $5 per room per night, which is recorded in this column.

"Office Use" records the room deposit received and the balance of the room tariff plus any extra meals or services.

The entries on the monthly revenue record are recorded, in chronological order, after each client has paid the bill and checked out. Note that columns 1 to 4 collect valuable business statistics on the sources of clients from different agencies. These statistics can be studied at the end of your business year to determine which agencies are economically worthwhile.

You can check the accuracy of your entries on your monthly revenue record by comparing column totals. For example, in Sample #22, the sum of columns 6, 7, and 8 equals the sum of columns 9, 12, and 13.

3. Revenue summary form

As you record your business revenues for each month of the year, you will accumulate 12 or more monthly revenue records. At the end of the business year, fill in a summary sheet showing each month's totals as shown in Sample #23. Again, as a check on the accuracy of this summary form, the total of columns 6, 7, and 8 should equal the total of columns 9, 12, and 13.

Stack all your monthly revenue records in correct order, place the revenue summary

SAMPLE #23
REVENUE SUMMARY

REVENUE SUMMARY FOR 199_

ENTRY NO.	MONTH	ROOM/DAYS BOOKED				MEALS INCL.	ROOM TARIFF	REVENUE		B. & B. ASSOC.		C of C	OFFICE USE		ENTRY NO.
		AGENCY A (1)	AGENCY B (2)	AGENCY C (3)	AGENCY D (4)	(5)	(6)	EXTRA MEALS (7)	EXTRA SERVICE (8)	DEPOSIT HELD (9)	BOOKING FEE (10)	BOOKING FEE (11)	DEPOSIT RECV'D (12)	BALANCE RECV'D (13)	
1	January														1
2	February				3	6	240						120	120	2
3	March		3	2	5	19	825			105	15	10	200	520	3
4	April	4	1	1	4	18	745			35	5		480	230	4
5	May	6	2	1	.3	23	1005	6		70	10	5	600	341	5
6	June	11	10	5	6	63	2690	12		350	50	25	1080	1272	6
7	July	10	11	6	5	63	2695	18		280	55	30	920	1513	7
8	August	9	18	12	12	99	4275	21		210	90	60	1345	2741	8
9	September	6	6	12	12	71	3000	18		210	30	60	1040	1768	9
10	October	4	10	2	2	35	1520	6		175	50	10	240	1111	10
11	November				3	6	240						40	120	11
12	December				1	1	80							40	12
13															13
14	Totals For 1992 --->	50	61	40	56	404	17315	81		1435	305	200	6185	9776	14
15															15
16															16
17	Total Bookings From All Agencies = 207														17
18															18
19															19
20															20
21															21
22															22
23															23
24															24
25															25
26															26

form on top, and staple them all together. This stapled package plus the 12 envelopes containing the monthly reservation slips represents your total revenue records for one business year.

By looking at Sample #23, you can get a good overall picture of the activity of this particular B & B. The number of bookings from each client source becomes evident, as do the customer visiting patterns. In chapter 13, we will show you how to record and analyze these bookings, so you can measure the success of your business.

e. AUDITS

At some time during the course of running your business, you may receive a notice from the tax authorities to submit to an audit. Quite often you will be randomly selected, and on other occasions the tax department will be questioning a specific deduction. If you have consulted a reliable accountant who has other B & Bs as clients, you should have no doubts about the legitimacy of your business records. The secret to passing an audit is to have proper documentation. Here are some suggestions:

(a) Enter *every* expense onto your expense records.

(b) Enter *every* revenue onto your revenue records.

(c) Make your financial records tidy and easy to understand.

(d) Keep a receipt for every expense. If you don't get a receipt from the vendor (for example at a garage sale), make out a memo with the date, purchase price, description of the item bought, purpose of purchase, and who you bought it from. Then sign the memo. Auditors live in the real world the same as you and I, and they know that receipts are not always given. They are more likely to accept the above memo rather than a vague verbal statement that you spent a certain amount on some furniture some time during the year.

(e) Complete and retain a reservation slip for every booking.

(f) If you are using the average method to calculate your food costs, be sure to keep a copy of your food-cost analysis.

(g) Keep a copy of all property tax bills and mortgage interest documents.

(h) Don't agree to same-day or surprise audits. Give yourself several days to collect all your documents together.

(i) Give the auditors only the financial records they require. Don't volunteer to hand over other business records such as client lists.

(j) If you are unsure of your position, it makes good business sense to seek the advice of your accountant before you submit to an audit.

f. DOCUMENT YOUR COSTS

Using a copy of Worksheet K, list any equipment and supplies needed to establish your financial records recording system. Remember to include technology, professional assistance, expense records, and revenue records.

Now turn to Cost Sheet 4 in Appendix 4; using the section labeled "Financial Recordkeeping," make a one-line entry for your worksheet. Do not total the cost sheet at this time because there are additional entries to be made later.

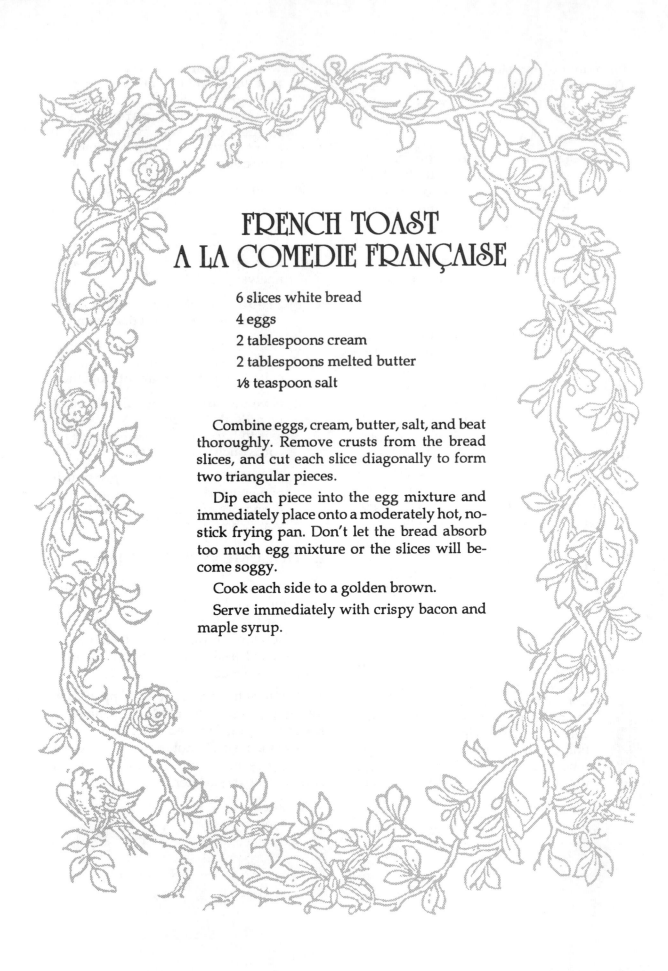

FRENCH TOAST
A LA COMEDIE FRANÇAISE

6 slices white bread

4 eggs

2 tablespoons cream

2 tablespoons melted butter

⅛ teaspoon salt

Combine eggs, cream, butter, salt, and beat thoroughly. Remove crusts from the bread slices, and cut each slice diagonally to form two triangular pieces.

Dip each piece into the egg mixture and immediately place onto a moderately hot, no-stick frying pan. Don't let the bread absorb too much egg mixture or the slices will become soggy.

Cook each side to a golden brown.

Serve immediately with crispy bacon and maple syrup.

12

ADVERTISING AND PROMOTION

Advertising and promotion are a part of any business, but no amount of advertising will save a business that is poorly run. Make sure your advertising campaign begins at home. The effort you put into your business, the cleanliness of your facilities, and the level of hospitality you give to your guests, will pay enormous dividends by creating large numbers of repeat and referred customers.

Satisfied customers may be the best form of advertising, but it takes at least one year of operation before you start to reap the rewards of this type of publicity. In the meantime, you need to seek other ways to advertise your B & B.

a. WORD OF MOUTH

Word-of-mouth advertising can be an effective way to get publicity. We often get new customers who are "friends of friends," or who have heard all about our B & B from one of their relatives.

There are many ways you can pass the word about your new business. Consider the following:

(a) *Family and friends.* Let all your family and friends know that you are operating a B & B and ask them to tell all their friends about your new venture. Provide family and friends with plenty of business cards and encourage them to distribute them freely to people they know.

(b) *Social groups.* If you belong to a church group, golf club, craft guild, or any other type of social group, tell the members about your B & B. Ask them to pass the word to their families and friends, and hand out plenty of business cards.

(c) *Professional organizations.* If you have been active in a professional organization, you should let them know that you are now operating a B & B. People often seek out B & B hosts who share a common interest, so you can expect to get some customers from your professional connections.

(d) *Networking.* Join your local B & B association and get to know the other operators in your immediate area. Tell them you will refer customers to them when you are fully booked, and they will likely offer to do the same. By networking with other B & B operators, you will not only receive additional customers, but you will be able to exchange useful information.

b. BUSINESS STATIONERY

1. Business cards

Business cards are essential for your business. They can be included in all your business correspondence and handed out to prospective customers.

Leave a business card in each guest room to encourage your customers to take one home. If you keep a supply of cards near the front door, departing guests will take a few extra cards to hand out to their friends.

You will probably get people coming to your door to enquire about your B & B If you can't accommodate them, you can give them one of your business cards, and ask them to contact you the next time they are in town.

Many small printing companies specialize in supplying business cards, so prices are quite competitive. Most printing companies can help you create the design and give advice on a suitable paper stock. Ask other B & B hosts for a copy of their cards. Study each card carefully to see what design features appeal to you before you go to the printers. Then, get at least three quotes from different printers and ask them for samples of their work.

Keep the following points in mind when ordering your business cards:

(a) Stay away from exotic or difficult-to-read print. Keep your written message simple. Your overall design should reflect the type of customer you are trying to attract.

(b) Include a logo or line drawing of your home, your business name, your own name, and your address and telephone number.

(c) Consider including one important feature of your business such as: "The closest B & B to _____ " or "Pick-up and drop-off service to the airport provided."

(d) A soft-colored paper stock is preferable to white. Black and white business cards are slightly cheaper, but they do not stand out in a crowd.

(e) Choose a standard 2" x 3½" (5 cm x 7.5 cm) flat card. Folded cards or non-standard sizes do not fit into card holders.

(f) Don't include your tariff structure on the card. Prices usually change from year to year and you want your cards to last longer than that. The setup cost for the press is the same regardless of the size of the order, so you can save a lot of money if you order enough cards to last for a few years.

Sample #24 shows our business card.

2. Brochures

Some B & Bs print brochures that describe the B & B in more detail. These brochures can be left in the guest rooms and sent out to prospective customers who are asking for a more detailed description of your home.

Brochures can be very expensive, especially if you want color photographs or other costly features, so you may decide to wait until your business expands before taking this step. We consider brochures optional advertising, particularly in the first year of operation.

If you do decide to have brochures printed, follow the same design principles as you did when printing your business cards. Get quotes from a number of printers and, again, ask for samples. Make sure that the size of brochure you choose will fit into a standard business envelope. Odd-sized envelopes cost more.

Include on the brochure some of your more important house rules, particularly the restrictive ones such as no smoking, no pets, etc. If you have pets, you should mention them. Many people are allergic to pets and will not want to stay anywhere that pets reside. Use "gentle" phrases such as "Our resident beagle, Sam, will greet you."

Try to describe your facilities and services in detail; giving a brief description of your food services would be useful. Some B & Bs find it helpful to print a map on the back of the brochure leading customers to their home, especially if they live off the beaten track.

Don't include your tariff structure on the brochure as you will probably want your brochures to last longer than your current prices will be in effect. You can write your rates in by hand or use a small pricing sheet which can be attached to the brochure.

Sample #25 shows the brochure from our B & B.

SAMPLE #24
BUSINESS CARD

239 WELLINGTON

Carnochan-Taylor House
1883

BED & BREAKFAST

Monica & Richard Taylor

Box 821, 239 Wellington Street
Niagara-On-The-Lake
Ontario, L0S 1J0

(416) 468-4081

SAMPLE #25
BROCHURE

239 WELLINGTON

Curnochan-Taylor House
1883

This Victorian home is situated in the Heritage District of the Old Town of Niagara-On-The-Lake on part of 1 3/4 acres bought by well known Niagara historian, Janet Curnochan in 1873.

In 1883 she sold 4575 square feet to her brother John for one dollar and he built the house that same year. Janet Carnochan rebought the property in 1891, retaining ownership until her death in 1926.

Located directly opposite the Shaw Theatre and one block from the main street, we offer private parking, double and twin rooms with shared bath, gracious sitting room, and a full breakfast in an elegant dining room.

Smoking is not permitted in the house, but our guests have the full use of the Victorian porch, patio and private gardens.

BED & BREAKFAST

Monica & Richard Taylor

Box 821, 239 Wellington Street
Niagara-On-The-Lake
Ontario, L0S 1J0

(416) 468-4081

117

3. Envelopes and letterhead

Some larger B & B operations have customized envelopes and letterhead for their business. This is a luxury that comes with a successful business, and is not normally found in the small B & B. A good alternative is to order a self-inking stamp that prints your business name, address, and telephone number. You can then purchase regular business stationery and mark it with your stamp.

4. Client forms

In chapter 9 we discussed two forms that you might send to your customers: deposit reminders (Sample #14) and booking confirmations (Sample #15). Any forms that you send to your customer should include some advertising about your B & B. The deposit reminder advertises tariff rates, the type of breakfast, and the types of rooms available. The booking confirmation advertises room types, cancellation policy, and check-in times.

Also, any time you mail forms such as these to your customers, you should enclose a business card.

5. Customer follow-up

Many B & Bs do some form of customer follow-up, which is a particularly useful practice in the first few years of operation when you are trying to develop repeat clientele.

You might send a year-end newsletter to any of your clients that you think are candidates for repeat business. The newsletter could highlight the year's activities and it could outline what additions or improvements you are planning for next year.

Keep the newsletter upbeat and amusing and no longer than one page (both sides). You can retain the home-made touch by composing, typing, and illustrating the newsletter yourself; then sign the newsletter yourselves. Include a holiday greeting and a few holiday recipes.

This kind of newsletter doesn't have to be sophisticated. Photocopies are adequate for a home-made newsletter.

If you don't want to create a newsletter, you could send holiday greeting cards instead. Again, choose the most promising repeat clientele. Sign each card personally and include a small personal greeting.

You can address your customers personally by referring to your reservation slips and recalling their first names as well as any useful information in the "details" section of the slip.

c. SIGNAGE

A well-designed and well-placed B & B sign can be a very effective form of advertising. On the other hand, a poorly designed sign or one in poor condition can deter prospective customers.

In some municipalities, there are strict sign bylaws that must be followed, so you may not have any choice in the matter. If you are allowed a sign, make sure it is easily seen from a passing automobile.

All the design criteria associated with business cards apply to the design of your sign. Make sure it is in good taste and that it will attract your target customers. It is equally important that your house number be visible from the road, and that it be illuminated after dark. Your customers should be able to locate your home easily — day or night.

d. ADVERTISING

The array of advertising choices available to even a small business can be quite daunting, but for you as a B & B operator, there are certain advertising options that are particularly productive and cost-effective. Here are a few ideas.

1. Booking agencies

A quick way to tap into an existing advertising network is to join a B & B booking agency. These agencies charge a fee to put you on their list and a booking fee for each room booked through them. A portion of those fees is used to advertise their services in selected magazines, government publications, tourist pamphlets, and travel brochures. By joining these established agencies, you may find your first few months of business easier.

2. Bed and breakfast guide books

There is a proliferation of B & B guide books on the market (see Appendix 2). You can apply to be listed in these books by writing to the authors or publishers. Some of them charge a fee for this service and others do not.

We recommend that you visit local bookstores to see which publications attract your attention. Look at the quality of the paper, the descriptions of the homes, and the overall appeal of the book. The procedures to get listed are usually included in the publications, so decide which books will best represent you and write to them for an application form. If any of your choices provide free listings, you should try them first. Free advertising is always a good investment.

3. Government publications

Most governments (provincial and state) have listings of bed and breakfast homes and/or booking agencies (see Appendix 1). You can obtain a copy of your government's brochure to determine if you wish to be listed. Government advertising is usually free.

4. Tourist attraction brochures

If there are major tourist attractions in your area, you should consider advertising in their brochures (if they will permit it). Get a copy of the brochure and see how other local businesses are represented. Make sure that the types of people who visit that attraction are the same types that you are trying to attract. In other words, you should target your advertising.

If you choose this type of advertising, you will have to make arrangements many months before the publishing date of the brochure.

5. Telephone directory

Telephone directories can be a good form of advertising, particularly if there is no listing for a B & B reservation service. You could list your home under "Bed and Breakfast" rather than your business name, so that potential customers can locate you easily.

You could either list your B & B's name in the white pages or advertise in the yellow pages — or both.

6. Magazines

Advertisements in magazines can be effective if your B & B relates in some way to the target audience of the magazine. A B & B in a farmhouse would appeal to readers of a "back-to-the-earth" type of magazine. An historic B & B might appeal to readers of an "antiques" magazine. You can use different magazines to target specific types of customers.

7. Newspapers

Newspaper advertising is difficult to target because newspapers are read by such a wide variety of people. Most people would not think to check the newspaper when looking for B & B accommodations.

However, some specialized newspapers aimed at ethnic groups or other special-interest groups could appeal to a narrower audience, and in these it might be worthwhile to place an advertisement.

8. Electronic mail

If you are a computer user and have joined an on-line database club, you can place your advertising on the electronic bulletin board. Most on-line databases will have a "travel and leisure" section, which would be an appropriate place to run an ad. The advertising is free, and you would attract other people who are members of the same on-line club.

e. MEASURING THE EFFECTIVENESS OF YOUR BOOKING SOURCES

When customers call to make reservations, make sure you ask them how they heard of your B & B. You will want this information to measure the effectiveness of all your booking sources, including your advertising. If you are advertising in several different publications, you will have to treat each one as a separate source of bookings.

1. Cost per booking

At the end of your business year, you should total the number of bookings you received from each booking source and each advertising resource. For each advertising resource, the cost of booking is calculated as the cost of placing the ad divided by the number of rooms booked through the ad. For example, if the cost of placing the advertisement was $200, and the number of bookings received as a result of the ad was 50, then the cost per booking is $200 ÷ by 50 = $4 per booking.

For a booking source such as an agency, the cost of booking is the fee for listing with the agency divided by the number of bookings obtained, plus the booking fee. For example, if the agency charges $50 to join and $5 per booking and you received 50 bookings through this agency, the cost of booking is ($50 + 50) + $5 = $6 per booking.

Every year, compare all your customer sources to see which produces the most bookings and which has the lowest cost per booking.

2. Break-even point

For each booking source, the break-even point is calculated as the cost of placing the advertisement divided by the profit made from one booking placed through the ad.

For example, if the cost of placing the ad was $200, and the profit obtained by one booking placed through the ad was $40, then the break-even point is 200 ÷ 40 = 5 bookings.

In other words, you would have to receive five bookings through this advertisement just to break even. Compare all your advertisements to see how effectively each one exceeded its break-even point.

If you find your paid advertising isn't reaching the break-even point, you might want to stay with free advertising through government brochures and some guide books. These sources are always a good investment, even if you only get a few bookings, because they cost you nothing. For the ads that you do pay for, make sure you keep accurate statistics on their effectiveness, and continue only with the ones that are "paying their way."

Note that calculating the break-even point does not provide a picture of how much money you *should* spend on advertising, it only provides a means of calculating the number of bookings required to cover the cost of placing a particular advertisement.

For more information on advertising, see *The Advertising Handbook for Small Business*, another title in the Self-Counsel Series.

f. DOCUMENT YOUR COSTS

Using a copy of Worksheet K provided in Appendix 3, list any costs associated with your advertising and promotion.

Now turn to Cost Sheet #4 in Appendix 4. Using the section labeled "Advertising Costs," make a one-line entry for your worksheet. Do not total the cost sheet at this time because there are additional entries to be made later.

"AS YOU LIKE IT" CODDLED EGGS

This receipe requires individual coddled egg cups which are small porcelain cups with screw lids. They are available at shops that sell English china. The following recipe is for two people — a unique way to serve eggs to your discriminating guests!

    2 coddled egg cups

    2 eggs

    Butter

    Pinch salt

    Pinch pepper

Guest's choices of the following toppings:

    grated cheese

    chopped chives

    finely chopped ham

Butter the inside of two coddled egg cups. Break eggs into cups, sprinkle salt and pepper on each, and top with the guests' choices of toppings.

Screw the lids onto the cups and place in a pan of cold water. Make sure that the water comes up to the top edge but not over the cup. Bring the water to a boil, then reduce heat and simmer for 3 to 5 minutes.

Remove the cups from the water and take off the lids. Be careful and use oven mitts — the cups will be hot!

Serve directly to your guests in the porcelain cups. Provide a small egg spoon.

13

FORECASTING YOUR BUSINESS SUCCESS

In the operation of any business, it is prudent to forecast and monitor the sales for the current year and to compare those sales to previous years. In this way, you can determine if the business is growing or shrinking, and if you need to make any adjustments to your business practices, marketing, or prices.

In the B & B business, your "sales" are reflected in the number of bookings you receive. By estimating your probable bookings, you can set and work toward achieving a realistic sales goal. A booking forecast is an estimate of the number of bookings you will receive for the current year. By forecasting and monitoring your bookings, you will be able to collect useful statistics that will enable you to measure the success of your business.

a. THE FIRST YEAR

A booking forecast is especially important for your first year in business because you must avoid setting an unrealistic sales goal. If you set an unattainable goal, you will likely become discouraged. Worse, an inaccurate booking forecast will throw off all your other plans such as cash-flow analysis (see chapter 14), and will probably land you into cash difficulties.

Unfortunately, a first-year booking forecast is considerably more difficult than a second- or third-year forecast because you don't have any of your own business statistics to refer to. To make up for the lack of these statistics, you will have to generate realistic estimates, based on as much information as possible. To achieve these estimates, you need to make three calculations:

(a) Estimate the booking days available to your B & B.

(b) Adjust the estimates to allow for various market conditions.

(c) Calculate your first-year booking forecast.

These calculations are discussed below and refer to Sample #26, which shows the first-year forecast for the Morris B & B. Worksheet L for your own calculations is provided in Appendix 3. Take the time to complete the worksheet in order to arrive at a realistic forecast of your first year's bookings.

1. Estimate the available booking days

(a) Review your final customer choices

In chapter 4, you summarized your final customer choices on your market research summary worksheet. You listed your customers in order of the total available booking days, and you estimated their available booking days for each month.

Now take all your final customer choices from your worksheet and calculate the average customer booking days available for each month of the year. You do this by adding all the figures for one month and then dividing that total by the number of final customer choices. Transfer your average calculations to Line 1 of your worksheet.

Sample #26 shows that the target customers for the Morris B & B are only available from the months of April to November. This shows that their business will be seasonal in nature.

SAMPLE #26
BOOKING FORECAST

REALISTIC BOOKING DAYS AVAILABLE — AVERAGE BOOKING DAYS EACH MONTH

	Total days	Jan	Feb	Mar	Apr	May	June	July	Aug	Sept	Oct	Nov	Dec
1. Final customers	105				2	6	17	30	30	11	8	1	
2. Local attractions	177			8	15	19	30	30	30	26	19		
3. Booking agencies	155	3	3	2	3	10	30	30	30	28	6	6	4
4. B & B associations	162	3	3	3	8	8	25	30	30	28	8	12	4
5. Average of 1 to 4 (Average Days Avail.)	151	2	2	3	7	11	26	30	30	23	10	5	2

ADJUSTMENTS TO BOOKING DAYS — ADJUSTMENTS TO AVERAGES EACH MONTH

	Total adjust	Jan	Feb	Mar	Apr	May	June	Jul	Aug	Sep	Oct	Nov	Dec
6. State of economy	+14					1	3	3	3	3	1		
7. Advertising	+24	2	2	2	2	2	2	2	2	2	2	2	2
8. Facilities/services	0												
9. Tariff structure	0												
10. Add Items 5 to 9 (Adj. booking days)	178	4	4	5	9	14	30	30	30	28	13	7	4
11. Adj. for vacations	-30	-15											-15
12. Adj. for days off	-14						-4	-4	-4	-2			
13. Total of 10 to 12 (Booking Days Avail.)	156	0	4	5	9	14	26	26	26	26	13	7	0

CALCULATE YOUR ROOM BOOKINGS — ROOM BOOKINGS EACH MONTH

	Totals	Jan	Feb	Mar	Apr	May	June	July	Aug	Sep	Oct	Nov	Dec
14. Max. Rm. Bookings Available (Line 13 x No. of Rms)	468	0	12	15	27	42	78	78	78	78	39	21	0
15. First-year adjustment (50% of Item 14)	232	0	6	7	13	21	39	39	39	39	19	10	0
16. Line 14 minus Line 15 (Booking Forecast)	236	0	6	8	14	21	39	39	39	39	20	11	0

123

(b) Review preferred attractions

Your market research summary that you completed in chapter 4 also shows the attractions that would be preferred by your chosen customers in their order of popularity. Now take all the preferred attractions shown on your worksheet and calculate the average operating days for each month of the year. Transfer your average calculations to Line 2 of Worksheet L.

Sample #26 shows that the average local attraction is open from March to October.

(c) Check local booking agencies

Contact local booking agencies to get their opinion on your first year's expected bookings. Make sure you tell them what types of customers you are targeting and what facilities and services you are offering. Agencies are always looking for new customers, and most of them will come out to your home and give you a realistic estimate of booking days, based on similar homes in the area. They can also advise on a suitable tariff rate for your home.

We recommend that you hire the services of a number of booking agencies in your first year. These agencies already have their advertising in place, and they can provide you with an immediate flow of clients.

Line 3 in Sample #26 shows that the booking agencies have estimated that Carol and Bob Morris should expect customers for most of the year, although the attendance does taper off at the beginning and the end of each calender year.

Interview several of your local booking agencies and get their estimates of booking days available for each month of the year. Calculate the average of their estimates for booking days and enter the figures onto Line 3 of Worksheet L.

(d) Check the local bed and breakfast association

Local B & B associations may have useful statistics, but you may have to join the association to get them. We recommend that you do join your local association. You will meet other local operators through these associations, and it is always beneficial to exchange ideas and information.

If there isn't a local association, ask a number of established operators for their estimates of your first year in business. They have already been down the road that you are facing. Take the average of their estimates, and transfer the figures onto Line 4 of Worksheet L.

Sample #26 shows that the B & B association predicts a similar operating season as reported by the booking agencies.

(e) Calculate the average booking days available

Complete Line 5 of Worksheet L by calculating the average of all entries on Lines 1 to 4. You now have a pattern of booking days available in each month, calculated by taking an average of all sources of information.

Sample #26 shows that some booking days are available for each month of the year. When you calculate the averages for Line 5, adjust any partial days to the next highest number.

2. Adjust the estimates for market conditions

(a) Check the state of the economy

As you forecast, you should ask yourself whether the economy is in a recession or in a period of business growth. How will this year's state of the economy affect the booking figures quoted by the booking agencies or local association, which are based on the previous year's business. You may have to adjust them slightly for this year's forecast.

Line 6 in Sample #26 shows that the economy is growing, and, therefore, Carol and Bob estimate that some additional booking days will probably occur during their busy months. They have arbitrarily added 14 more booking days to their calculations. In your first year of business, it is wise to be conservative in any adjustments you make.

Estimate the impact of the state of the economy on your existing calculations. If it is growing, add a few booking days to compensate. If the economy is shrinking, subtract a few booking days. If it is stable, do not make any entries on Line 6.

(b) How aggressive will your advertising be?

Well-placed and selective advertising is a good tool to attract customers to your business. If you are hiring one booking agent and printing business cards and/or brochures, make no adjustments on Line 7. If you have multiple booking agents or plan to place one or more advertisements, add a few booking days on Line 7 to compensate. If you have no booking agent, subtract a few booking days on Line 7.

Sample #26 shows that Carol and Bob plan to advertise aggressively, and they have arbitrarily added 24 booking days, spread evenly over the entire year.

(c) How unique are your facilities or services?

What are you offering that the competition isn't? If you can offer unique facilities and/or services, you can expect to attract additional customers.

During your market research, you closely examined your local competition, which you summarized on Worksheet F. Compare their facilities and services to your establishment, and make a modest adjustment on Line 8 of your Worksheet L. If your facilities are above average, add a few booking days. If they are below average, subtract a few booking days.

Sample #26 shows that Carol and Bob Morris provide average facilities and services, so no adjustments were made on Line 8.

(d) Compare your tariff structure

Refer back to Worksheet F and note the minimum and maximum tariff structures of your competitors. Compare your proposed tariff structure to these figures. If your tariff is higher, subtract a few booking days on Line 9 on Worksheet L. If your tariff is lower, add a few booking days to Line 9.

(e) Calculate the adjusted booking days available

Add the figures on Lines 5 to 9, and enter the totals on Line 10. Remember to keep the maximum days available in each month to no more than 30. Sample #26 shows that July and August started with 30 days on Line 5, so they remained at 30 days on Line 10 (even though they total 35).

(f) Allow time for vacations and days off

If you are running your B & B by yourself or as a team, you will probably have to shut the business down to take a vacation. Subtract these days in the months that are affected, using Line 11 on Worksheet L.

As well, you should plan for some time off during your busy season. Everyone needs some time off during a working week. Subtract enough days from every month to bring the adjusted booking days on Line 10 down to a maximum of 26. For months that have fewer than 26 adjusted booking days, you will be able to take some days off in between bookings.

If you employ people to run your B & B, you may decide to keep the business running during your vacation and time off. If this is the case, then do not subtract any days on Lines 11 and 12.

As Carol and Bob have decided to close the B & B and take their vacation in the slack months of December and January, they subtracted 15 days from these months on Line 11 of Sample #26.

(g) Calculate the booking days available

Calculate the total of Lines 10, 11, and 12, and enter the results on Line 13. If a month adds up to a negative number, enter a zero in that month.

In Sample #26, December and January have dropped to zero due to the 15 days of vacation in each month.

3. Calculate your first-year booking forecast

(a) Calculate the maximum room bookings available

Multiply the number of booking days available on Line 13 by the number of rooms you will be renting. Enter the result onto Line 14.

(b) Do a first-year adjustment

Since this is your first year in business, you should not expect all the bookings shown on Line 14. We suggest that you set your first-year goal at 50% of the bookings shown on Line 14. This is a realistic goal and one that you can confidently work toward. Most successful businesses have learned to set realistic goals, and then move heaven and earth to achieve them. If you set excessive and unrealistic goals, you will never reach them.

Calculate 50% of the bookings on Line 14, and enter the results on Line 15.

(c) Calculate your booking forecast.

Subtract Line 15 from Line 14 and place the results on Line 16. This total represents your best estimate of a realistic booking forecast for your first year in business.

b. SUBSEQUENT YEARS' FORECASTS

As you progress through your first year of business, you should collect and keep statistics on advance bookings, actual bookings, and sources of bookings (discussed below). With these statistics, you can build a data base that can be used for your second and subsequent years' forecasting.

For example, in your second year of business, you can use the actual bookings that you received in each month of the first year, and divide them by the number of rooms you are renting. This calculation will give you the average days available which should be entered onto Line 5 of your second-year forecast. You can then continue with your calculations for the other lines on the forecast. You should anticipate additional bookings through repeat and referred customers and add bookings to each month based on your estimates of this additional business.

As each year passes, and you gather more statistics, you will find your forecasting will become increasingly accurate.

c. STATISTICS

1. Advance bookings

Depending on your location and your target customers, a certain percentage of your bookings will be reserved in advance. Customers will contact you weeks, months, or even a year ahead of time to arrange for accommodations. It is useful to document these advance reservations so that you can compare subsequent years' advance booking patterns.

Sample #27 shows the advance bookings for the Morris B & B as they were received during the year. At the start of each month, Carol and Bob counted the reservations they had received for each of the remaining months of the year. They started counting advance reservations on January 1 and in Sample #27 you can see that they had already received 27 advance bookings spread over a number of different months.

On February 1, they again counted their advance bookings, but because January had already passed, they began counting from February onwards. They continued this routine until they had built up an advance booking pattern for the entire year.

If you have a computer that can generate graphs, you may want to display your figures in graphic form, or you can draw graphs manually on graph paper. The lower half of Sample #27 shows a graph of the total advance bookings at the start of each month. Graphs are not necessary, but sometimes a "picture" can help you analyze a table of figures.

When Carol and Bob start collecting next year's statistics, they will refer to this advance booking pattern to try to forecast next year's success.

2. Actual bookings

At the *end* of every month, you can count the number of bookings you actually received during that month. This is a true measure of the success of the current operating year.

In Sample #28, Carol and Bob have recorded the total bookings received in each month, and on each day of the week. They have also recorded the maximum possible bookings by multiplying the number of days in the month times three (the number of rooms they rent). To help them visualize their actual booking pattern, they have drawn a graph as well.

From their analysis, Carol and Bob found that the majority of business occurs from May to October, a six-month season. They therefore considered the following options:

(a) Open the business for only six months of the year (and lose 50% of their tax advantages)

(b) Offer off-season rates and extra services to increase the business in the slow months

(c) Change their target customers during the slow months to attract customers who are willing to travel in those months

They noticed that even during the peak month of August, the business attracted only 51 bookings out of a possible 93, slightly over 50% of capacity. Looking at these statistics, Carol and Bob should consider increasing their advertising and the number of booking agencies they belong to, providing extra services to attract more customers, and reviewing their tariff structure compared to their competitors.

They determined that as Monday is the least popular day for this area, they would take Monday as their "day off." Everybody needs a day off, and Monday would be the least damaging to the business.

Tuesday, Wednesday, and Thursday also need improvement. Carol and Bob should consider offering mid-week special rates to attract more customers, or marketing these three days as a "package deal."

The Morrises discovered that the total actual bookings for the year was 207. The maximum possible bookings were 1,095, calculated by multiplying 3 rooms by 365 days. However, they reminded themselves of the following:

(a) 1,095 bookings are virtually impossible to achieve, and they could not possibly stand the physical strain.

(b) 207 bookings for a three-room B & B operating for only six reasonably active months is quite good for the first year in business.

(c) The maximum possible bookings for May through October is 552, but the summer business peaks only at August with the other months showing fewer bookings. Even with good booking agents and aggressive advertising, it is realistic to expect only 300 to 350 bookings over these 6 months.

(d) Given the poor performance of November to May, they should not expect more than 400 to 500 bookings if they stay open for 12 months.

MORRIS B & B ADVANCE BOOKINGS

START OF MONTH	ADVANCE BOOKINGS FOR 199-												TOTAL ADVANCE
---	JAN	FEB	MAR	APR	MAY	JUN	JUL	AUG	SEP	OCT	NOV	DEC	---
JAN	0	2	1	0	3	4	6	6	3	2	0	0	27
FEB		3	3	2	4	6	7	6	4	0	0	0	35
MAR			4	6	5	6	8	8	6	3	0	0	46
APR				7	7	9	9	10	8	5	1	0	56
MAY					8	14	12	15	11	7	1	0	68
JUNE						19	18	20	16	9	1	0	83
JULY							24	26	19	10	1	0	80
AUG								30	21	11	2	0	64
SEP									25	13	2	0	40
OCT										14	2	1	17
NOV											2	1	3
DEC												1	1

ADVANCED BOOKINGS FOR 199-

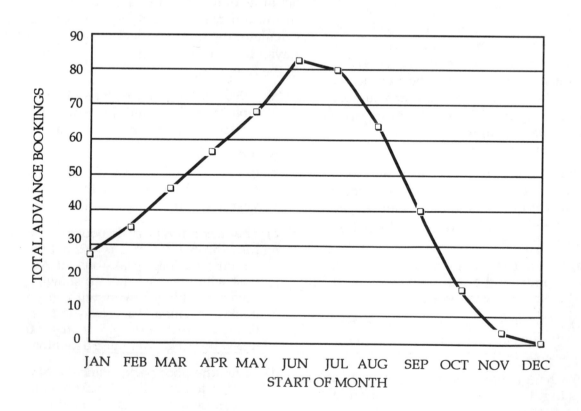

SAMPLE #28
MORRIS B & B ACTUAL BOOKINGS

ACTUAL BOOKINGS FOR 199-

END OF MONTH	DAYS OF THE WEEK							ACTUAL BOOKINGS	MAXIMUM POSSIBLE BOOKINGS
	SU	MO	TU	WE	TH	FR	SA		
JAN								0	93
FEB							3	3	84
MAR	1					4	5	10	93
APR	2					2	5	9	90
MAY	1					4	7	12	93
JUNE	6			2	6	8	10	32	90
JULY	6	1	1	3	7	6	8	32	93
AUG	8	3	8	6	8	9	9	51	93
SEP	7	1	3	3	4	8	10	36	90
OCT	4		1	1	2	4	6	18	93
NOV							3	3	90
DEC							1	1	93
YEAR TOTALS =	35	5	13	15	27	45	67	207	1,095

ACTUAL BOOKINGS FOR 199-

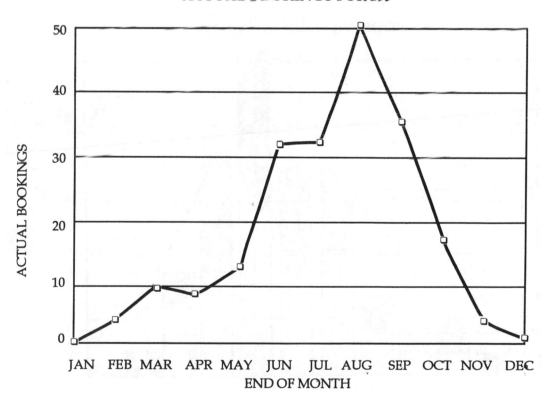

ACTUAL BOOKINGS

END OF MONTH

SAMPLE #29
MORRIS B & B BOOKING SOURCES
BOOKING SOURCES FOR 199-*

MONTH	A	B	C	D	TOTAL
JAN					0
FEB				3	3
MAR		3	2	5	10
APR	4	1		4	9
MAY	6	2	1	3	12
JUNE	11	10	5	6	32
JUL	10	11	6	5	32
AUG	9	18	12	12	51
SEPT	6	6	12	12	36
OCT	4	10	2	2	18
NOV				3	3
DEC				1	1
BOOKING TOTALS =	50	61	40	56	207

*BOOKING SOURCES
A = Advertising   B = B & B Association
C = Chamber of Commerce D = Direct Customers

Source	Listing fee	No. of bookings	Booking fee	Cost per booking
A	$100.00	50	$0.00	$2.00
B	$100.00	61	$5.00	$6.63
C	$100.00	40	$5.00	$7.50
D	$ 0.00	56	$0.00	$0.00

BOOKING SOURCES FOR 199-

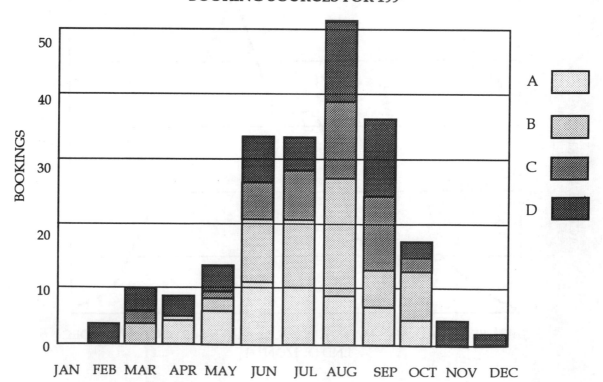

(e) They can expect their client volume to increase each year. Their repeat and referred customers will help fill in the gaps.

3. Sources of bookings

When you open for business, you will probably have booking agencies, signage, and other advertising attracting customers to your B & B. The Morris B & B has four sources of bookings:

(a) A = Advertising in a local attraction brochure

(b) B = The Bed and Breakfast Association (booking agency)

(c) C = The local chamber of commerce (booking agency)

(d) D = Direct calls to the hosts (repeat clients or referrals)

Sample #29 shows the statistics on booking sources for the Morris B & B. Most of these statistics are found on the revenue summary form (Sample #23 in chapter 11). Carol and Bob have also drawn a graph to help them analyze the figures.

These statistics are used to monitor the relative effectiveness of the different booking sources. As their repeat and referred clients increase, the hosts will rely less and less on the other sources of bookings.

In examining these statistics, Carol and Bob notice the following:

(a) Source A (Advertising) costs $100 with zero cost for each room booked. Since this source produced 50 bookings, the cost is 100 divided by 50 = $2 per booking.

(b) Source B (B & B Association) costs $100 to list plus $5 per room booked. Since this source produced 61 book-

ings, the cost is $100 divided by 61 + $5 = $6.63 per booking.

(c) Source C (chamber of commerce) costs $100 to list plus $5 per room booked. Since this source produced 40 bookings, the cost is $100 divided by 40 + $5 = $7.50 per booking.

(d) Source D has no listing or booking costs to produce 56 bookings, so there is no cost per booking.

Carol and Bob should consider promoting Sources A and D as much as possible. Source A (advertising) can be promoted by targeting advertising to attract more customers of the type that they desire. Source D (direct) can be promoted by running an efficient, friendly, and high-quality B & B.

Because this is their first year in business, Carol and Bob should probably continue the services of agencies B and C for at least one more year and monitor them to see if the number of bookings increases. As their business expands, they will reach the point where the booking agencies will not be sending enough clients to make the listing fee worthwhile. At that time, Carol and Bob may decide to drop the services of one or both of their booking agencies.

d. DOCUMENT YOUR COSTS

Using a copy of Worksheet K provided in Appendix 3, list any equipment and supplies needed to do your forecasting and statistics (e.g., drafting supplies, note books, calculator, etc.)

Now turn to Cost Sheet #4 in Appendix 4; using the section labeled "Forecasts and Statistics," make a one-line entry for your worksheet.

You can now total Cost Sheet #4.

"TOO GOOD TO BE TRUE" MARMALADE

6 bitter (Seville) oranges, seeds removed
and cut into thin pieces

1 lemon, cut into thin pieces with
seeds removed

14 cups water

5 lbs sugar

Add oranges, lemon, and their juices to the water. Cover and let stand for 24 hours.

Bring mixture to a boil. Boil mixture down to about ½ quantity, stirring occasionally. Add sugar and continue boiling and occasionally stirring for about 1 hour or until the mixture becomes thick.

Pour into sterilized jars.

14

FINANCIAL PLANNING

In this chapter, we discuss the financial implications of starting and running a B & B business. As you have progressed through this book, you have recorded your start-up costs on four cost sheets. Now it is time for you to total these sheets, and then examine various sources of start-up capital.

We also discuss the importance of financial forecasting, and we show you how to do a first-year forecast of revenue and expenses. You can use this information to create your first-year cash-flow analysis.

a. CALCULATE YOUR START-UP COSTS

Review the cost sheets you have completed:

(a) Cost Sheet #1: Market Research

(b) Cost Sheet #2: Rules and Regulations

(c) Cost Sheet #3: Facilities Cost Estimates

(d) Cost Sheet #4: Miscellaneous

Total each of the individual cost sheets, and transfer their totals onto Cost Sheet #5, the Start-up Cost Summary. Add the four totals together to get your start-up subtotal. Calculate 10% of the subtotal, and enter that amount as a contingency to take care of any unknown or unexpected costs that you might encounter during your business start-up. Add the subtotal and the 10% contingency to arrive at your "Total Bed and Breakfast Start-up Cost."

You have already spent the money for market research, but it does not represent a major expenditure. The remainder of the money represents the capital outlay that you will need to start your business. This money will be needed "up front" to get your establishment ready for your first customer.

You must now decide whether the amount you need is within your budget or whether you need to seek outside financing. If you do have to have to borrow, keep the amount as small as possible. When you start your B & B, you will have enough to occupy your thoughts without the added burden of worrying about large loan repayments.

b. REVIEW YOUR START-UP COSTS

If you do have to consider outside financing, now is a good time to review your start-up costs to see if you could start your B & B with less capital and without hurting the overall level of service or the ambience of your facilities. Take the time to review your cost sheets and their associated worksheets with a view to eliminating unnecessary costs. Perhaps some of the "nice-to-have" items could be acquired later on, and you could limit your purchases to "must-have" items.

As you review your costs, keep the following points in mind.

(a) Don't skimp on market research. You must have detailed and accurate market research information to properly focus your business. Also, the amount you spend on market research is quite small compared to the other start-up costs.

(b) You can't get around rules and regulations, so don't attempt to bypass any of these costs. You must make sure that your B & B is properly licensed and registered with the various levels of government.

(c) Facilities might be a source of start-up savings, but be careful where you cut back. You would be wise to concentrate on family and office areas. Do you really need that new computer now or could it wait? Could your office be temporarily housed in a part of an existing room, rather than getting involved in renovations? Look at all your family and office areas carefully to see if you could trim these start-up costs.

(d) There may be some room to save on miscellaneous costs, but again, be careful where you cut back. Anything that improves the efficiency of your record keeping and day-to-day operations should not be compromised. Similarly, housekeeping is very important, so tread softly there. Advertising should be reviewed to see if such items as customized stationery or expensive brochures should be reserved for your second year in business. Don't reduce any necessary items such as booking agencies, business cards, or any advertising that is targeted at your customers.

After reviewing your individual worksheets and eliminating any unnecessary items, adjust the totals on each of your cost sheets. Recalculate the total start-up cost at the bottom of Cost Sheet #5. This adjusted total is the minimum amount necessary to start your B & B. Hopefully, you have reduced or eliminated the amount of capital that you will need to borrow.

c. SOURCES OF START-UP CAPITAL

Everyone reacts differently to debt. Some people love to be in debt because they need some motivation to keep them working toward their goals. Other people dislike debt because it causes worry and depression. You must decide how much debt you can comfortably tolerate and plan your borrowing accordingly.

There are a number of sources of start-up capital that you may want to consider. If you have to borrow money, we suggest that you consult your accountant first. He or she will have useful suggestions on types of loans that can be treated as "business loans," which allow you to deduct the interest as a business expense.

1. Personal savings

If you use your existing funds, you won't have the stress of a loan hanging over your head. You will be able to concentrate on running your B & B without the worry of loan repayments. If you are running your B & B as a team (e.g., with friends or other family members), all team members should contribute to the start-up fund. In that way, all partners will have a financial stake in the business, which will be an added incentive to succeed.

2. Personal financing

If you obtain a personal loan, you can avoid the hassle of preparing a business plan for the bank, which is necessary for a business loan. Ask your accountant for advice on documenting the loan so that it can be considered as a business loan for tax purposes.

(a) Personal loans

Most banks will extend a personal line of credit or loan to their customers as long as you can offer some collateral or prove that you can repay the loan. Home improvement loans are particularly suited to the type of upgrading that may be required for a B & B.

(b) Credit card

A credit card can be another quick source of funds, but the interest rate is very high. Don't use this method for large sums of money, but keep it in mind as a quick source of back-up cash in an emergency.

(c) Family or friends

Borrowing from family or friends is generally not a good idea. There are exceptions, however, and only you can be the judge. There is a great tendency to treat a friendly loan as a less-important loan, and your repayments might fall behind. This inevitably results in bad feelings all around and your personal relationship with the lender will suffer.

If you are considering a loan from family or friends, make sure it is properly documented, particularly the repayment schedule. Stick to the schedule, and treat the loan with the same respect as a bank loan. It would also be wise to have a back-up source of funds available in case you have trouble meeting your payments. Paying back loans from family and friends should get top priority if you value the relationship.

3. Business loan

Most banks will consider a B & B as a suitable candidate for a business loan, but they require fairly extensive documentation before they process your request.

Different banks have different approaches to business loans, and competition for your business is brisk, so shop around for the best deal. Banks will ask you to prepare a "business plan," so we suggest that you consult your accountant to get his or her advice on the layout and substance of your business plan document.

Alternatively, you could ask your bank what documents they require. You might also want to refer to *Preparing a Successful Business Plan*, another title in the Self-Counsel Series.

All of these sources will suggest that the business plan include a cash-flow analysis of your first year in business. How to prepare your own cash flow analysis is discussed later in this chapter.

4. Private investor

If you plan to raise start-up capital through a private investor, be careful. This area of financing is full of dangers so ask your accountant for guidance. Private investors generally want high interest rates or "a piece of the action." Your accountant may have some reliable contacts that can be approached for start-up capital.

5. Government loan

The chance of getting any funding from government for your B & B is slim. Generally, the government provides loan guarantees only as a last resort if you have been turned down by all other lending institutions. They require a full business plan, and they usually want the business to be incorporated.

Government loan departments can be useful sources of business information and educational material, however, so it would be worthwhile to contact the appropriate authorities. Also, governments are constantly changing their business assistance programs, so you may find programs useful to your situation.

In the United States, you should contact the Small Business Administration office in your area. In Canada, you contact the small business development department of your provincial government. They will be able to send you information about assistance programs for small businesses.

d. WHAT IS FINANCIAL FORECASTING?

Financial forecasting means estimating your business revenues and expenses ahead of time. Most small businesses will do financial forecasting for one year in advance, but larger corporations routinely forecast up to five years ahead.

Regardless of your size, it is good business practice to get into the habit of financial forecasting. Forecasts will help you make informed business decisions, and they will highlight potential trouble spots before they occur. First-year financial forecasts are particularly important because new businesses have no previous years' statistics to refer to. A first-year forecast will help you see your new business "on paper" before you begin.

To develop your financial forecast, you must estimate your revenues and expenses for your first year in business and then incorporate these figures into a cash-flow analysis, which will show the flow of cash into and out of your business for each month of your business year. This process is examined in the following pages by showing how Carol and Bob Morris prepared their financial estimates.

e. ESTIMATING REVENUE

Sample #30 shows the financial estimates for the Morris Bed and Breakfast. Let's study this example, and see how the hosts have arrived at their first-year estimates of revenues.

1. Booking forecast and revenue

Earlier (see chapter 13), Carol and Bob Morris prepared a forecast of their first-year bookings. Recall that this forecast was obtained by taking the data that they had collected during their market research and adding or subtracting bookings based on the extent of their proposed advertising, facilities and services, tariff structure, days off, vacations, etc. They transferred these figures to the top of their financial estimate form.

Next, they convert their booking forecast into booking revenue by multiplying the forecast by their room tariff. Carol and Bob propose to charge $80 per night for each booking, so they have multiplied each month's forecast by 80 to get their estimated booking revenue for each month of the year. Although they will charge extra for customers coming through booking agents, they decided to be conservative in their estimates and use the $80 figure for all customers.

Carol and Bob then estimated any additional revenue for extra meals and services provided. They made an assumption that 10% of their guests would like a packed picnic lunch during the hot summer months of May to October. They estimated a price of $3 per person or $6 per booking. They decided not to anticipate any revenue from additional services for their first year in business; instead, they want to wait and see what their customers' requirements are, and they will keep track of these revenues for next year's financial forecast.

Finally, Carol and Bob considered any revenues from other sources. Since this is their first year in business, they will be injecting some start-up capital into their business to cover their calculated start-up costs. They estimate that $5,000 would be adequate start-up capital. Since this money is required "up front," they have entered the entire amount in the first month of their business year.

2. Second- and subsequent-year revenue estimates

Carol and Bob plan to collect statistics during their first business year, which will be very helpful when estimating subsequent-year revenues. They will have a much clearer picture of their booking patterns, and they will have a good idea of the type of extra meals and services their customers prefer.

One of the statistics they will collect is advance bookings. Once they have a predictable pattern, they will be able to count on the deposit money that will arrive ahead of the actual booking. These room deposits will help their cash flow during the early months of each business year. Next year, they will enter their estimates for advance deposits, under "Other Revenues."

f. ESTIMATING EXPENSES

1. First-year expense estimates

The remainder of Sample #30 shows the first-year estimates of expenses for the Morris B & B. The first three expenses are associated with the direct servicing of the guests, which are proportional to the number of guests booked. Fees charged by the

SAMPLE #30
FINANCIAL ESTIMATES

	Jan	Feb	Mar	Apr	May	June	July	Aug	Sep	Oct	Nov	Dec
Booking Forecast	0	6	8	14	21	39	39	39	39	20	11	0
REVENUES												
Booking Revenue	0	480	640	1120	1680	3120	3120	3120	3120	1600	880	0
Extra Meals	0	0	0	0	12	23	23	23	23	12	0	0
Extra Services	0	0	0	0	0	0	0	0	0	0	0	0
Other Revenues	5000	0	0	0	0	0	0	0	0	0	0	0
EXPENSES												
Booking Fees	0	15	20	35	50	100	100	100	100	50	25	0
Guest Food	0	72	96	168	252	468	468	468	468	240	132	0
Guest Supplies	0	18	24	42	63	117	117	117	117	60	33	0

	AMOUNT	PRORATED	MONTHLY	QUARTERLY	OTHER
Gas	110	55	✓		
Electric Bi-monthly	110	50			Bi-monthly
Water/Sewer	34	17	✓		
Telephone	80	40	✓		
Cable TV	20	10	✓		
Property Taxes	216	108	✓		
Mortgage Interest	80	40	✓		
House Repairs	60	30	✓		
House Insurance	300	150			May
Bank Charges	15		✓		
Office Expenses	30		✓		
Accounting & Legal	180				March
Business Insurance	100				May
Advertising					
Agent Listing Fees					
Licences					
Loan Repayments	50		✓		
Other Expenses	4400				Jan.

booking agencies, the cost of guest food, and the cost of non-food guest supplies are included in guest expenses.

To estimate the booking fees, the hosts remembered that they will have four sources of bookings: advertising, B & B association, chamber of commerce, and direct calls. Only the chamber of commerce and the B & B association charge a booking fee, so Carol and Bob estimate that one-half of their bookings would cost $5 each. They then used the booking forecast to estimate their monthly booking-fee expense.

To estimate the guest food cost, Carol and Bob use their calculation of the average food cost for each guest, which is $4.89 for breakfast plus $1.11 for room refreshments or $6.00 per guest. Since the average booking has two guests, the food costs per booking is $12. They then multiplied their monthly booking forecast figure by $12 to get their estimate of the monthly guest food expenses.

To estimate the guest supply expenses, they arbitrarily assigned $3 per booking. This figure represents the cost of non-food items such as toilet paper, facial tissue, paper towels and cups, guest soap, laundry detergent, cleaning supplies, etc. Three dollars per booking should prove to be a reasonably accurate estimate for a three-bedroom B & B. They then multiplied their monthly booking forecast figure by $3 to get their estimate of the monthly guest supply expenses.

Utility bills and house-related expenses can be partially charged (or prorated) to the B & B. Carol and Bob have calculated the business portion of their house to be 50% of the total house, which means they can charge 50% of all utilities and house-related expenses to the business. They also note when these utility bills come due during the year.

It's worthwhile to note that utilities such as gas, electric, water, and telephone will be substantially higher once you open your

doors to business. You'll be using more of these utilities to service your customers, so it is wise to adjust your utility estimates upward. Expenses such as property taxes, mortgage interest, normal house repairs, and conventional house insurance will not be affected by your business.

Direct expenses are all costs that can be directly charged to the business without prorating. These include all costs that are a direct result of running a B & B. Carol and Bob estimate their bank charges, office expenses, accounting and legal fees, and their business insurance cost. Because this is their first year in business, advertising costs, agent listing fees, and licenses have already been included in their start-up costs, so no additional amounts appear under these three headings.

Because Carol and Bob arranged a $1,000 business loan to help with their start-up costs, they have included the $50-per-month loan repayment in their expense estimates.

Finally, because this is their first year in business, Carol and Bob have entered their start-up costs under "Other Expenses." They totalled their four cost sheets and added a 10% contingency to arrive at a total start-up cost of $4,400. This is an "up front" expense, so the hosts have charged the entire amount in the first month of their business year.

2. Second- and subsequent-year expense estimates

As Carol and Bob gain experience, they will fine-tune their estimates of expenses. Start-up costs will not be a factor after the first year, so advertising, agent listing fees, and licenses will be shown as separate entries. The entry for "Other Expenses" can be used for estimates of capital purchases, equipment rentals, wages, car expenses, etc.

Worksheet M has been provided in Appendix 3 to help you estimate what your first-year revenue and expenses will be. Follow the same procedures as described above. Start by transferring Line 16 from your Worksheet L onto the top of Worksheet M, then proceed to fill in the remainder of the worksheet. Try to be as realistic as possible in your estimates of revenues and expenses because these estimates will be transferred to your cash-flow analysis.

g. CASH FLOW ANALYSIS

You have probably often heard people say "We had a cash flow problem and went out of business." This means that the flow of cash going out of the business was greater than the flow of cash coming into the business. Most businesses can survive a few months of this type of cash flow, but a lengthy period of negative cash flow will spell disaster for a small business. It is important, therefore, to do a cash-flow analysis of your first business year before you begin in order to forecast the probable success or failure of your B & B business plan.

On Worksheet M, you have already collected an estimate of all your anticipated revenues and expenses for your first year and these are the figures you will use in your analysis — but in a format that is more easily understood.

Sample #31 shows the cash-flow analysis for the first year of the Morris B & B. The various revenues and expenses are listed down the left side of the page, and the 12 months of the business year are listed across the top. After calculating total monthly revenues (Line 4) and total monthly expenses (Line 22), Carol and Bob were able to calculate a monthly surplus or shortage (Line 24). Note that in February, March, and December, the business was spending more than it was taking in. In most small B & Bs, there will be slack periods that will result in monthly shortages. If the business is otherwise strong, it should be able to weather these slack months.

The most important figures on this cash-flow analysis sheet are found on lines 26 and 27. Line 26 shows the cash at the start of each month, and line 27 shows the cash at the end of each month. In other words, these figures show the monthly flow of cash into and out of the Morris B & B. If either of these figures drop to zero, the business has run out of cash.

The cash-flow analysis should be taken seriously; it will prove to be a reasonably accurate picture of what will actually happen when you begin your operation. By studying theirs, Carol and Bob can see, for example, that their business will lose money during January, February, March, and December (four months). Clearly, they should not plan to make any major purchases during these months. When their business is at its lowest point in March, they should plan for sources of emergency money (just in case). Alternatively, they could increase their start-up fund to create a larger cash reserve. By monitoring line 27, they can look ahead to see if their business can maintain a reasonable cash reserve during the year. In their case, the business year starts with $5,000 and ends with $10,127, so they should be able to pay back their start-up fund, pay themselves a small salary, and create a cash reserve fund. Not bad for one year in business!

Now, it is time to do your own cash-flow analysis. You will find it easiest to use a 13-column ledger sheet similar to the sheets used for your financial records, which can be purchased in any stationery store. Alternatively, if you have a spreadsheet program on a computer, you can easily generate your analysis with that.

Use the figures you collected on Worksheet M to fill in your cash-flow analysis. If you do not run your business January to December, cross out the months that appear across the top of the worksheet, and enter the correct months.

When you have completed your cash-flow analysis, review the following:

(a) Are your start-up funds adequate? Will they carry the business until it starts to make a profit?

SAMPLE #31
CASH FLOW ANALYSIS

MORRIS BED AND BREAKFAST CASH FLOW ANALYSIS — FROM JANUARY 199_ TO DECEMBER 199_ — Page 1 of 1

ENTRY NO.	REVENUE OR EXPENSE ITEM	JAN. 1	FEB. 2	MAR. 3	APR. 4	MAY 5	JUNE 6	JULY 7	AUG. 8	SEPT. 9	OCT. 10	NOV. 11	DEC. 12	YEAR TOTALS 13	ENTRY NO.
1	Booking Revenue	0	480	640	1120	1680	3120	3120	3120	3120	1600	880	0	18880	1
2	Extra Meals & Services	0	0	0	0	12	23	23	23	23	12	0	0	116	2
3	Other Revenues	5000	0	0	0	0	0	0	0	0	0	0	0	5000	3
4	TOTAL MONTHLY REVENUES	5000	480	640	1120	1692	3143	3143	3143	3143	1612	880	0	23996	4
5															5
6	Booking Fees	0	15	20	35	50	100.	100	100	100	50	25	0	595	6
7	Guest Food & Supplies	0	90	120	210	315	585	585	585	585	300	165	0	3540	7
8	Utilities	105	155	122	155	105	172	105	155	122	155	105	172	1628	8
9	Property Taxes	108	108	108	108	108	108	108	108	108	108	108	108	1296	9
10	Mortgage Interest	40	40	40	40	40	40	40	40	40	40	40	40	480	10
11	House Repairs	30	30	30	30	30	30	30	30	30	30	30	30	360	11
12	House Insurance	0	0	0	0	150	0	0	0	0	0	0	0	150	12
13	Bank Charges	15	15	15	15	15	15	15	15	15	15	15	15	180	13
14	Office Expenses	30	30	30	30	30	30	30	30	30	30	30	30	360	14
15	Accounting & Legal	0	0	180	0	0	0	0	0	0	0	0	0	180	15
16	Business Insurance	0	0	0	0	100	0	0	0	0	0	0	0	100	16
17	Advertising	0	0	0	0	0	0	0	0	0	0	0	0	0	17
18	Agents Listing Fees	0	0	0	0	0	0	0	0	0	0	0	0	0	18
19	Licenses	0	0	0	0	0	0	0	0	0	0	0	0	0	19
20	Loan Repayments	50	50	50	50	50	50	50	50	50	50	50	50	600	20
21	Other Expenses	4400	0	0	0	0	0	0	0	0	0	0	0	4400	21
22	TOTAL MONTHLY EXPENSES	4778	533	715	673	993	1130	1063	1113	1080	778	568	445	13869	22
23															23
24	MONTHLY SURPLUS OR SHORTAGE	222	-53	-75	447	699	2013	2080	2030	2063	834	312	-445	10127	24
25															25
26	CASH AT THE START OF THE MONTH	5000	222	169	94	541	1240	3253	5333	7363	9426	10260	10572		26
27	CASH AT THE END OF THE MONTH	222	169	94	541	1240	3253	5333	7363	9426	10260	10572	10127	10127	27

(b) Where is your break-even point? (cash in equals cash out)

(c) How much cash do you have at the end of the year?

(d) How many debts do you have at the end of the year? (include start-up capital, business loan balances, etc.) How much of this debt do you plan to pay off?

(e) How much cash will you set aside for the start of next year?

(f) What salary can you collect?

(g) Does your business plan look feasible?

Item (f) is one that should not be overlooked. Your cash-flow analysis will predict what your first year's profit will be, so you should decide what portion of that profit should be set aside for you to "pay yourself." Some operators choose to forego any salary during their first year in business in order to get the business up and running. Other operators set a minimum hourly or daily wage rate that they wish to achieve. Whatever your salary demands, check that your cash-flow analysis can support them. As your business expands, you can adjust your salary level accordingly.

Your cash-flow analysis will paint a realistic picture of the financial health of your business, and it will point out the strengths and the weaknesses of your business plan. Get into the habit of doing a cash-flow analysis each year. As you gain experience in the B & B business, you will find yourself creating surprisingly accurate financial forecasts, which will prove invaluable in planning financial decisions and in monitoring the health of your business.

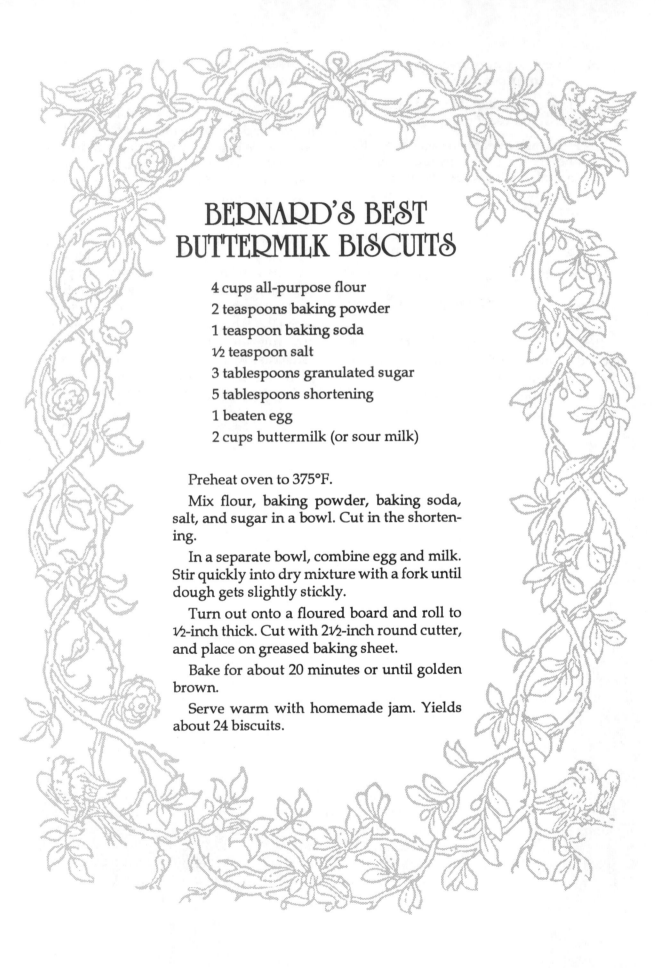

BERNARD'S BEST BUTTERMILK BISCUITS

4 cups all-purpose flour
2 teaspoons baking powder
1 teaspoon baking soda
½ teaspoon salt
3 tablespoons granulated sugar
5 tablespoons shortening
1 beaten egg
2 cups buttermilk (or sour milk)

Preheat oven to 375°F.

Mix flour, baking powder, baking soda, salt, and sugar in a bowl. Cut in the shortening.

In a separate bowl, combine egg and milk. Stir quickly into dry mixture with a fork until dough gets slightly stickly.

Turn out onto a floured board and roll to ½-inch thick. Cut with 2½-inch round cutter, and place on greased baking sheet.

Bake for about 20 minutes or until golden brown.

Serve warm with homemade jam. Yields about 24 biscuits.

15

YOUR START-UP PROJECT PLAN

a. WHY DO PROJECT PLANNING?

Think about the activity when a large office building is renovated. An army of different trades swarm all over the site; people are going in many different directions; and trucks seem to arrive with materials in a haphazard fashion. Somehow, all these random activities produce a renovated building that looks exactly like the architect's plans.

In reality, all of those activities are not random, they are planned. All the different trades are coordinated, and the delivery of materials to the site is strictly controlled. Many hundreds of hours have gone into careful planning to enable the contractor to renovate the building on time and within the budget. Any construction company that does not do project planning won't be in business very long.

Any renovations that are required for your B & B will be considerably smaller in scope than a major office building, but the problems and confusion that can arise are just as real. If you invest a little effort in doing basic "project planning," you will eliminate potential problems that could cost you both time and money.

b. ORGANIZING YOUR PLAN

1. Gather your paperwork

Now is the time to gather together all copies of Worksheets H and K you have diligently completed throughout this book. Separate them into two piles and, using the space labeled "Sheet #" at the top of each, label the worksheets numerically. These worksheets detail the labor and materials needed for your renovations and the equipment and supplies that you need to purchase before opening for business.

2. Determine the extent of renovations

Looking at your copies of Worksheet H, consider whether the renovations you plan are simple or complex.

Simple renovations involve tasks such as painting and minor refurbishing of one to three rooms. If you have only a few copies of Worksheet H, you should have no problems coordinating the tasks on those worksheets. You could tape the worksheets to a convenient wall and, as each task is completed, check it off or mark it with a highlighter pen.

Your completed copies of Worksheet K, which involve purchasing only, you could treat in the same way.

Complex renovations involve tasks like plastering, carpentry, electrical work, or major refurbishing of four or more rooms. Your copies of Worksheet H that describe complex renovations will contain many tasks, and these tasks will require very careful planning.

If you are going to have a general contractor do all the work, then let him or her do the project planning. If you are doing most of the work yourself, you will need to create your own project plan. To put each of the dozens of tasks that are listed on all of your worksheets in proper sequence, you will find it helpful to transfer each task onto a task form (see Sample #32).

SAMPLE #32
TASK FORMS

WORKSHEET _H_
SHEET # _1_ TASK # _1A_
TITLE _Bedroom - twin beds_
TASK _Remove furniture_
and room contents
_____
_____
TOTAL HRS. EST. _____1_____ HRS.
ACTUAL HRS. _____ HRS.
TOTAL COSTS EST. $ _0_
ACTUAL COSTS $_____

WORKSHEET _H_
SHEET # _1_ TASK # _1B_
TITLE _Bedroom - twin beds_
TASK _Repair and repaint_
ceiling, walls, and
woodwork
_____
TOTAL HRS. EST. _____10_____ HRS.
ACTUAL HRS. _____ HRS.
TOTAL COSTS EST. $ _72_
ACTUAL COSTS $_____

WORKSHEET _H_
SHEET # _1_ TASK # _3_
TITLE _Bedroom - twin beds_
TASK _Replace outlets,_
plates, and fixture
_____
_____
TOTAL HRS. EST. _3.5_ HRS.
ACTUAL HRS. _____ HRS.
TOTAL COSTS EST. $ _75_
ACTUAL COSTS $_____

WORKSHEET _H_
SHEET # _1_ TASK # _2_
TITLE _Bedroom - twin beds_
TASK _Purchase + install rug_
_____
_____
_____
TOTAL HRS. EST. _7.5_ HRS.
ACTUAL HRS. _____ HRS.
TOTAL COSTS EST. $ _600_
ACTUAL COSTS $_____

WORKSHEET _H_
SHEET # _1_ TASK # _4_
TITLE _Bedroom - twin beds_
TASK _Replace bookcase,_
bedside table, and
table lamp
_____
TOTAL HRS. EST. _3_ HRS.
ACTUAL HRS. _____ HRS.
TOTAL COSTS EST. $ _170_
ACTUAL COSTS $_____

WORKSHEET _K_
SHEET # _1_ TASK #_____
TITLE _Interior housekeeping_
TASK _Purchase equipment_
and supplies
_____
_____
TOTAL HRS. EST. _8_ HRS.
ACTUAL HRS. _____ HRS.
TOTAL COSTS EST. $ _945_
ACTUAL COSTS $_____

3. Complete task forms

Sample #32 shows task forms made out by Carol and Bob Morris for their B & B. The tasks listed are drawn from their completed copies of Worksheets H and K. They have identified each task by the worksheet letter, the sheet number, and, in the case of renovations, the task number. This helps keep everything organized.

Each task form then describes the task and estimates the labor and cost needed to complete it. Actual hours will be filled in after the task is complete. You'll see in Sample #32 that although there will be one hour spent on the first task, they do not charge any labor because they plan to do the task themselves. (When owners of a business do the work, no labor can be charged as a business expense.)

Blank task forms are provided in Appendix 3 (Worksheet N). Make as many photocopies as you will require to document all the tasks contained on all your copies of Worksheets H and K.

Note that in most cases, you can amalgamate all the jobs listed on a copy of Worksheet K into one task that covers all the hours and costs required for all the purchases listed. In Sample #32, Carol and Bob have made out one task form to cover all the estimated costs and hours associated with purchasing the equipment and supplies for interior housekeeping. They will continue to make out a task form for each remaining completed Worksheet K.

As a final step, the hosts took two blank task forms and labeled one as "Project Start," and the other as "Project End."

4. Designing your start-up plan

Once all your task forms are completed, find or buy a roll of paper that you can tape each form to. You'll want to make room for this organizational activity — somewhere in your house where you can lay out all your forms and leave them there undisturbed. A large table that is not used regularly is ideal.

Cut out each individual task form and place all your task forms face up on the paper and position the "Project Start" form at the extreme left-hand edge of the paper. Slowly and thoughtfully create your project plan by placing each task in the order that you want them to occur. Keep in mind the following helpful points:

(a) Prior to room renovations or decorations, remove as many of the contents as possible. Any extra time required will be made up by a speedier job. Also the possibility of furniture damage is less.

(b) Get all the dirty jobs in all the rooms done first to avoid tracking dirt into freshly cleaned areas.

(c) When you are planning outside tasks, have some inside tasks standing by in case of inclement weather.

(d) Schedule your purchasing tasks as filler jobs, or assign them to another member of your project team. Carol and Bob did their purchasing whenever they were momentarily held up, for example when they were waiting for the contractor to install the carpets.

(e) If you have more than one source of labor, such as relatives, friends, or outside contractors, you can shorten your project time by scheduling several tasks to be done at the same time.

(f) Don't hesitate to rearrange your tasks as many times as you want during this planning stage. Some extra time spent in anticipating problems will be amply rewarded in a smoother-running start-up plan.

When you are satisfied that all your tasks are positioned in the most logical and efficient way, put your "Project End" form as the last task in your project. Fasten all your task forms to the paper backing with adhesive tape. Draw lines to join the tasks together, similar to the project plan shown in Sample #33.

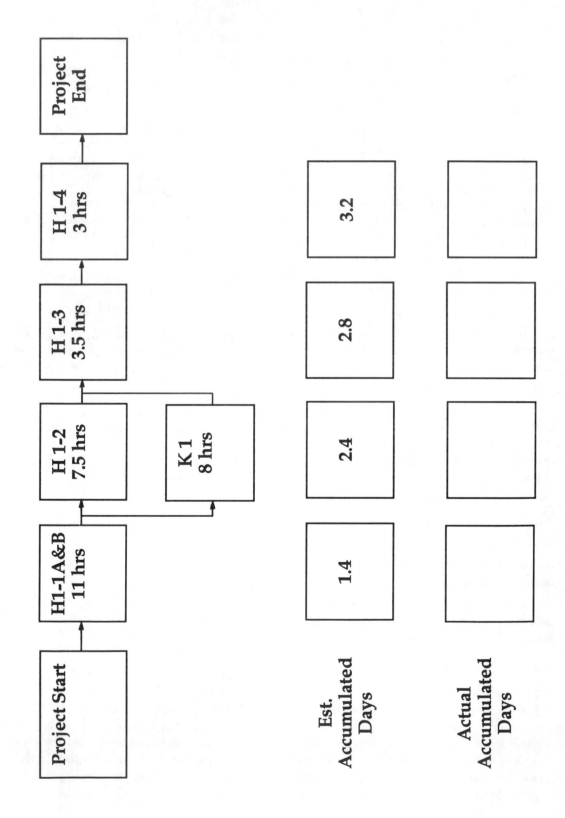

Along the bottom of your paper backing, place time lines that show the estimated accumulated days needed to reach various points in your project. Below these estimated figures leave room to insert the actual accumulated days used to evaluate your day-to-day progress. If you fall behind the estimated targets, you could choose to work some overtime to put yourselves back "on track."

Sample #33 shows a very short project plan created from the task forms shown in Sample #32. In reality, the entire start-up plan would contain many more tasks.

c. IMPLEMENT YOUR START-UP PROJECT PLAN

1. Review your financial planning

Before you make any purchases, it is always prudent to check your wallet or purse to see if you have enough money. This approach should be taken before you begin your start-up project. Take the time to review the financial planning that you did in the preceding chapter. Also, it is worthwhile to total the dollars needed for all your tasks and compare that figure with your start-up subtotal on Cost Sheet #5. The figures should agree, and if they don't, then find out why.

When you are certain that the required funds are in place, you can confidently proceed to the next step.

2. Review your start-up project plan

Do one last review of your project plan. Take a fresh look at the overall logical flow of tasks from the beginning of the project to the end. Don't hesitate to shuffle the tasks again if you see a better way to complete the project. If you are satisfied with the plan, then consider it final.

3. Start

Tape your project plan to a convenient wall where you can refer to it often. Begin your project by starting the first task on your plan.

Keep a running total of your actual accumulated days and compare them to the estimated, accumulated days. Adjust your working schedule to keep yourself on track. If you continue to work toward these targets, you will complete your project on time.

It is also wise to keep a record of the actual dollars spent on each task. In this way you will be instantly alerted to any potential cash problems well before they materialize. Remember that as long as you are within your 10% contingency on any task overrun, you should arrive at the end of the total project within your estimated budget.

As you complete each task, check it off or use a highlighter pen to identify that the task is done. Enter the actual hours and actual dollars used. If the project stalls because of labor or material problems, substitute other tasks that can go ahead until the problem is resolved. The secret is to be flexible in the execution of your project plan. By consulting your plan you will be able to more easily identify those tasks that could be substituted.

EPIFANIA'S APRICOT LOAF

½ cup dried apricots

1 large orange

½ cup raisins, chopped

½ cup chopped walnuts

2 cups flour

2 teaspoons baking powder

½ teaspoon baking soda

1 cup white sugar

¼ teaspoon salt

1 beaten egg

2 tablespoons melted shortening

1 teaspoon vanilla

Preheat oven to 350°F.

Chop apricots and cover with boiling water. Let stand ½ hour, then drain. Reserve liquid.

Grate the rind of orange into a large bowl. Add raisins, nuts, and drained apricots.

Sift flour, baking powder, baking soda, sugar, and salt over top of fruit and fold together.

Squeeze orange; add reserved liquid drained from apricots, plus water if needed to make up 1 cup of liquid. Add to flour mixture and blend.

Add egg, shortening, and vanilla and blend well.

Pour into greased 9½ x 4½ loaf pan and bake for about 1 hour.

Slice and serve either warm or cold.

16

SETTING AND MAINTAINING YOUR LEVEL OF SERVICE

A major hotel chain in the United States recently conducted a survey of the traveling public to find out what features they disliked about their hotel accommodations. The results of the survey are very interesting because they point out the weaknesses of your competition and highlight the areas that should receive your extra care and attention.

The survey listed the results in their order of importance, starting with the most common complaint:

(a) Rooms that smell stale

(b) Inefficient and unfriendly front-desk personnel

(c) Late or missed wake-up calls

(d) Showers with low water pressure

(e) Inefficient or unfriendly service personnel

(f) Not being able to get an outside phone line

(g) Room keys that don't work

(h) Cheap and uncomfortable pillows

(i) Too long to check out

(j) Thin, poor-quality bath towels

(k) Inflexible check-out times

(l) Too long to check in

We have discussed all of these points in the preceding chapters of this book, and we have made numerous suggestions on how you can provide a high level of service for each of the items mentioned above. When you open for business, make sure that your B & B establishment does not reflect any of the above problems.

a. SETTING YOUR LEVEL OF SERVICE

You should start out the way you intend to go on. In other words, offer only the basic services initially. Keep in mind that most of the routines will be new to you, and therefore it will take time to become efficient at these basic routines.

Decide on the level of service that you can comfortably handle. Don't offer a huge selection of services to your guests only to discover you can't cope.

After your first year in operation, you will become more at ease with your guests, and you will find that the basic routines are more easily handled. You can then decide if you want to increase the services offered to your customers.

Don't be in a hurry to add a large number of new services to your establishment. Add them one at a time and evaluate the success of each. The cardinal rule is: Always increase your services, never decrease them. Your repeat customers will welcome any increase in services, but they will resent any decrease. If you must withdraw any service, you should substitute another one in its place.

When you are establishing your standards, don't burn yourself out trying to be all things to all people. No matter how many services you offer to your customers, you will find some people want something else. Tell your guests exactly what range of services you offer and let them decide if they wish to stay at your establishment. Don't compromise your standards or your house rules.

b. MAINTAINING YOUR LEVEL OF SERVICE

Make sure your facilities provide the atmosphere expected by your targeted customers. Cleanliness is of the utmost importance, as reflected in the hotel survey above.

Hospitality and efficiency are the key ingredients for quality service. Again, the survey discussed above shows that many travelers are dissatisfied with hospitality in hotels.

Review the sections in this book if you have any lingering questions about applying quality service and offering good facilities to your targeted customers.

The ability to establish good customer relations is one of the most important duties of a B & B host. You must be able to communicate effectively with your customers and you must be a good listener.

You also must be sensitive to the different standards and expectations of different people. Don't impose your own moral standards onto your guests. Don't be judge and jury to every customer that crosses your threshold. However, if a customer breaks one of your house rules, ask him or her to comply. Remember to establish your house rules before you open for business and make sure your customers are informed about them.

Always keep the relationship between you and your guests as strictly business. Don't ever let yourself get emotionally involved with a paying guest. Be sympathetic and supportive by all means, but keep the relationship at arms length. There is a world of difference between "being friendly," and "being intimate." Make sure that your behavior can never be misinterpreted.

c. IN CONCLUSION

Running a bed and breakfast can be a very rewarding experience, especially when you develop a loyal following of repeat customers. Your first year in business will be the most difficult because you will be dealing with brand new people for every booking. As you build up a clientele, you will come to recognize repeat customers as friends and it is always more relaxing to provide hospitality to friends.

As you gain more experience in dealing with your customers, you will find yourself looking for more ways to increase your services. Tasks that once seemed difficult will become easier to manage, and any fears or apprehensions that you might have had will disappear.

We are constantly amazed at the variety of interesting customers that frequent our B & B. Every person is different and everyone has a story to tell. Our clientele have taught us a great deal about the world we live in, and we have gained a better appreciation of their many wonderful and diverse cultures. Our guests have become our friends and have reinforced our belief that the vast majority of humans are decent and caring people.

We hope that you will decide to operate your own B & B so that you can share in this wonderful experience. If you decide to go ahead, we know that you will soon discover:

"THERE ARE NO STRANGERS, ONLY FRIENDS YOU HAVE NOT MET."

Good luck in your new bed and breakfast business!

APPENDIX 1
HELPFUL PUBLICATIONS

The publications listed under the following addresses list B & B homes, reservations services, or both. Write for a copy of the publications or for more information.

a. CANADA

ALBERTA

Alberta Tourism, Government of Alberta, Box 2500, Edmonton, Alberta
T5J 2Z4
1-800-661-8888
Accommodation Guide

BRITISH COLUMBIA

Ministry of Tourism
Parliament Buildings
Victoria, B.C.
V8V 1X4
1-800-663-6000
Accommodations

MANITOBA

Travel Manitoba
7-1455 Waverley Street
Winnipeg, Manitoba
R3T 0P7
1-800-665-0040
Accommodation and Travel Services

NEW BRUNSWICK

Tourism, Recreation and Heritage
Box 12345
Fredericton, New Brunswick
E3B 5C3
1-800-561-0123
New Brunswick Bed and Breakfast Association Guide

NEWFOUNDLAND

Department of Development, Tourism Branch
P.O. Box 8730
St. John's, Newfoundland
A1B 4K2
1-800-563-6353
Newfoundland & Labrador Travel Guide

NORTHWEST TERRITORIES

Travel Arctic
Department of Economic Development and Tourism
Government of Northwest Territories
Yellowknife, N.W.T.
X1A 2L9
1-800 661-0788
Explorers' Guide

NOVA SCOTIA

Department of Tourism and Culture
P.O. Box 130
Halifax, Nova Scotia
B3J 2M7
1-800-565-0000
Complete Guide to the Festival Province of Canada

ONTARIO

Ministry of Tourism and Recreation
Queen's Park
Toronto, Ontario
M7A 2E5
1-800-668-2746
Bed and Breakfast Associations

PRINCE EDWARD ISLAND

Visitor Services
P.O. Box 940
Charlottetown, P.E.I.
C1A 7M5
1-800-565-0267
Bed and Breakfast, Country Inns

QUEBEC

Tourism Quebec
P.O. Box 20000
Quebec City, Quebec
G1K 7X2
1-800-363-7777
Gites du Passant

SASKATCHEWAN

Tourism Saskatchewan
1919 Saskatchewan Drive
Regina, Saskatchewan
S4P 3V7
1-800-667-7191
Country Vacations and Bed & Breakfast

b. UNITED STATES

ALABAMA

State of Alabama Bureau of Tourism and
Travel
532 South Perry Street
Montgomery, AL 36104
1-800-ALABAMA
Official Alabama Lodging Guide

ALASKA

Alaska Tourism Marketing Council
P.O. Box E-501
Juneau, AK 99811
907-465-2010
Alaska Official State Vacation Planner

ARIZONA

Arizona Office of Tourism
1100 West Washington
Phoenix, AZ 85007
602-542-TOUR
Arizona Accommodations Directory lists
B & B homes. It also gives the addresses
and phone numbers of regional Chambers
of Commerce to obtain specific B & B listings in each of their areas.

ARKANSAS

Arkansas Department of Parks
and Tourism
1 Capital Mall
Little Rock, AR 72201
501-682-7777
Arkansas Bed and Breakfast

CALIFORNIA

California Office of Tourism
1121 L Street
Sacramento, CA 95814
916-322-1396
Discover the Californias

COLORADO

Colorado Tourism Board
P.O. Box 38700
Denver, CO 80238
Official State Vacation Guide lists B & B res-
ervation services and *Colorado Planning
Supplement* lists B & B homes.

CONNECTICUT

Connecticut Department of Economic
Development
865 Brook Street
Rocky Hill, CT 06067
1-800-CT BOUND
Classic Connecticut

DELAWARE

Delaware Development Office
99 Kings Highway
P.O. Box 1401
Dover, DE 19903
302-739-4271
Delaware, The Quiet Resorts lists one B & B
home and *Rehoboth Beach, Dewey Beach,
Map & Visitors Guide*

DISTRICT OF COLUMBIA

Washington Convention and Visitors
Association
1212 New York Avenue, Suite 600
Washington DC 20005
202-789-7000
Washington DC Accommodations

FLORIDA

Department of Commerce, Visitor Inquiry
126 Van Buren Street
Talahassee, FL 32399-2000
904-487-1462
See Florida provides the addresses and telephone numbers of regional Chambers of Commerce to obtain specific B & B listings in each of their areas. *Bed & Breakfast Listing* is a photocopied seven-page listing of B & B homes.

GEORGIA

Georgia Department of Industry and Trade
P.O. Box 1776
Atlanta, GA 30301
404-656-3590
Georgia on my Mind

HAWAII

Hawaii Visitors Bureau
2270 Kalakaua Avenue
Honolulu, HI 96815
1-808-923-1811
Accommodation and Car Rental Guide lists an All Islands B & B reservation service: 1-800-542-0344

IDAHO

Idaho Travel Council
Department of Commerce
700 West State Street
Boise, ID 83720
1-800-635-7820
Official Idaho State Travel Guide

ILLINOIS

Illinois Department of Commerce and Community Affairs
Tourist Information Center
310 South Michigan Avenue
Suite 108
Chicago, IL 60604
312-793-2094
A Guide to Illinois Bed & Breakfasts & Country Inns

INDIANA

Indiana Department of Commerce
One North Capitol, Suite 700
Indianapolis, IN 46204-2288
317-232-8860
Indiana Lodging Guide

IOWA

Iowa Department of Economic Development
200 East Grand Avenue
Des Moines, IA 50309
515-281-3251
Bed and Breakfast, Keys to Iowa's Hidden Treasures

KANSAS

Department of Commerce
400 West 8th Street, 5th Floor
Topeka KS 66603
913-296-5055
Kansas Directory Bed & Breakfast Homes & Small Inns

Kansas Bed & Breakfast Association
Rt. 1, Box 93, WaKeeney, KS 67672
Welcome to Kansas Bed & Breakfasts

KENTUCKY

Kentucky Department of Travel Development
Capital Plaza Tower
Frankfort, KY 40601
1-800-225-TRIP
Kentucky Traveller's Guide and *Bed and Breakfast Inns, Homes, and Little out-of-the-way Places*

LOUISIANA

Louisiana Office of Tourism
P.O. Box 94291
Baton Rouge, LA 70804
1-800-231-4730
Antebellum Homes, Bed and Breakfast, Historic Houses

MAINE

Maine Tourism Information Services
97 Winthrop Street
P.O.Box 2300
Hallowell, ME 04347
207-289-2423
Exploring Maine

MARYLAND

Office of Tourism Development
217 East Redwood Street
Baltimore, MD 21202
1-800-543-1036
Maryland Travel and Outdoor Guide

MASSACHUSETTS

Massachusetts Division of Tourism
Department of Commerce
100 Cambridge Street, 13th Floor
Boston, MA 02202
1-800-343-9072
The Spirit of Massachusetts Guidebook lists B
& B homes and reservation services.

MICHIGAN

The West Michigan Tourist Association
136 Fulton East
Grand Rapids, MI 49503
616-456-8557
*West Michigan Bed and Breakfast & Country
Inns* and *Michigan Bed and Breakfast*

MINNESOTA

Minnesota Office of Tourism
375 Jackson Street
250 Skyway Level
St. Paul, MN 55101
1-800-657-3700
Minnesota Bed and Breakfast and Historic Inns

MISSISSIPPI

Mississippi Department of Economic &
Community Development
1200 Walter Sillers Building
Box 849
Jackson, MS 39205
601-359-3297
Mississippi Bed and Breakfast Guide

MISSOURI

Missouri Division of Tourism
Truman State Office Building
P.O. Box 1055
Jefferson City, MO 65102
Missouri Accommodations Directory

MONTANA

Travel Montana
Department of Commerce
Helena, MT 59620
1-800-548-3390
Montana Travel Planner

NEBRASKA

Nebraska Department of Economic
Development
Division of Travel and Tourism
301 Centennial Mall S.
Box 94666
Lincoln, NE 68509
1-800-228-4307
Nebraska Lodging Directory

NEVADA

Nevada Commission on Tourism
Capital Complex
Carson City, NV 89710
702-687-4322
Nevada Visitors Guide

NEW HAMPSHIRE

Office of Vacation Travel
Box 856
Concord, NH 03301-0856
603-271-2666
New Hampshire Guidebook

NEW JERSEY

Division of Travel and Tourism
CN 826
Trenton, NJ 08625
1-800-JERSEY 7
Discover New Jersey.

NEW MEXICO

Economic Development and Tourism
Department
Joseph Montoya Building
P.O. Box 20003
1100 St. Francis Drive
Santa Fe, NM 87503
1-800-545-2040
New Mexico Vacation Guide

NEW YORK

Department of Economic Development
1 Commerce Plaza
Albany, NY 12245
1-800 CALL-NYS (in U.S.A.); 518-474-4116
(in Canada)
Travel Guide with Map of New York State.

NORTH CAROLINA

Division of Travel and Tourism
430 N. Salsbury Street
Raleigh, NC 27611
1-800-VISIT NC
North Carolina Accommodations Directory

NORTH DAKOTA

North Dakota Tourism Promotion
Capitol Grounds
Bismark, ND 58505
1-800-437-2077 (in U.S.A.); 1-800-537-8879
(in Canada)
Discover The Spirit, North Dakota and *North
Dakota B & B Operators*

OHIO

Division of Travel and Tourism
P.O. Box 1001
Columbus, OH 43266-0101
1-800-BUCKEYE
Ohio Pass — State of Ohio Travel Planner and
Bed and Breakfast Homes and Inns

OKLAHOMA

Tourism and Recreation Department
500 Will Rogers Building
Oklahoma City, OK 73105
1-800-652-6552
Oklahoma Bed and Breakfast Inns

OREGON

Oregon Economic Development
Department
775 Summer Street N.E.
Salem, OR 97310
1-800-547-7842
Where to Stay in Oregon

PENNSYLVANIA

Department of Commerce
P.O. Box 61
Warrendale, PA 15086
1-800-VISIT PA
Write for the following three brochures:

Experience Gettysburg Pa
Gettysburg Travel Council
Dept. 10K
25 Carlisle Street
Gettysburg, PA 17325
717-334-6274

Pennsylvania Dutch Country Visitors Guide
Pennsylvania Dutch Convention &
Visitors Bureau
501 Greenfield Road
Lancaster, PA 17601
717-299-8901

Cumberland Valley PA Visitors' Guide
Cumberland Valley Visitors' Council
1235 Lincoln Way E.
Chambersburg, PA 17201
717-261-1200

RHODE ISLAND

Department of Economic Development
7 Jackson Walkway
Providence, RI 02903
1-800-556-2484
Visitor's Guide, Rhode Island

SOUTH CAROLINA

Division of Tourism
P.O. Box 71
Columbia, SC 29202-0071
803-734-0235
*South Carolina's Historic Inns, Country Inns,
and Bed and Breakfast*

SOUTH DAKOTA

South Dakota Department of Tourism
711 Wells Avenue
Pierre, SD 57501-3335
1-800-843-1930
South Dakota Vacation Guide

TENNESSEE

Tennessee Tourist Development
P.O. Box 23170 Nashville, TN 37202
615-741-2158
Tennessee Bed and Breakfast Homes & Country Inns

TEXAS

Bed and Breakfast Texas Style Inc. is a reservation service that publishes a descriptive directory for $3. Send a self-addressed stamped legal size envelope to:

4224 W. Red Bird Lane
Dallas, TX 75237

UTAH

Utah Travel Council
Council Hall, Capital Hill
Salt Lake City, UT 84114
801-533-5681
Utah's Bed and Breakfast Establishments

VERMONT

Department of Travel and Tourism
Chamber of Commerce
Box 37,
Montpelier, VT 05601
802-223-3443
Vermont Country Inns

VIRGINIA

Division of Tourism
1021 E. Cary Street
Richmond, VA 23219
804-786-4484
A Guide to Virginia's Bed and Breakfasts

WASHINGTON

Trade & Economic Development
General Administration Building
Olympia, WA 98504
1-800-541-9274
Destination Washington

WEST VIRGINIA

Department of Commerce, Labor &
Environmental Resources
State Capitol
Charleston, WV 25305
1-800-CALL WVA
West Virginia Bed and Breakfast Inns

WISCONSIN

Division of Tourism Development
123 W. Washington Avenue
P.O. Box 7606
Madison, WI 53707
1-800-432-TRIP
Where to Stay in Wisconsin

WYOMING

Wyoming Travel Commission
1-25 at College Drive
Cheyenne, WY 82002
307-777-7777
Wyoming Vacation Guide

APPENDIX 2
BED AND BREAKFAST GUIDE BOOKS

a. NORTH AMERICA

Featherston, Phyllis and Barbara Ostler. *The Official Bed And Breakfast Guide: (U.S.A., Canada, Bermuda, Puerto Rico, Virgin Islands)*. Norwalk, Connecticut: National Bed & Breakfast Association, 1989. 1,517 listings, 102 reservation services, 483 pages.

Knight, Diane. *Bed and Breakfast Homes Directory: (California, Oregon, Washington, British Columbia)*. Vancouver: Whitecap Books, 1990. Over 250 listings, 319 pages.

Lanier, Pamela. *Complete Guide to Bed & Breakfasts, Inns, Guesthouses*. Santa Fe, New Mexico: John Muir Publications, 1991. 4,800 listings, 499 pages.

Rundback, Betty and Nancy Kramer. *Bed And Breakfast U.S.A.: (All 50 States Plus Canada)* Toronto: Fitzhenry and Whiteside Ltd, 1987. 650 pages.

Thaxton, John. *The Great American Guest House Book: (Bed & Breakfast U.S.A. and Canada)*. New York: Burt Franklin & Co. Inc., 1984. 294 listings, 70 reservation services, 325 pages.

b. CANADA

Higgins, Janette. *The Best Places to B & B in Ontario: (An Independent Guide to Bed and Breakfast)*. Toronto: Juno Press, 1990. 189 pages.

Nova Scotia Bed and Breakfast. Margaree Valley, Nova Scotia: Normaway Books, 1990. 200 pages of B & Bs, inns, restaurants, museums, etc.

Pantel, Gerda. *The Canadian Bed & Breakfast Guide*. Markham, Ontario: Fitzhenry and Whiteside, 1990. 378 pages.

Wilson, Patricia. *The Ontario Bed and Breakfast Book: (with a Quebec supplement)*. Staffa, Ontario: William Street Press, 1990. Over 450 listings, 187 pages.

c. U.S.A.

Chesler, Bernice. *Bed And Breakfast In The Northeast: (From Maine to Washington D.C.)*. Chester, Connecticut: The Globe Pequot Press, 1983. 300 listings, 509 pages.

Rose, Corinne Madden. *The New England Guest House Book*. Charlotte, North Carolina: The Eastwoods Press Books, 1979. 156 listings, 192 pages.

Worth, Courtia and Terry Berger. *The West Coast Bed and Breakfast Guide: (California, Oregon, Washington)*. New York: Simon and Schuster, 1984. 86 listings, 20 reservation services, 128 pages.

Zahn, Laura. *Room At The Inn — Wisconsin: (Guide to Wisconsin's Historic B & Bs & Country Inns)*. St. Paul, Minnesota: Down to Earth Publications, 1987. 87 listings, 224 pages.

APPENDIX 3
WORKSHEETS

The following worksheets have been provided for your convenience as you work through this book. Each worksheet corresponds to a particular sample in the text. Read the book and follow the text and the samples to help guide you through completing your own worksheets.

In many cases, more than one copy of a worksheet is provided. If you need more copies than appear here, photocopy as many as you need. The forms have been perforated for easy removal.

The Cost Sheets referred to in the book can be found in Appendix 4 on page 201.

WORKSHEET A
SKILL ASSESSMENT

SKILL GROUP	SKILL STATEMENTS	No	Yes	TEAM
FRIENDLINESS	You prefer to be around people.	❑	❑	
	You enjoy talking to strangers.	❑	❑	
	You usually speak first.	❑	❑	
	You are always ready to smile.	❑	❑	
TOLERANCE	You tolerate all age groups.	❑	❑	
	You tolerate religions & races.	❑	❑	
	You are open minded and flexible.	❑	❑	
	You help people in distress.	❑	❑	
CLEANLINESS	You are a tidy person.	❑	❑	
	You don't mind housework.	❑	❑	
	You have good personal hygiene.	❑	❑	
	You are always well groomed.	❑	❑	
DIPLOMACY	You seldom lose your temper.	❑	❑	
	You can accept criticism.	❑	❑	
	You are a peacemaker.	❑	❑	
	You can be firm if necessary.	❑	❑	
HOSPITALITY	You like to entertain guests.	❑	❑	
	You anticipate their needs.	❑	❑	
	You seldom moan and groan.	❑	❑	
	You are a good cook.	❑	❑	
ORGANIZATION	You like to be organized	❑	❑	
	You like to make lists.	❑	❑	
	You like record keeping.	❑	❑	
	You like to work with figures.	❑	❑	
PREPARATION	You plan for emergencies.	❑	❑	
	You know First Aid and C.P.R.	❑	❑	
	You can put out a grease fire.	❑	❑	
	You act calmly in an emergency.	❑	❑	
COMMUNICATION	You think before you speak.	❑	❑	
	You speak clearly.	❑	❑	
	You are a good listener.	❑	❑	
	You enjoy letter writing.	❑	❑	
INFORMATION	You are interested in history.	❑	❑	
	You know your area businesses.	❑	❑	
	You are aware of local events.	❑	❑	
	You know public transportation.	❑	❑	
MOTIVATION	You are a self starter.	❑	❑	
	You set goals & deadlines.	❑	❑	
	You always meet those goals.	❑	❑	
	You want to operate a B & B.	❑	❑	
WORK ETHIC	You don't mind hard work.	❑	❑	
	You don't mind extra duties.	❑	❑	
	You are in good health.	❑	❑	
	You maintain high standards.	❑	❑	

WORKSHEET A
SKILL ASSESSMENT

SKILL GROUP	SKILL STATEMENTS	No	Yes	TEAM
FRIENDLINESS	You prefer to be around people.	❏	❏	
	You enjoy talking to strangers.	❏	❏	
	You usually speak first.	❏	❏	
	You are always ready to smile.	❏	❏	
TOLERANCE	You tolerate all age groups.	❏	❏	
	You tolerate religions & races.	❏	❏	
	You are open minded and flexible.	❏	❏	
	You help people in distress.	❏	❏	
CLEANLINESS	You are a tidy person.	❏	❏	
	You don't mind housework.	❏	❏	
	You have good personal hygiene.	❏	❏	
	You are always well groomed.	❏	❏	
DIPLOMACY	You seldom lose your temper.	❏	❏	
	You can accept criticism.	❏	❏	
	You are a peacemaker.	❏	❏	
	You can be firm if necessary.	❏	❏	
HOSPITALITY	You like to entertain guests.	❏	❏	
	You anticipate their needs.	❏	❏	
	You seldom moan and groan.	❏	❏	
	You are a good cook.	❏	❏	
ORGANIZATION	You like to be organized	❏	❏	
	You like to make lists.	❏	❏	
	You like record keeping.	❏	❏	
	You like to work with figures.	❏	❏	
PREPARATION	You plan for emergencies.	❏	❏	
	You know First Aid and C.P.R.	❏	❏	
	You can put out a grease fire.	❏	❏	
	You act calmly in an emergency.	❏	❏	
COMMUNICATION	You think before you speak.	❏	❏	
	You speak clearly.	❏	❏	
	You are a good listener.	❏	❏	
	You enjoy letter writing.	❏	❏	
INFORMATION	You are interested in history.	❏	❏	
	You know your area businesses.	❏	❏	
	You are aware of local events.	❏	❏	
	You know public transportation.	❏	❏	
MOTIVATION	You are a self starter.	❏	❏	
	You set goals & deadlines.	❏	❏	
	You always meet those goals.	❏	❏	
	You want to operate a B & B.	❏	❏	
WORK ETHIC	You don't mind hard work.	❏	❏	
	You don't mind extra duties.	❏	❏	
	You are in good health.	❏	❏	
	You maintain high standards.	❏	❏	

WORKSHEET A
SKILL ASSESSMENT

SKILL GROUP	SKILL STATEMENTS	No	Yes	TEAM
FRIENDLINESS	You prefer to be around people.	❏	❏	
	You enjoy talking to strangers.	❏	❏	
	You usually speak first.	❏	❏	
	You are always ready to smile.	❏	❏	
TOLERANCE	You tolerate all age groups.	❏	❏	
	You tolerate religions & races.	❏	❏	
	You are open minded and flexible.	❏	❏	
	You help people in distress.	❏	❏	
CLEANLINESS	You are a tidy person.	❏	❏	
	You don't mind housework.	❏	❏	
	You have good personal hygiene.	❏	❏	
	You are always well groomed.	❏	❏	
DIPLOMACY	You seldom lose your temper.	❏	❏	
	You can accept criticism.	❏	❏	
	You are a peacemaker.	❏	❏	
	You can be firm if necessary.	❏	❏	
HOSPITALITY	You like to entertain guests.	❏	❏	
	You anticipate their needs.	❏	❏	
	You seldom moan and groan.	❏	❏	
	You are a good cook.	❏	❏	
ORGANIZATION	You like to be organized	❏	❏	
	You like to make lists.	❏	❏	
	You like record keeping.	❏	❏	
	You like to work with figures.	❏	❏	
PREPARATION	You plan for emergencies.	❏	❏	
	You know First Aid and C.P.R.	❏	❏	
	You can put out a grease fire.	❏	❏	
	You act calmly in an emergency.	❏	❏	
COMMUNICATION	You think before you speak.	❏	❏	
	You speak clearly.	❏	❏	
	You are a good listener.	❏	❏	
	You enjoy letter writing.	❏	❏	
INFORMATION	You are interested in history.	❏	❏	
	You know your area businesses.	❏	❏	
	You are aware of local events.	❏	❏	
	You know public transportation.	❏	❏	
MOTIVATION	You are a self starter.	❏	❏	
	You set goals & deadlines.	❏	❏	
	You always meet those goals.	❏	❏	
	You want to operate a B & B.	❏	❏	
WORK ETHIC	You don't mind hard work.	❏	❏	
	You don't mind extra duties.	❏	❏	
	You are in good health.	❏	❏	
	You maintain high standards.	❏	❏	

WORKSHEET B
SKILLS ACTION PLAN

STATEMENTS NEEDING IMPROVEMENT	ACTION PLAN FOR IMPROVEMENT
1. _____	_____
_____	_____
2. _____	_____
_____	_____
3. _____	_____
_____	_____
4. _____	_____
_____	_____
5. _____	_____
_____	_____
6. _____	_____
_____	_____
7. _____	_____
_____	_____
8. _____	_____
_____	_____
9. _____	_____
_____	_____
10. _____	_____
_____	_____
11. _____	_____
_____	_____
12. _____	_____
_____	_____

WORKSHEET B
SKILLS ACTION PLAN

STATEMENTS NEEDING IMPROVEMENT	ACTION PLAN FOR IMPROVEMENT
1.	
2.	
3.	
4.	
5.	
6.	
7.	
8.	
9.	
10.	
11.	
12.	

WORKSHEET C
TOURIST ATTRACTION SURVEY

LOCAL ATTRACTION NAME DISTANCE & GATE TOTAL	TARGET CUSTOMERS		
	LENGTH OF STAY	AGE RANGES	INTERESTS
1._____ _____ Distance_____ Gate Total_____	Few Hours ❑ Day Tour ❑ Overnight ❑ Long Stay ❑	Children ❑ Teenagers ❑ Adults ❑ Elderly ❑	Sporting ❑ Artistic ❑ Cultural ❑ General ❑
2._____ _____ Distance_____ Gate Total_____	Few Hours ❑ Day Tour ❑ Overnight ❑ Long Stay ❑	Children ❑ Teenagers ❑ Adults ❑ Elderly ❑	Sporting ❑ Artistic ❑ Cultural ❑ General ❑
3._____ _____ Distance_____ Gate Total_____	Few Hours ❑ Day Tour ❑ Overnight ❑ Long Stay ❑	Children ❑ Teenagers ❑ Adults ❑ Elderly ❑	Sporting ❑ Artistic ❑ Cultural ❑ General ❑
4._____ _____ Distance_____ Gate Total_____	Few Hours ❑ Day Tour ❑ Overnight ❑ Long Stay ❑	Children ❑ Teenagers ❑ Adults ❑ Elderly ❑	Sporting ❑ Artistic ❑ Cultural ❑ General ❑
5._____ _____ Distance_____ Gate Total_____	Few Hours ❑ Day Tour ❑ Overnight ❑ Long Stay ❑	Children ❑ Teenagers ❑ Adults ❑ Elderly ❑	Sporting ❑ Artistic ❑ Cultural ❑ General ❑
6._____ _____ Distance_____ Gate Total_____	Few Hours ❑ Day Tour ❑ Overnight ❑ Long Stay ❑	Children ❑ Teenagers ❑ Adults ❑ Elderly ❑	Sporting ❑ Artistic ❑ Cultural ❑ General ❑

VISITOR PATTERNS TO LOCAL ATTRACTIONS
OPERATING DAYS

LOCAL ATTRACTIONS	Jan	Feb	Mar	Apr	May	Jun	Jul	Aug	Sep	Oct	Nov	Dec
1._____												
2._____												
3._____												
4._____												
5._____												
6._____												

WORKSHEET D
CUSTOMER SURVEY FORM

Potential Customer_____Age Range_____

CUSTOMER
AVAILABILITY

Month	Est. Days	Reasons for Estimate of Days
January	_____	_____
February	_____	_____
March	_____	_____
April	_____	_____
May	_____	_____
June	_____	_____
July	_____	_____
August	_____	_____
September	_____	_____
October	_____	_____
November	_____	_____
December	_____	_____

Booking Days Avail._____Actual No._____

OVERNIGHT
FACILITIES
NEEDED

REASONS

FOOD
SERVICES
NEEDED

REASONS

OTHER
FACILITIES
NEEDED

REASONS

PREFERRED ATTRACTIONS   1.   2.   3.   4.   5.   6.

WORKSHEET D
CUSTOMER SURVEY FORM

Potential Customer_____Age Range_____

CUSTOMER
AVAILABILITY

Month	Est. Days	Reasons for Estimate of Days
January	_____	_____
February	_____	_____
March	_____	_____
April	_____	_____
May	_____	_____
June	_____	_____
July	_____	_____
August	_____	_____
September	_____	_____
October	_____	_____
November	_____	_____
December	_____	_____

Booking Days Avail._____Actual No._____

OVERNIGHT
FACILITIES
NEEDED

_____ | REASONS
_____ | _____
_____ | _____
_____ | _____
_____ | _____

FOOD
SERVICES
NEEDED

_____ | REASONS
_____ | _____
_____ | _____
_____ | _____
_____ | _____

OTHER
FACILITIES
NEEDED

_____ | REASONS
_____ | _____
_____ | _____
_____ | _____
_____ | _____

PREFERRED ATTRACTIONS   1.   2.   3.   4.   5.   6.

WORKSHEET D
CUSTOMER SURVEY FORM

Potential Customer_____Age Range_____

CUSTOMER AVAILABILITY

Month	Est. Days	Reasons for Estimate of Days
January	_____	_____
February	_____	_____
March	_____	_____
April	_____	_____
May	_____	_____
June	_____	_____
July	_____	_____
August	_____	_____
September	_____	_____
October	_____	_____
November	_____	_____
December	_____	_____

Booking Days Avail._____Actual No._____

OVERNIGHT FACILITIES NEEDED

REASONS

_____ | _____

_____ | _____

_____ | _____

_____ | _____

_____ | _____

FOOD SERVICES NEEDED

REASONS

_____ | _____

_____ | _____

_____ | _____

_____ | _____

OTHER FACILITIES NEEDED

REASONS

_____ | _____

_____ | _____

_____ | _____

_____ | _____

_____ | _____

PREFERRED ATTRACTIONS   1.   2.   3.   4.   5.   6.

173

WORKSHEET D
CUSTOMER SURVEY FORM

Potential Customer_____Age Range_____

CUSTOMER
AVAILABILITY

Month	Est. Days	Reasons for Estimate of Days
January		
February		
March		
April		
May		
June		
July		
August		
September		
October		
November		
December		

Booking Days Avail._____Actual No._____

OVERNIGHT
FACILITIES
NEEDED

	REASONS

FOOD
SERVICES
NEEDED

	REASONS

OTHER
FACILITIES
NEEDED

	REASONS

PREFERRED ATTRACTIONS   1.   2.   3.   4.   5.   6.

WORKSHEET E
COMPETITOR SURVEY

ESTABLISHMENT | Name _____ B & B home ☐
Small inn ☐
Commercial ☐

HOST/MANAGER | Name_____
Address_____
Phone (___)_____ Postal/Zip code_____

STYLE | _____

FACILITIES AND SERVICES

Air conditioning	☐	Handicap access	☐
Swimming	☐	Walk to shops	☐
Sauna or gym	☐	Child play area	☐
Tennis court	☐	Patio or gardens	☐
Guest lounge	☐	Television	☐
Public transit	☐	Fax service	☐
Taxi service	☐	Babysitting	☐
Parking	☐	Pet sitting	☐
Boat mooring	☐	Laundry service	☐
Other_____		Room service	☐

BEDROOMS

Numbers	Upstairs _____	No. of stairs up _____	
	Downstairs_____	No. of stairs down _____	
	Main floor _____	Adjoining rooms _____	
Beds	King _____	Single _____	Other_____
	Queen _____	Crib _____	_____
	Double _____	Roll-out _____	_____
	Twin _____	Waterbed _____	_____

BATHROOMS

En-suite	_____	Bathtubs	_____
Private	_____	Showers	_____
Shared	_____	Other_____	

BREAKFAST

Menu	Continental ☐	Buffet ☐
	Hot food ☐	Served by host ☐
	Cold food ☐	Cook your own ☐
	Other_____	
Location	Dining room ☐	Kitchen ☐
	Guest room ☐	Lounge or lobby ☐
	Other_____	

OTHER FOODS AVAILABLE

Extra meals	☐	Hot/cold drinks	☐
Snacks	☐	Special diets	☐
Packed lunch	☐	Ethnic	☐
Fruit	☐	Other_____	

OPERATING RULES

Min. stay (days)	_____	No children	☐
Check-in time	_____	No pets	☐
Check-out time	_____	No alcohol	☐
Season from_____to_____		No smoking	☐

ROOM TARIFFS

Single occupancy	_____	Group rate	☐
Double occupancy	_____	Weekly rate	☐
Personal checks	☐	Off season	☐
		Extra person_____	

Credit cards: MC ☐ Visa ☐ AE ☐ Other_____

WORKSHEET E
COMPETITOR SURVEY

ESTABLISHMENT | Name _____ B & B home ❏
Small inn ❏
Commercial ❏

HOST/MANAGER | Name_____
Address_____
Phone (___)_____ Postal/Zip code_____

STYLE | _____

FACILITIES AND SERVICES

Air conditioning	❏	Handicap access	❏
Swimming	❏	Walk to shops	❏
Sauna or gym	❏	Child play area	❏
Tennis court	❏	Patio or gardens	❏
Guest lounge	❏	Television	❏
Public transit	❏	Fax service	❏
Taxi service	❏	Babysitting	❏
Parking	❏	Pet sitting	❏
Boat mooring	❏	Laundry service	❏
Other_____		Room service	❏

BEDROOMS

Numbers	Upstairs _____	No. of stairs up	_____	
	Downstairs_____	No. of stairs down	_____	
	Main floor_____	Adjoining rooms	_____	
Beds	King _____	Single _____	Other_____	
	Queen _____	Crib _____	_____	
	Double _____	Roll-out _____	_____	
	Twin _____	Waterbed _____	_____	

BATHROOMS

En-suite	_____	Bathtubs	_____
Private	_____	Showers	_____
Shared	_____	Other_____	

BREAKFAST

Menu	Continental	❏	Buffet	❏
	Hot food	❏	Served by host	❏
	Cold food	❏	Cook your own	❏
	Other_____			
Location	Dining room	❏	Kitchen	❏
	Guest room	❏	Lounge or lobby	❏
	Other_____			

OTHER FOODS AVAILABLE

Extra meals	❏	Hot/cold drinks	❏
Snacks	❏	Special diets	❏
Packed lunch	❏	Ethnic	❏
Fruit	❏	Other_____	

OPERATING RULES

Min. stay (days)	_____	No children	❏
Check-in time	_____	No pets	❏
Check-out time	_____	No alcohol	❏
Season from_____to_____		No smoking	❏

ROOM TARIFFS

Single occupancy	_____	Group rate	❏
Double occupancy	_____	Weekly rate	❏
Personal checks	❏	Off season	❏
		Extra person_____	
Credit cards: MC ❏ Visa ❏ AE ❏ Other_____			

WORKSHEET E
COMPETITOR SURVEY

ESTABLISHMENT	Name _____ B & B home ❑
	Small inn ❑
	Commercial ❑
HOST/MANAGER	Name_____
	Address_____
	Phone (___)_____ Postal/Zip code_____
STYLE	_____

FACILITIES AND SERVICES

Air conditioning	❑	Handicap access	❑
Swimming	❑	Walk to shops	❑
Sauna or gym	❑	Child play area	❑
Tennis court	❑	Patio or gardens	❑
Guest lounge	❑	Television	❑
Public transit	❑	Fax service	❑
Taxi service	❑	Babysitting	❑
Parking	❑	Pet sitting	❑
Boat mooring	❑	Laundry service	❑
Other_____		Room service	❑

BEDROOMS

Numbers Upstairs	_____	No. of stairs up	_____
Downstairs	_____	No. of stairs down	_____
Main floor	_____	Adjoining rooms	_____
Beds King	_____	Single _____	Other_____
Queen	_____	Crib _____	_____
Double	_____	Roll-out _____	_____
Twin	_____	Waterbed _____	_____

BATHROOMS

En-suite	_____	Bathtubs	_____
Private	_____	Showers	_____
Shared	_____	Other_____	

BREAKFAST

Menu	Continental ❑	Buffet	❑
	Hot food ❑	Served by host	❑
	Cold food ❑	Cook your own	❑
	Other_____		
Location	Dining room ❑	Kitchen	❑
	Guest room ❑	Lounge or lobby	❑
	Other_____		

OTHER FOODS AVAILABLE

Extra meals	❑	Hot/cold drinks	❑
Snacks	❑	Special diets	❑
Packed lunch	❑	Ethnic	❑
Fruit	❑	Other_____	

OPERATING RULES

Min. stay (days)	_____	No children	❑
Check-in time	_____	No pets	❑
Check-out time	_____	No alcohol	❑
Season from____to____		No smoking	❑

ROOM TARIFFS

Single occupancy	_____	Group rate	❑
Double occupancy	_____	Weekly rate	❑
Personal checks	❑	Off season	❑
		Extra person_____	
Credit cards: MC ❑ Visa ❑ AE ❑ Other_____			

WORKSHEET E
COMPETITOR SURVEY

ESTABLISHMENT | Name _____ B & B home ❑
Small inn ❑
Commercial ❑

HOST/MANAGER | Name_____
Address_____
Phone (___)_____ Postal/Zip code_____

STYLE | _____

FACILITIES AND SERVICES

Air conditioning	❑	Handicap access	❑
Swimming	❑	Walk to shops	❑
Sauna or gym	❑	Child play area	❑
Tennis court	❑	Patio or gardens	❑
Guest lounge	❑	Television	❑
Public transit	❑	Fax service	❑
Taxi service	❑	Babysitting	❑
Parking	❑	Pet sitting	❑
Boat mooring	❑	Laundry service	❑
Other_____		Room service	❑

BEDROOMS

Numbers	Upstairs _____	No. of stairs up _____	
	Downstairs_____	No. of stairs down _____	
	Main floor_____	Adjoining rooms _____	
Beds	King _____	Single _____	Other_____
	Queen _____	Crib _____	_____
	Double _____	Roll-out _____	_____
	Twin _____	Waterbed _____	_____

BATHROOMS

En-suite _____	Bathtubs _____	
Private _____	Showers _____	
Shared _____	Other_____	

BREAKFAST

Menu	Continental	❑	Buffet	❑
	Hot food	❑	Served by host	❑
	Cold food	❑	Cook your own	❑
	Other_____			
Location	Dining room	❑	Kitchen	❑
	Guest room	❑	Lounge or lobby	❑
	Other_____			

OTHER FOODS AVAILABLE

Extra meals	❑	Hot/cold drinks	❑
Snacks	❑	Special diets	❑
Packed lunch	❑	Ethnic	❑
Fruit	❑	Other_____	

OPERATING RULES

Min. stay (days)	_____	No children	❑
Check-in time	_____	No pets	❑
Check-out time	_____	No alcohol	❑
Season from_____to_____		No smoking	❑

ROOM TARIFFS

Single occupancy	_____	Group rate	❑
Double occupancy	_____	Weekly rate	❑
Personal checks	❑	Off season	❑
		Extra person_____	

Credit cards: MC ❑ Visa ❑ AE ❑ Other_____

WORKSHEET F
MARKET RESEARCH SUMMARY

FINAL CUSTOMER CHOICE   AVAILABLE BOOKING DAYS

BY AVAILABILITY	Total	Jan	Feb	Mar	Apr	May	Jun	Jul	Aug	Sep	Oct	Nov	Dec
a)													
b)													
c)													
d)													
e)													
f)													
g)													
h)													
i)													

PREFERRED ATTRACTIONS Gate   OPERATING DAYS

BY POPULARITY	Totals	Jan	Feb	Mar	Apr	May	Jun	Jul	Aug	Sep	Oct	Nov	Dec

SUMMARY OF COMPETITORS OF SIMILAR SIZE

Total surveyed _____
B & B homes _____
Small inns _____
Historic _____
Quaint _____
Modern _____

Air conditioning _____
Swimming _____
Sauna or gym _____
Tennis court _____
Guest lounge _____
Public transit _____
Taxi service _____
Parking _____
Boat mooring _____
Handicap access _____
Walk to Shops _____
Child play area _____
Patio or gardens _____
Television _____
Fax service _____
Babysitting _____
Pet sitting _____
Laundry service _____
Room service _____

Bedrooms up _____
Bedrooms down _____
Bedrooms main _____

King size _____
Queen size _____
Double size _____
Twin beds _____
Single bed _____
Crib _____
Rollout _____
Waterbed _____

Ensuite bath _____
Private bath _____
Shared _____
Tubs _____
Showers _____

Continental _____
Hot food _____
Cold food _____

Buffet _____
Served by host _____
Cook your own _____

Dining room _____
Guest room _____
Kitchen _____
Lounge/lobby _____

Extra meals _____
Snacks _____
Packed lunch _____
Fruit _____
Hot/Cold drink _____
Special diets _____
Ethnic _____

No children _____
No pets _____
No alcohol _____
No smoking _____
Min. single rate _____
Max. single rate _____
Min. double rate _____
Max. double rate _____

Discount rates _____
Credit cards _____
Personal checks _____

WORKSHEET G
HOSPITALITY RATING FORM

HOUSE NAME _____ DATE VISITED _____

		Poor	Fair	Good			Poor	Fair	Good
EXTERIOR	Signage	❑	❑	❑	BATHROOM	Fixtures	❑	❑	❑
	Parking	❑	❑	❑		Lighting	❑	❑	❑
	House condition	❑	❑	❑		Decoration	❑	❑	❑
	Landscaping	❑	❑	❑		Cleanliness	❑	❑	❑
	Trash & garbage	❑	❑	❑		Towels	❑	❑	❑
	Ext. guest areas	❑	❑	❑		Ventilation	❑	❑	❑
	Neighborhood	❑	❑	❑		Privacy	❑	❑	❑
CHECK IN	Welcome	❑	❑	❑		Convenience	❑	❑	❑
	Baggage	❑	❑	❑	BREAKFAST	Welcome	❑	❑	❑
	Tariff payment	❑	❑	❑		Time slot	❑	❑	❑
	Check in routine	❑	❑	❑		Presentation	❑	❑	❑
	Tour of facilities	❑	❑	❑		Food variety	❑	❑	❑
	House rules	❑	❑	❑		Food quality	❑	❑	❑
	Advice offered	❑	❑	❑		Cleanliness	❑	❑	❑
	Host attitude	❑	❑	❑		Host hygiene	❑	❑	❑
BEDROOM	Layout	❑	❑	❑		Host attitude	❑	❑	❑
	Cleanliness	❑	❑	❑	CHECK OUT	Routine	❑	❑	❑
	Decoration	❑	❑	❑		Time slot	❑	❑	❑
	Comfortable chairs	❑	❑	❑		Baggage	❑	❑	❑
	Clothes storage	❑	❑	❑		Host attitude	❑	❑	❑
	Bed comfort	❑	❑	❑		Travel advice	❑	❑	❑
	Reading material	❑	❑	❑	HOSPITALITY RATING		❑	❑	❑
	Writing space	❑	❑	❑					
	Lighting	❑	❑	❑					
	Privacy	❑	❑	❑					
	Security	❑	❑	❑					
	Room refreshments	❑	❑	❑					

COMMENTS:

_____

_____

_____

_____

_____

_____

_____

_____

WORKSHEET G
HOSPITALITY RATING FORM

HOUSE NAME _____ DATE VISITED _____

		Poor	Fair	Good			Poor	Fair	Good
EXTERIOR	Signage	❏	❏	❏	BATHROOM	Fixtures	❏	❏	❏
	Parking	❏	❏	❏		Lighting	❏	❏	❏
	House condition	❏	❏	❏		Decoration	❏	❏	❏
	Landscaping	❏	❏	❏		Cleanliness	❏	❏	❏
	Trash & garbage	❏	❏	❏		Towels	❏	❏	❏
	Ext. guest areas	❏	❏	❏		Ventilation	❏	❏	❏
	Neighborhood	❏	❏	❏		Privacy	❏	❏	❏
CHECK IN	Welcome	❏	❏	❏		Convenience	❏	❏	❏
	Baggage	❏	❏	❏	BREAKFAST	Welcome	❏	❏	❏
	Tariff payment	❏	❏	❏		Time slot	❏	❏	❏
	Check in routine	❏	❏	❏		Presentation	❏	❏	❏
	Tour of facilities	❏	❏	❏		Food variety	❏	❏	❏
	House rules	❏	❏	❏		Food quality	❏	❏	❏
	Advice offered	❏	❏	❏		Cleanliness	❏	❏	❏
	Host attitude	❏	❏	❏		Host hygiene	❏	❏	❏
BEDROOM	Layout	❏	❏	❏		Host attitude	❏	❏	❏
	Cleanliness	❏	❏	❏	CHECK OUT	Routine	❏	❏	❏
	Decoration	❏	❏	❏		Time slot	❏	❏	❏
	Comfortable chairs	❏	❏	❏		Baggage	❏	❏	❏
	Clothes storage	❏	❏	❏		Host attitude	❏	❏	❏
	Bed comfort	❏	❏	❏		Travel advice	❏	❏	❏
	Reading material	❏	❏	❏	HOSPITALITY RATING		❏	❏	❏
	Writing space	❏	❏	❏					
	Lighting	❏	❏	❏					
	Privacy	❏	❏	❏					
	Security	❏	❏	❏					
	Room refreshments	❏	❏	❏					

COMMENTS:

_____

_____

_____

_____

_____

_____

_____

_____

_____

182

WORKSHEET H
RENOVATION SURVEY

ROOM _____   SHEET # _____

Task #	Renovation	Labor Required	Hours	Materials Required	Costs	Accumulated Costs
		Total Labor for Task #		Total Costs for Task #		
		Total Labor for Task #		Total Costs for Task #		
		Total Labor for Task #		Total Costs for Task #		
		Total Labor for Task #		Total Costs for Task #		

183

WORKSHEET H
RENOVATION SURVEY

ROOM   SHEET #

Task #	Renovation	Labor Required	Hours	Materials Required	Costs	Accumulated Costs
		Total Labor for Task #		Total Costs for Task #		
		Total Labor for Task #		Total Costs for Task #		
		Total Labor for Task #		Total Costs for Task #		
		Total Labor for Task #		Total Costs for Task #		

WORKSHEET H
RENOVATION SURVEY

SHEET #

ROOM

Task #	Renovation	Labor Required	Hours	Materials Required	Costs	Accumulated Costs
		Total Labor for Task #		Total Costs for Task #		
		Total Labor for Task #		Total Costs for Task #		
		Total Labor for Task #		Total Costs for Task #		
		Total Labor for Task #		Total Costs for Task #		

WORKSHEET H
RENOVATION SURVEY

ROOM _____   SHEET # _____

Task #	Renovation	Labor Required	Hours	Materials Required	Costs	Accumulated Costs
		Total Labor for Task #		Total Costs for Task #		
		Total Labor for Task #		Total Costs for Task #		
		Total Labor for Task #		Total Costs for Task #		
		Total Labor for Task #		Total Costs for Task #		

WORKSHEET I
FOOD SERVICES BULLETIN

WE ARE PLEASED TO OFFER THE FOLLOWING FOOD SERVICES FOR YOUR ENJOYMENT

BREAKFAST

SPECIAL DIETS
AND
ALLERGIES

EXTRA MEALS

REFRESHMENTS

WORKSHEET J
FOOD COST ANALYSIS

FOOD SERVICE_____DATE_____

DESCRIPTION	SIZE	PURCHASE PRICE	# OF UNITS IN PACKAGE	UNITS PER SERVING	PRICE PER SERVING

AVERAGE INDIVIDUAL SERVING COST_____

WORKSHEET J
FOOD COST ANALYSIS

FOOD SERVICE_____DATE_____

DESCRIPTION	SIZE	PURCHASE PRICE	# OF UNITS IN PACKAGE	UNITS PER SERVING	PRICE PER SERVING

AVERAGE INDIVIDUAL SERVING COST_____

190

WORKSHEET K
START-UP EQUIPMENT AND SUPPLIES

AREA_____SHEET #_____

ITEM #	EQUIPMENT AND SUPPLIES	EST. COST	EST. HOURS
	TOTAL		

WORKSHEET K
START-UP EQUIPMENT AND SUPPLIES

AREA_____SHEET #_____

ITEM #	EQUIPMENT AND SUPPLIES	EST. COST	EST. HOURS
		TOTAL	

WORKSHEET K
START-UP EQUIPMENT AND SUPPLIES

AREA_____SHEET #_____

ITEM #	EQUIPMENT AND SUPPLIES	EST. COST	EST. HOURS
	TOTAL		

WORKSHEET K
START-UP EQUIPMENT AND SUPPLIES

AREA_____ SHEET #_____

ITEM #	EQUIPMENT AND SUPPLIES	EST. COST	EST. HOURS
	TOTAL		

WORKSHEET L
BOOKING FORECAST

REALISTIC BOOKING DAYS AVAILABLE

AVERAGE BOOKING DAYS EACH MONTH

	Total days	Jan	Feb	Mar	Apr	May	June	July	Aug	Sept	Oct	Nov	Dec
1. Final customers													
2. Local attractions													
3. Booking agencies													
4. B & B associations													
5. Average of 1 to 4 (Average Days Avail.)													

ADJUSTMENTS TO BOOKING DAYS

ADJUSTMENTS TO AVERAGES EACH MONTH

	Total adjust	Jan	Feb	Mar	Apr	May	June	Jul	Aug	Sep	Oct	Nov	Dec
6. State of economy													
7. Advertising													
8. Facilities/services													
9. Tariff structure													
10. Add Items 5 to 9 (Adj. booking days)													
11. Adj. for vacations													
12. Adj. for days off													
13. Total of 10 to 12 (Booking Days Avail.)													

CALCULATE YOUR ROOM BOOKINGS

ROOM BOOKINGS EACH MONTH

	Totals	Jan	Feb	Mar	Apr	May	June	July	Aug	Sep	Oct	Nov	Dec
14. Max. Rm. Bookings Available (Line 13 x No. of Rms)													
15. First-year adjustment (50% of Item 14)													
16. Line 14 minus Line 15 (Booking Forecast)													

WORKSHEET L
BOOKING FORECAST

REALISTIC BOOKING DAYS AVAILABLE

AVERAGE BOOKING DAYS EACH MONTH

	Total days	Jan	Feb	Mar	Apr	May	June	July	Aug	Sept	Oct	Nov	Dec
1. Final customers													
2. Local attractions													
3. Booking agencies													
4. B & B associations													
5. Average of 1 to 4 (Average Days Avail.)													

ADJUSTMENTS TO BOOKING DAYS

ADJUSTMENTS TO AVERAGES EACH MONTH

	Total adjust	Jan	Feb	Mar	Apr	May	June	Jul	Aug	Sep	Oct	Nov	Dec
6. State of economy													
7. Advertising													
8. Facilities/services													
9. Tariff structure													
10. Add Items 5 to 9 (Adj. booking days)													
11. Adj. for vacations													
12. Adj. for days off													
13. Total of 10 to 12 (Booking Days Avail.)													

CALCULATE YOUR ROOM BOOKINGS

ROOM BOOKINGS EACH MONTH

	Totals	Jan	Feb	Mar	Apr	May	June	July	Aug	Sep	Oct	Nov	Dec
14. Max. Rm. Bookings Available (Line 13 x No. of Rms)													
15. First-year adjustment (50% of Item 14)													
16. Line 14 minus Line 15 (Booking Forecast)													

WORKSHEET M
FINANCIAL ESTIMATES

FINANCIAL ESTIMATES WORKSHEET

	Jan	Feb	Mar	Apr	May	June	July	Aug	Sep	Oct	Nov	Dec
Booking Forecast												
REVENUES												
Booking Revenue												
Extra Meals												
Extra Services												
Other Revenues												
EXPENSES												
Booking Fees												
Guest Food												
Guest Supplies												

	AMOUNT	PRORATED	MONTHLY	QUARTERLY	OTHER
Gas					
Electric Bi-monthly					
Water/Sewer					
Telephone					
Cable TV					
Property Taxes					
Mortgage Interest					
House Repairs					
House Insurance					
Bank Charges					
Office Expenses					
Accounting & Legal					
Business Insurance					
Advertising					
Agent Listing Fees					
Licences					
Loan Repayments					
Other Expenses					

WORKSHEET M
FINANCIAL ESTIMATES

FINANCIAL ESTIMATES WORKSHEET

	Jan	Feb	Mar	Apr	May	June	July	Aug	Sep	Oct	Nov	Dec
Booking Forecast												
REVENUES												
Booking Revenue												
Extra Meals												
Extra Services												
Other Revenues												
EXPENSES												
Booking Fees												
Guest Food												
Guest Supplies												

	AMOUNT	PRORATED	MONTHLY	QUARTERLY	OTHER
Gas					
Electric Bi-monthly					
Water/Sewer					
Telephone					
Cable TV					
Property Taxes					
Mortgage Interest					
House Repairs					
House Insurance					
Bank Charges					
Office Expenses					
Accounting & Legal					
Business Insurance					
Advertising					
Agent Listing Fees					
Licences					
Loan Repayments					
Other Expenses					

WORKSHEET N
TASK FORMS

WORKSHEET_____

SHEET #_____TASK #_____

TITLE _____

TASK _____

_____

_____

_____

TOTAL HRS. EST.	_____HRS.
ACTUAL HRS.	_____HRS.
TOTAL COSTS EST.	$_____
ACTUAL COSTS	$_____

WORKSHEET_____

SHEET #_____TASK #_____

TITLE_____

TASK_____

_____

_____

_____

TOTAL HRS. EST.	_____HRS.
ACTUAL HRS.	_____HRS.
TOTAL COSTS EST.	$_____
ACTUAL COSTS	$_____

WORKSHEET_____

SHEET #_____TASK #_____

TITLE _____

TASK _____

_____

_____

_____

TOTAL HRS. EST.	_____HRS.
ACTUAL HRS.	_____HRS.
TOTAL COSTS EST.	$_____
ACTUAL COSTS	$_____

WORKSHEET_____

SHEET #_____TASK #_____

TITLE_____

TASK_____

_____

_____

_____

TOTAL HRS. EST.	_____HRS.
ACTUAL HRS.	_____HRS.
TOTAL COSTS EST.	$_____
ACTUAL COSTS	$_____

WORKSHEET_____

SHEET #_____TASK #_____

TITLE _____

TASK _____

_____

_____

_____

TOTAL HRS. EST.	_____HRS.
ACTUAL HRS.	_____HRS.
TOTAL COSTS EST.	$_____
ACTUAL COSTS	$_____

WORKSHEET_____

SHEET #_____TASK #_____

TITLE_____

TASK_____

_____

_____

_____

TOTAL HRS. EST.	_____HRS.
ACTUAL HRS.	_____HRS.
TOTAL COSTS EST.	$_____
ACTUAL COSTS	$_____

WORKSHEET N
TASK FORMS

WORKSHEET_____

SHEET #_____TASK #_____

TITLE _____

TASK _____

_____

_____

_____

TOTAL HRS. EST. _____HRS.

ACTUAL HRS. _____HRS.

TOTAL COSTS EST. $_____

ACTUAL COSTS $_____

WORKSHEET_____

SHEET #_____TASK #_____

TITLE_____

TASK_____

_____

_____

_____

TOTAL HRS. EST. _____HRS.

ACTUAL HRS. _____HRS.

TOTAL COSTS EST. $_____

ACTUAL COSTS $_____

WORKSHEET_____

SHEET #_____TASK #_____

TITLE _____

TASK _____

_____

_____

_____

TOTAL HRS. EST. _____HRS.

ACTUAL HRS. _____HRS.

TOTAL COSTS EST. $_____

ACTUAL COSTS $_____

WORKSHEET_____

SHEET #_____TASK #_____

TITLE_____

TASK_____

_____

_____

_____

TOTAL HRS. EST. _____HRS.

ACTUAL HRS. _____HRS.

TOTAL COSTS EST. $_____

ACTUAL COSTS $_____

WORKSHEET_____

SHEET #_____TASK #_____

TITLE _____

TASK _____

_____

_____

_____

TOTAL HRS. EST. _____HRS.

ACTUAL HRS. _____HRS.

TOTAL COSTS EST. $_____

ACTUAL COSTS $_____

WORKSHEET_____

SHEET #_____TASK #_____

TITLE_____

TASK_____

_____

_____

_____

TOTAL HRS. EST. _____HRS.

ACTUAL HRS. _____HRS.

TOTAL COSTS EST. $_____

ACTUAL COSTS $_____

200

APPENDIX 4
COST SHEETS

The following five cost sheets are referred to throughout this book for documenting your costs. Read the book and follow the text to help guide you through completing your own cost sheets. The forms have been perforated for easy removal.

COST SHEET #1
MARKET RESEARCH COSTS

CATEGORY	ITEM DESCRIPTION	COST
REFERENCE MATERIAL	Reference books, guide books, listings, statistics, etc.	
(Chapter 3)		
OFFICE SUPPLIES	Stationery, postage, typewriter ribbons, pens, etc.	
(Chapter 3)		
COMMUNICATIONS	Telephone charges, fax, etc.	
(Chapter 3)		
OTHER	Transportation, parking, tariffs, miscellaneous	
(Chapter 3)		
TRIAL B & B VISIT	Transportation, tariffs, etc.	
(Chapter 4)		

TOTAL COSTS	SUBTOTAL	
	State or Provincial Taxes	
	GST or Other Taxes	
	TOTAL COST FOR MARKET RESEARCH	

COST SHEET #2
RULES AND REGULATION COSTS

CATEGORY	ITEM DESCRIPTION	COST
CONSULTING AND REFERENCE (Chapter 5)	Accounting, legal, reference books, etc.	
GOVERNMENT REQUIREMENTS (Chapter 5)	Registration, licenses, permits, etc.	
INSURANCE (Chapter 5)	Appraisals, inspections, premiums, etc.	
OTHER (Chapter 5)	Office supplies, transportation, parking, etc.	

TOTAL COSTS		
	SUBTOTAL	
	State or Provincial Taxes	
	GST or Other Taxes	
	TOTAL COST FOR RULES AND REGULATIONS	

COST SHEET #3
FACILITIES COST ESTIMATES

HOUSE AREA	RENOVATION	WORKSHEETS	LABOR AND MATERIALS COSTS
Guest Bedrooms (Chapter 6)	_____ _____ _____	_____ _____ _____	_____ _____ _____
Guest Bathrooms (Chapter 6)	_____ _____ _____	_____ _____ _____	_____ _____ _____
Hallways and Stairways (Chapter 6)	_____ _____	_____ _____	_____ _____
Sitting Area (Chapter 6)	_____ _____	_____ _____	_____ _____
Exterior Areas (Chapter 6)	_____ _____ _____	_____ _____ _____	_____ _____ _____
Private Family Areas and Office (Chapter 6)	_____ _____ _____ _____ _____	_____ _____ _____ _____ _____	_____ _____ _____ _____ _____
Guest Breakfast and Other Food Facilities (Chapter 7)	_____ _____ _____ _____	_____ _____ _____ _____	_____ _____ _____ _____
Food Handling Facilities (Chapter 7)	_____ _____	_____ _____	_____ _____

TOTAL COSTS   Labor & Materials Totals

SUBTOTAL _____

State or Provincial Taxes _____

GST or Other Taxes _____

TOTAL ESTIMATED COST FOR FACILITIES _____

COST SHEET #4
MISCELLANEOUS START-UP COSTS

START-UP COSTS	WORKSHEETS	EQUIPMENT/SUPPLIES
EXT. & INT. HOUSEKEEPING (Chapter 8)	_____ _____ _____ _____	_____ _____ _____ _____
CLIENT RECORDKEEPING (Chapter 9)	_____ _____ _____ _____	_____ _____ _____ _____
OPERATING OPTIONS (Chapter 10)	_____ _____ _____ _____	_____ _____ _____ _____
FINANCIAL RECORD KEEPING (Chapter 11)	_____ _____ _____ _____	_____ _____ _____ _____
ADVERTISING COSTS (Chapter 12)	_____ _____ _____ _____	_____ _____ _____ _____
FORECASTS AND STATISTICS (Chapter 13)	_____ _____ _____ _____	_____ _____ _____ _____

SUBTOTAL

State or Provincial Taxes _____

GST or Other Taxes _____

TOTAL MISCELLANEOUS START-UP COSTS _____

COST SHEET #5
START-UP COST SUMMARY

1. MARKET RESEARCH

        (Cost Sheet No.1, Chapter 3)

        (Chapter 14)   _____

2. RULES AND REGULATIONS

        (Cost Sheet No.2, Chapter 5)   _____

3. FACILITIES

        (Cost Sheet No.3, Chapter 6)   _____

4. MISCELLANEOUS

        (Cost Sheet No.4, Chapter 8)   _____

START-UP SUBTOTAL   _____

ADD 10% CONTINGENCY   _____

TOTAL BED AND BREAKFAST START-UP COST   _____